THE TITLE

THE STORY OF THE FIRST DIVISION

SCOTT MURRAY

BLOOMSBURY

LONDON · OXFORD · NEW YORK · NEW DELHI · SYDNEY

Bloomsbury Sport
An imprint of Bloomsbury Publishing Plc

50 Bedford Square   1385 Broadway
London   New York
WC1B 3DP   NY 10018
UK   USA

www.bloomsbury.com

BLOOMSBURY and the Diana logo are trademarks of Bloomsbury Publishing Plc

First published 2017

British Library Cataloguing-in-Publication Data
A catalogue record for this book is available from the British Library.

Library of Congress Cataloguing-in-Publication data has been applied for.

ISBN: HB: 978-1-4729-3661-5
ePub: 978-1-4729-3662-2

2 4 6 8 10 9 7 5 3 1

Typeset in Adobe Garamond Pro by Deanta Global Publishing Services, Chennai, India
Printed and bound in Great Britain by CPI Group (UK) Ltd, Croydon CR0 4YY

To find out more about our authors and books visit www.bloomsbury.com.
Here you will find extracts, author interviews, details of forthcoming events
and the option to sign up for our newsletters.

Dedicated to the memory of Sandy Murray and the Nethy Bridge side of the 1950s, three-in-a-row Strathspey & Badenoch title winners.

Contents

Preface

'Football began in 1992.' It's one of the great running jokes, variations on a theme trotted out by the patter merchants whenever a caption is flashed up on the television: highest scorer in Premier League history, biggest-ever Premier League away win, most miles run by a player in a Premier League match. A wry, knowing nod to an awkward fact: that the self-styled greatest league in the world hasn't always been the top division of English football; that these records, while correct by strict definition, should really stretch a wee bit further back than year zero. To 1888, in fact, so we can factor in the years when the First Division of the Football League was the ultimate prize. That period in time, to borrow another zinger from the banter boys, before Sky invented football.

It's not as though histories of the English game completely avoid reference to events preceding the genesis of the Football Association's great usurper. Herbert Chapman's all-conquering Arsenal, five-time winners of the First Division during the 1930s, are still one of the most famous sides in the sport. Ditto the Busby Babes and the Manchester United of Best, Law and Charlton; Don Revie's Leeds; Brian Clough's championship sides at Derby and Forest; the domineering Liverpool of the seventies and eighties. But these are the rule-proving exceptions, and the century-long story of the old First Division, starring all those glorious winners

(Preston! Sunderland! Manchester City!) and abject losers (Glossop! Orient! Manchester City!) has been curiously underrepresented. That was already the case decades ago, when the Football League was still the top prize; now we're over a quarter of a century into the brave new Premier League era, the epic saga of the Football League is in danger of being lost completely in the vague mists of time.

This cannot stand! So here's an attempt to snatch the long-forgotten tale of the First Division back from the darkness, shine a light in a few corners, and give it the love and attention it so richly deserves. Homer will have nothing on this odyssey.

Introduction:
Old Mac pours a cup of coffee
(206BC to 1888–89)

Ts'u Chu was invented in ancient China, a pastime popular among the genteel elite of the Han dynasty. The game was played on the courts of the imperial palace, where nimble athletes of both sexes would attempt, with their elegant, privileged feet, to caress a ball made of feathers through a hole in a silk sheet suspended between bamboo poles. The goal swayed softly in the breeze. Close your eyes and drift away: you can almost hear the wind flicking the branches of the cherry blossom, the delicate oscillations of a wood flute, the ethereal glissando of the chimes.

Two millennia later, the British got involved and . . . what ho! There's a voluminous, rumbling, cartoon cloud of dust with arms, legs, fists, stovepipe hats and big degenerate hobnail boots sticking out of it. Hey, we're nothing if not passionate.

It was a perfect storm. A craze for organised sport swept Victorian Britain, thanks partly to the invention of the lawn mower, which meant folk didn't require a flock of sheep to maintain and manicure playing fields, and partly to recent child-labour legislation, which ensured a modern generation spent their formative years gambolling rather than working up chimneys. In particular, a mania for the strangely beguiling practice of hoofing a ball around took hold, and a battle for control of this new game soon raged.

In 1846, some blue-sky thinkers at Trinity College, Cambridge, took a first pass at some standardised rules, and set about wrapping their fingers like bindweed around the administrative tiller. Some more salt-of-the-earth types from Sheffield committed a few laws of their own to parchment in 1860. They went as far as forming the world's first football-only clubs, Sheffield and Hallam, everything that came before having been affiliated to public schools, universities or cricket clubs. But the southerners refused to cede control, regaining the momentum in 1862 when J.C. Thring, one of the young dandies behind the Trinity College gambit, tweaked his old work into a new set of laws called The Simplest Game. A year later, a gaggle of public-school hoorays met in a Covent Garden drinker, buffed up Thring's rewritten rulebook, and the Football Association – and Association Football – was born!

The FA and Sheffield codes co-existed for a while, but the FA were better equipped to print and send out copies of their rulebook, and the 1871 launch of their eponymous Challenge Cup was the killer blow. Sixteen teams from across Britain entered the tournament. The favourites for the first FA Cup were Queen's Park of Glasgow, who since forming in 1867 had yet to concede a goal in competitive play. They didn't let one in during their FA Cup run either, though that enviable defensive record wasn't enough to secure them the trophy. Queen's Park had been given a bye to the semi-finals, at which point they would face Wanderers – formerly Forest-Leytonstone, the London club of FA secretary Charles Alcock – at The Oval cricket ground. The match ended goalless. Queen's Park turned out their pockets to find nothing but brass bawbees, hope and dust; with no money left for food or board, they were forced to withdraw and head back home. Nobody appears to have considered a replay in Glasgow. Wanderers went on to beat Royal Engineers in the first final. Queen's Park finally let one slip past the keeper three years later in a Hampden friendly against Vale of Leven. Some defence, but they never won the Cup.

An amateurish shambles, all told. Which was fair enough in one respect: these people *were* amateurs, after all. The FA – drawing on the self-righteous moral certainty only the moneyed classes can afford – insisted the sport remain an idyllic jolly-hockey-sticks pastime. Not a pragmatic profession open to all. But the balance of power was shifting. Most of the best players were working men from Scotland, while in the Midlands and industrial north the penny had dropped with a few savvy entrepreneurial types that hard brass could be forged from the game: thousands and thousands were flocking to their new clubs to watch. And so a new movement prepared to cut a swashbuckling swathe through the bourgeois nonsense.

Sidney Yates, owner of a Blackburn ironworks, decided to start pumping money into his local club Olympic. Talented players were all given reputable day jobs: dental assistants, plumbers, staff at cotton mills and the Yates iron foundry. Success soon followed, and upon reaching the 1883 FA Cup final, Olympic were packed off on a pre-match training beano to Blackpool. Enjoying what was effectively a paid week's holiday, the players rose each day at 6 a.m., necked a refreshing glass of port mixed with two raw eggs, then took a bracing stroll up and down the beach before spending the rest of the day wolfing down porridge and haddock for breakfast, mutton for lunch, and oysters for tea. Arsène Wenger's healthy-eating revolution of the late 1990s had nothing on this. Olympic beat the Old Etonians 1–0 after extra time to become the first northern – more importantly, the first *proudly proletariat* – team to lift the Cup. Class war! Class war now!

The toffs of the FA attempted to pull up the drawbridge in a futile bid to stop the unwashed masses storming the castle. In January 1884, amateur southerners Upton Park visited Preston North End in the FA Cup. They came away from Deepdale with a 1–1 draw. But before a replay could be contested, Upton Park lodged a complaint with the FA, claiming Preston were illegally fielding professionals. That was, in a roundabout way, almost certainly the case: Preston were shelling out over £1,000 a year on wages, and while the FA could not prove this cash was being directly trousered by the players, the club was found guilty of enticing Scottish talent to the town by finding them suspiciously highly paid work in the mill run by team manager William Sudell. Preston were disqualified from the Cup. Sudell, defiant and unbowed, simply organised a boycott and threw down a gauntlet: if professionalism wasn't legalised, politically muscular North End, along with several other newly powerful northern clubs, would form their own breakaway association. The FA capitulated to their demands.

This didn't stop other competitions being set up anyway. The FA's trump card – the FA Cup – also proved to be its joker. It had given fans around the country the taste for proper competition, games that *really* meant something. Demand outstripped supply: a couple of FA Cup ties each year couldn't slake the thirst. Aston Villa had become one of the best sides in the country during the 1880s, winning the vast majority of the friendly matches they contested. Their supporters, though, were tiring of these monotonous non-events. One fan, Joe Tillotson, ran a coffee shop next door to Villa board member William McGregor's drapery shop in Aston, and the pair would often put the world to rights over a cup or two. Tillotson, high on java, was not afraid to regularly harangue his friend Old Mac, expressing extreme boredom at watching Villa batter local nonentities for the purposes of . . . well, what, exactly?

McGregor eventually took the hint. In early 1888 he wrote to the chairmen of Preston North End, Blackburn Rovers, Bolton Wanderers and West Bromwich Albion with a fine idea for a new competition. His plan was for 'ten or twelve of the most prominent clubs in England [to] combine to arrange home and away fixtures each season'. This 'fixity of fixtures' would be called, he suggested, 'the Association Football Union'. Hey, you can't expect to get everything right in the first draft. But in a whirlwind of organisational brilliance, Accrington, Burnley, Derby County, Everton, Notts County, Stoke and Wolverhampton Wanderers were invited by the Big Five to make up the numbers. The rebranded Football League was formed after a resolution was passed at the Royal Hotel in Manchester on 17 April 1888 and the whole shebang was up and running within five months. Old Mac was sworn in as president.

The genius of McGregor's Football League scheme should not be understated. While the watertight logic of home and away fixtures seems glaringly obvious now, it wasn't so clear back then. A mere ten days after the plan for the League was announced, a meeting was held at the Royal Hotel in Crewe. In attendance were representatives of several other clubs – among them such luminaries as Notts Rangers, Leek, Witton, Long Eaton Rangers and Bootle – piqued at not being part of McGregor's plan. They decided to launch an alternative competition, denouncing the Football League as unrepresentative of the game as they saw it.

The Football Combination would be a 20-club affair, with each team playing eight matches against other sides in the division. It made little sense in the first place, even less when it eventually got under way and fixtures remained unfulfilled, the Combination bigwigs having left it to the clubs to make their own arrangements, with predictable consequences. The competition descended into farce, and the opening season was left uncompleted, much to the chagrin of Manchester outfit Newton Heath, the form team when it all went south. Ah well, maybe they'd have their time in the sun some other day.

The Football League was the original and best, and Preston North End went into the inaugural season as favourites for the title. William Sudell's side were by this point firmly established as the best team in the country. They had recently enjoyed a 42-game unbeaten run, a stretch which included a 26–0 FA Cup win over Hyde, still the heaviest win in English football history. That came to an abrupt end in the 1888 FA Cup final, a match they unexpectedly lost to West Bromwich Albion. Upon arriving at The Oval for the big game, Sudell had shamelessly requested his team's picture be taken with the Cup before kick-off, so their crisp white shirts would be recorded, unsullied, for posterity. 'Hadn't you better win it first?' asked the ref. Liverpool's cream Armani duds of 1996 had nothing on this hubristic disgrace.

To be fair to Preston, their confidence, while misplaced, was understandable at the time. Battering the minnows of Hyde by 26 goals during the run-up to the final had been no great surprise; but walloping Bolton Wanderers, one of the top teams, 9–1 in the next round had sent a few jaws dropping. Preston also beat

McGregor's Aston Villa during their sashay to the final. And they dominated the final against West Brom in the modern sterile fashion, but succumbed to a late sucker punch from Albion's George Woodhall.

Lessons were learned, and on 8 September 1888, Preston set about the very first day of the very first Football League season in a focused, professional style. Fred Dewhurst scored within three minutes of their opening fixture, at home against Burnley, and they went on to win 5–2. Dewhurst's early strike was not enough to give him the honour of scoring the first Football League goal: Preston's game kicked off at 3.50 p.m., three minutes after Kenny Davenport of Bolton Wanderers scored the opener two minutes into his team's 3.45 p.m. kick-off against Derby.

Five matches were staged on the day the curtain went up (Blackburn Rovers were busy losing a prearranged friendly in Manchester against Newton Heath, so they and Notts County missed out on a little history):

Bolton Wanderers 3–6 Derby County
Everton 2–1 Accrington
Preston North End 5–2 Burnley
Stoke 0–2 West Bromwich Albion
Wolverhampton Wanderers 1–1 Aston Villa

The pattern of the season was set. Preston won the first Football League with remarkable ease, winning all but four of their matches, losing none. While the organisation of the League was considerably better than that of the Combination, it was still far from perfect. Initially, it was thought the League would be ordered by number of wins alone, until the system of two points for a victory and one for a draw was worked out in November. And there was no trophy for Preston to lift when they finally wrapped up the first title on 5 January 1889 with a 4–1 win over Notts County.

Never mind. Preston could wave the 1889 FA Cup about instead, as they completed a League and Cup Double in the League's very first season. Having not lost a single game in League or Cup, this Preston team – fuelled by the goals of Jimmy Ross and John Goodall – went down in history as The Invincibles. And yet a month after their Cup-final win, these supposed immortals among men found themselves on the end of a very significant thrashing. Sunderland had been desperate to join the new League, but were blackballed simply because all the other clubs didn't fancy the long trudge to the remote north-east. They proved a point by thrashing so-called invincible Preston 4–1 in a showpiece friendly.

A year later, in another one-off occasion, Sunderland battered Aston Villa 7–2. Old Mac, smarting yet sporting and smitten, described his club's vanquishers as 'talented men in every position', a quote which was soon mangled, in the folk tradition, into 'Team of All the Talents'. This new talent was about to barge its way into the Football League with a view to taking over as the premier club in the land. Close your eyes and drift away again, and you may hear another of those ethereal glissandi: the sound of Preston's hearts dissolving slowly towards their boots.

1

Tom and George set a high bar (1888–89 to 1900–01)

The roll call of managerial greats throws up the same old names: Herbert Chapman, Matt Busby, Bill Nicholson, Alf Ramsey, Bill Shankly, Don Revie, Brian Clough, Bob Paisley, Kenny Dalglish, Alex Ferguson, Arsène Wenger, José Mourinho. Yet two of the most successful of all, gentlemen whose achievements would knock most of our aforementioned heroes into a cocked hat, rarely get the recognition they deserve. The relentless march of time has not been a friend to Tom Watson or George Ramsay.

Only Alex Ferguson has won more English league titles than George Ramsay. Only Ferguson, Ramsay and Bob Paisley have made a bigger mark on the roll of honour than Tom Watson. Between them, Watson and Ramsay won nine of the first 13 Football League championships, ending their careers with five and six titles respectively. The problem is, the bulk of their achievements were done and dusted when Victoria still sat on the throne, and so few outside a partisan *cognoscenti* pay them much heed these days. Time to right some wrongs.

Tom Watson was usually captured on new-fangled photographic paper sporting a bowler hat. Sometimes he chose a straw boater, though neither headpiece was ever worn at a jaunty angle. Watson had a big, round, chubby face, the centrepiece a luxuriously waxed handlebar moustache. Also influenced by the fashions of the age was a very stern expression. He looked about 55, though that seems to have been the way of things back in the late 1880s. In fact, as a mere twentysomething, he was quite the tyro.

Watson became manager of Sunderland in 1888, aged just 29, having already proved his capabilities 15 miles north of Wearside. As secretary-manager of Newcastle West End, he was influential in helping the Geordies find a ground to play on. A notorious charmer, Watson sweet-talked the local council and several city freemen into leasing St James' Park – previously used by an outfit called Newcastle Rangers – to West End. His wife was the only woman present at the ground's official opening, a soirée that generated receipts of eight shillings. Watson was enticed across the city to rivals Newcastle East End, who in turn lost him to Sunderland. (East End launched a reverse takeover of West End in 1892, moving in at St James' and rebranding the merged club as Newcastle United.)

The logistical problem of Sunderland's extreme northerly location (as viewed by the new Football League, based exclusively in Lancashire and the Midlands) was offset by the city's close proximity to Scotland, which made it easy for the club to dip into a rich reservoir of talent. Their first big signing was striker Johnny Campbell from 1888 Scottish Cup winners Renton. Another forward, Jimmy Millar, along with midfield enforcer Hughie Wilson and defender John Auld, soon followed. The Team of All the Talents was taking shape.

After Preston were thrashed 4–1 in the April 1889 friendly, and Aston Villa went down 7–2 a year later, the Football League had little choice but to allow Sunderland to become the first new club admitted to their fold. They were lined up to replace underperforming Stoke for the start of the 1890–91 season, albeit only after agreeing to cover travelling expenses of every visiting team. Sunderland celebrated the news by once again beating Preston, 6–3 in a pre-season friendly. It seemed another significant marker: Preston had just retained their title in the League's second season, the signature result of that 1889–90 campaign a breezy 5–1 victory over nearest challengers Everton.

But if Sunderland – now the proven bosses of the two-time champions – thought life in the League would be a cakewalk, they were quickly disabused of the notion. Their first two League matches were at their spanking-new Newcastle Road stadium. They were beaten 3–2 by Burnley, then 4–3 by Wolverhampton Wanderers having led 3–0 at half-time. Watson took immediate action, signing goalkeeper Ned Doig from Arbroath. Doig cut a slightly eccentric figure. Extremely sensitive over his receding hairline, he wore a cap during matches. This in itself wouldn't have been particularly noteworthy, except that he secured it tightly with a strap below his chin, and on the many occasions the cap worked its way loose from its moorings and flew off, Doig would scurry after it in an embarrassed panic as it danced around on the breeze. He would give chase regardless of whether the opposition was on the attack or not.

Doig was also a brilliant keeper. Despite his tendency to vacate his goal while in hot pursuit of his lid, his presence otherwise calmed Sunderland's shaky defence. They won their third game of the season 4–0 at West Bromwich Albion. However, these first League points were soon taken off them, and the club was fined £50 when it transpired Doig had yet to be registered properly and was technically ineligible to play. Sunderland eventually recovered from this beyond-hapless start to finish a season of consolidation in seventh place.

Everton won the championship that season. The 1890–91 title was effectively secured around Christmas and New Year with a burst of hot activity at their home ground, Anfield: 19 goals spread over four matches saw off Accrington, Burnley, Aston Villa and Notts County. Preston North End put an end to that sequence by turning up and winning by a single goal, but by this point Everton had stockpiled too many points for the reigning champions to make up. They were worthy winners, star striker Fred Geary netting 20 goals in 22 starts, Alf Milward and Edgar Chadwick chipping in with 12 and 10 respectively from the wings. Yet Everton's first title proved somewhat pyrrhic, in so much as it sparked off a chain of events leading to the birth of the bane of their existence. Club president John Houlding was also their Anfield landlord, and he raised the rent the minute Everton tasted success. A brewer by trade, he demanded that Everton's fans sup his suds, and his suds alone, at the ground. Leaving no commercial stone unturned, he also insisted Everton use his Sandon Hotel as a changing room before each fixture, in order to give his hostelry free publicity. The rest of Everton's board quickly tired of this carry-on, and upped sticks for a new ground at Mere Green on Goodison Road. Houlding was left with an empty stadium and nothing to fill it. The subsequent formation of Liverpool Football Club seemed an obvious way to solve the problem.

Sunderland meanwhile began their second season in the Football League as dismally as they had the first. They lost three of their first four games in 1891–92, copping for a little payback: Preston, vexed having surrendered their title, beat them 3–1 at Deepdale; Aston Villa prevailed 5–3 at Perry Barr. Villa went top, Sunderland plunged to the bottom. This time, however, early-season form was deceptive. Villa were slowly putting together a mighty fine side, but they weren't there quite yet: inconsistency set in, and they finished fourth. Sunderland, however, clicked into a higher gear, because even their slow start had offered hope. They'd scored 12 goals in those first four matches, and soon enough the attack overpowered all. Johnny Campbell scored 28 goals in 25 games. Jimmy Hannah and Jimmy Millar both chipped in with 16, while John Scott also reached double figures. Sunderland found the net 93 times in all, easily surpassing the 74 scored by the Preston Invincibles of 1888–89. At one point they won 13 games in a row, a top-flight record only broken in 2002 by Arsenal. They won all of their games at home, a feat still to be matched in the English top flight. They *romped* it.

Their penultimate match of the season was a celebratory 7–1 jig at League new boys Darwen. Three weeks earlier, the hapless Lancastrian virgins had lost 12–0 at West Bromwich Albion, still the heaviest defeat in top-flight history (though Leicester Fosse, now City, came a similar cropper against Nottingham Forest in 1909). As a result of shipping 112 goals in 26 games, Darwen finished bottom, and were shunted into a new Second Division, the Football League's runaway popularity having necessitated an expansion.

Sunderland surpassed themselves in 1892–93, the first season under the new First Division banner. They became the first team to score 100 times in a season, reaching the mark with their third and final goal of their last match at Burnley. They hit five on four occasions, six five times, and eight once. Campbell helped himself to 30 this time. Sunderland's scoring record, set over 30 matches, would not be beaten until 1919–20, by which time the League had been extended and West Bromwich Albion had a dozen extra matches in which to surpass it. Preston, runners-up for the third season in a row, stumbled home 11 points off the pace. Their Double-winning Invincibles team already seemed a speck in the rear-view mirror; Watson and Sunderland had taken things up a notch.

Serendipity played a big role in the early development of Aston Villa. One misty winter's morning, late in 1876, 21-year-old clerical worker George Ramsay took a stroll through the grounds of Jacobean pile Aston Hall. He spotted a few chaps enjoying a kick-about. After asking a couple of times whether it was possible to join in – his thick Glaswegian brogue took a little deciphering – he was soon bossing the game with his almost comically superior close control, dribbling, body swerves and feints. Without knowing it, he had just made a complete show of the entire Villa team, who had been practising the more basic hoof-and-rush style. Not too proud to look a gift horse in the mouth, the Villa players begged for some on-the-spot tuition. Ramsay was persuaded to join the club. He was unanimously elected as a member, and quickly installed as captain.

Ramsay was a graduate of the Glasgow school, well versed in the more-refined Scottish passing game. Under his tutelage, Villa became one of the top teams in England during the 1880s, and their lust for proper competition had, of course, inspired director William McGregor to set up the League. Villa's star man was Archie Hunter, who like Ramsay ended up at the club by accident rather than design (having, like McGregor, moved to Birmingham from Scotland to start a drapery business). Hunter had once faced local side Calthorpe while playing as a striker for Ayr Thistle, so decided to pay the West Midlands club a visit in the hope of getting a game. But he got lost on his way to the ground and doubled back. Before he could plan another odyssey, a business associate persuaded him to try out for Villa instead, pointing out that quite a few Scotsmen were already at the club, most notably the main man Ramsay. Hunter was instantly up to speed with Villa's quick-passing philosophy, and eventually took over as captain when Ramsay quit playing to concentrate on a secretarial-managerial role.

Hunter was the complete package. He could run, dribble and shoot hard. His twin specialities were spraying long passes out to the wingers – then a novel tactic – and fending off challenges by turning and sticking out his ample backside, a bootylicious skill copied much later by Kenny Dalglish and Mark Hughes. Hunter scored in every round of the FA Cup as Villa won the competition in 1887. The only thing he couldn't boast was good health. He suffered a stroke on the field against Everton in 1890 and never played again. Four years later he fell victim to consumption, aged 35. He passed away in a hotel room near Perry Barr. One of his last wishes, during a Saturday hubbub, was to insist his heavy brass bed be pushed towards the window so he could see and hear the Villa faithful traipsing to the match.

At least Villa's beloved former captain lived to see the club's first title. By 1893–94, Villa boasted three new heroes: free-scoring striker and captain Jack Devey, tricky winger Charlie Athersmith, and statesmanlike defender James Cowan. All were exceptional; all had their eccentricities. During one match against Sheffield United in 1894, a sleet storm was so biting that Devey pulled on an overcoat borrowed from a spectator; Athersmith patrolled his wing holding an umbrella. Cowan meanwhile was a superb organiser who calmly played out from the back. He regularly embarked on long dribbles upfield, and from overly ambitious distances would blooter shots miles over the bar. The crowd affectionately referred to these comedic efforts as Cowan's Skyscrapers.

Cowan could also shift like greased lightning, and at one point decided to earn some extra money competing in the Powderhall

Sprint, a famous handicap race held in Edinburgh every New Year. Correctly surmising that Villa would not want their star defender running for prizes when there were football matches to play, Cowan devised a fictional back injury and swanned off to his native Scotland to 'recuperate'. He won the race in 12.5 seconds and pocketed £80, but was hit with a four-week suspension upon his return to the club. His winnings offset the fine levied by some distance. His teammate Athersmith wasn't so fortunate: he ended up out of pocket as a result of the caper, having placed a large sum on Cowan with an Edinburgh bookmaker who subsequently disappeared rather than paying up.

Villa won the 1893–94 title at a canter. A run of nine wins in ten games between late October and the middle of December sent them clear at the top. Only reigning champions Sunderland kept up the pretence of a challenge, but they still ended six points off the pace. Down at the bottom, Preston, who during the first five years of the League were either champions or runners-up, finished 14th out of 16, their golden years over with a jolt. They survived relegation to the Second Division by the skin of their teeth, winning a Test Match – a play-off to determine divisional status – with Notts County.

On the opening day of the 1894–95 season, new champions Villa faced newly promoted Small Heath, later to become Birmingham City. The Football League's very first second-city derby started in sensational fashion, Small Heath scoring within a minute, though Villa bounced back for a 2–1 win. But up north, Sunderland's Team of All the Talents made quite a statement of intent against Derby County. The match had kicked off 20 minutes late under the auspices of a stand-in official, the appointed referee Tom Kirkham having missed his train. Sunderland led 3–0 at half-time, at which point Kirkham belatedly arrived and pompously ordered the game to be restarted with him on whistle duty. A miffed Sunderland went on to replicate the 3–0 half-time scoreline, before scoring five more in the second against a clearly knackered Derby. Eleven goals scored in an 8–0 win played over three halves. Go figure.

Sunderland won 12 of their first 15 matches, then eight of their last ten, to regain their title. It was a last hurrah for the Team of All the Talents. Having become the first club to win three championships, Sunderland struggled for goals in 1895–96, and inspirational manager Watson upped sticks for upwardly mobile Liverpool. Sunderland's form fell off a cliff. They finished 15th out of 16 in 1896–97, surviving relegation only via the Test Matches. Still, they'd set that bar high.

But Villa were preparing to take a run at clearing it. George Ramsay's side secured their second title in 1895–96, then became the second team to win the League and FA Cup Double in 1896–97, finishing top of the table, clear of second-placed Sheffield United by a hefty 11 points. A hat-trick of titles would prove beyond them, though sixth place in 1897–98 proved to be merely a brief interregnum: Villa were midway through a run of dominance which has subsequently been matched only by Arsenal in the 1930s, Liverpool in the 1970s and 1980s, and Manchester United during the Premier League era.

The plot of land where the old Adelphi Hotel used to stand, on Arundel Street in Sheffield, is one of the sacred sites of sport. It's now the location of the Crucible Theatre, host venue of the Snooker World Championships since 1977. Steve Davis against Dennis Taylor, Alex Higgins against Ray Reardon, Stephen Hendry against Jimmy White, Ronnie O'Sullivan against himself: those battles alone are enough to qualify it as one of the most famous locations in the history of competitive endeavour, along-side Wembley, the Maracanã, Lord's and the Colosseum in Rome. But the old Adelphi had a big role in the story too: it was where Yorkshire County Cricket Club, The Wednesday Football Club, and the Sheffield United Cricket Club were formed. The latter led to the building of the Bramall Lane cricket and football stadium, which in turn begat a soccer team, also called Sheffield United.

The first-ever football match between two separate clubs took place in Sheffield: in a Boxing Day snowstorm, Sheffield FC beat Hallam 2–0 in 1860. A couple of years later, the same teams met in a charity match to raise funds for soldiers who had fought in the ongoing American Civil War. The game ended in a dukes-up fistfight after Sheffield's star player Major Nathaniel Creswick – one of the men behind the Sheffield Rules – clattered opposite number William Waterfall in the face in an attempt to win the ball. Waterfall threw down his waistcoat in a fit of pique and rained blows upon Creswick, who reportedly remained indifferent throughout. Never forget Sheffield's envelope pushing in football's early days: one of the first rulebooks, the first club match, the first hot-faced brawl. Thank you, Steel City!

But there was no Sheffield representation when the Football League was formed: William McGregor's baby was a stitch-up between the Midlands and the north-west. The Wednesday – named after the cricket club from which it sprung, in turn named after the day it played its matches – had to make do with joining the Football Alliance, another League-a-like confection launched in 1889. The Wednesday won the first staging of the Alliance, then came bottom a year later, before finishing fourth in what proved to be the third and final season of the competition. The Alliance was disbanded in 1892, effectively merging with the expanding Football League. Most of its members joined the new

Second Division, though winners Nottingham Forest and two of that season's other high finishers – The Wednesday and erstwhile Combination toppers Newton Heath – went into the newly re-titled First Division.

Sheffield United were not available for selection as a founding member of the League, formed a year too late in 1889. They were then overlooked for a place in the Alliance. So they spent their first three years juggling friendlies with stints in the Midland Counties and Northern leagues. An ambitious application to join the First Division of the expanded Football League in 1892 was predictably turned down, though a place in the new Second wasn't a bad consolation for a club not inclined to faff about.

The dashing young Blades won instant promotion. Their early moxie was personified by small but powerful striker Harry Hammond, who played one match for Everton during the 1889–90 season, and seemed determined not to waste his second chance of glory. Hammond claimed a hat-trick in United's first League fixture, a 4–2 win over Lincoln; not long after, he rattled up five in an 8–3 victory against Bootle. United went to Burslem Port Vale and, in a snowstorm, won 10–0, a score which still stands as a League record away victory. Hammond scored four this time, though was upstaged by a former Vale player who, refreshed from a lunchtime session in the drinker and incensed at what was unfolding in front of his increasingly flushed face, rushed the pitch three times in order to demonstrate the art of dribbling to his inept successors. Blades captain Billy Hendry eventually apprehended the interloper, lifting him off the ground and dumping him head-first into a pile of pitchside snow.

Hammond's will to win sometimes got the better of him, and he was sent off during a 4–0 win at Crewe for needlessly toe-punting an opponent up the jacksie. The home fans invaded the pitch in order to avenge their stricken player. Hammond avoided their grasp with a couple of slippery swerves, turned tail, hopped over a wall at one end of the ground, and made off into the town. He resurfaced a couple of hours later at the train station, where his teammates were waiting to make their journey back home. Hammond was still in his kit; whether any of his pals had remembered to gather up his civvies is not recorded. United went on to finish second and made the First Division via a play-off with League founder member Accrington, who having made very little impression in the five seasons since 1888, resigned from the League altogether rather than take up a place in the Second.

After three seasons of top-flight consolidation, United finished runners-up to Double-winning Aston Villa in 1896–97. They trailed the champions by 11 points, but laid down a marker nonetheless, for their defence had become exceptionally hard to breach. With 21-stone William 'Fatty' Foulke in goal, United conceded just 29 times, by some distance the best record in the division. They were clearly a resilient bunch, something they proved conclusively during their championship season of 1897–98, in which they successfully faced down the League's two big beasts, wriggling off the ropes when all looked lost.

United built up an early lead, thanks to a run of five wins in October, only to stumble during the fall: no wins during November or December frittered away their cushion. Champions Villa were coming up on the rail, and could take over the leadership if they prevailed in back-to-back January fixtures between the clubs. But United beat them 1–0 at Bramall Lane, then willed their way to a staunch victory at Perry Barr, where the home side had not lost all season. In front of 40,000 punters, generating a record-breaking gate of £1,300, United lost striker Ralph Gaudie to a broken nose and fell behind early in the second half. But their defence characteristically stood strong as Villa pressed hard for a second. Gaudie was thrown back on, and his determined presence slowly changed the momentum. An equaliser was scrambled against the run of play, Gaudie claimed the decider late on, and suddenly there was daylight again between the teams.

Having seen off Villa, United moved seven points clear at the top. But now Sunderland were in pursuit, and the pressure of being hunted by another three-time title winning club looked like telling. Three defeats in four, including a sound 3–1 beating at Sunderland, saw United's lead evaporate. Sunderland came to Bramall Lane in early April knowing that a win would take them top; United went into this crucial return without their captain and all-purpose hero Ernest Needham, away helping England to victory over Scotland. No matter! United ground out a 1–0 win, a result which removed all the wind from Sunderland's sails. Needham returned for a Good Friday fixture at Bolton, scoring the only goal with a dazzling dribble. Sunderland meanwhile lost at Bury, and United were champions.

This Blades team had more to prove. They would beat Scottish champions Celtic in a prestigious friendly; finish second behind Villa in 1899–1900; and reach the FA Cup final three times in four seasons between 1899 and 1902, winning the old pot twice. But as far as League titles went, it was a one-off. Villa re-emerged from the pack, and set about claiming another pair of back-to-back titles. 'One can safely say that no team will set aside such a record as that,' opined one William McGregor. Give it time, Old Mac, give it time.

The first of those championships, in 1898–99, was claimed in extraordinary circumstances. Liverpool should have won it. Tom

Watson, during his first couple of years on Merseyside since his big-money move from Sunderland, built Liverpool into a formidable unit. He implemented much the same design strategy so successful in the north-east: plunder Scotland for the best talent and send them out to do their thing. Tom Robertson and John Walker came in from Heart of Midlothian to offer width, strikers George Allan and Hugh Morgan arrived from Celtic and St Mirren, and domineering box-to-box genius Alex Raisbeck, the Souness/Gerrard of his day, was sourced from Hibernian. Jack Cox, a zippy winger, offered a dash of local spirit.

Between mid-January and mid-March, Liverpool won seven successive matches. They reached the top of the League, and the semi-finals of the FA Cup. But their exploits in the knockout competition would prove their undoing. They faced reigning League champions Sheffield United, and were 20 minutes from the final before shipping an equaliser. The subsequent replay was an unmitigated fiasco. Liverpool twice found themselves two goals clear – only to let United claw themselves level on both occasions. At 4–2 up, and with eight minutes to play, their goalkeeper Harry Storer went into meltdown, gifting United forward Fred Priest two goals in three minutes. The 4–4 draw severely dented Liverpool's confidence. Storer was dropped by a livid Watson and replaced by 35-year-old Matt McQueen, who was far from a specialist in the position, having spent half of his career as a winger. McQueen picked the ball out of the net repeatedly as Liverpool lost their next two League fixtures, plus the second semi-final replay.

Bill Perkins, newly signed from Luton Town, took over in goal, and his arrival helped Liverpool regain a sense of equilibrium. The ship seemingly steadied, they won their next four games, a run that took them two points clear of second-placed Villa with one match left. They also had a superior goal average. But Villa had a game in hand, and boy would they make it count.

Villa's form during February, March and most of April had been little short of appalling: one win in ten. But they suddenly clicked into action when it mattered. In their antepenultimate fixture, they battered Notts County 6–1. Next up, in the game they held in hand, West Bromwich Albion were trounced 7–1. That win allowed Villa to squeak into pole position, level on points with Liverpool but 0.02 of a goal ahead. Suspicions were raised at Villa's sudden upturn in form. The man from the *Sporting Life* paper opined that it 'did look as if somebody had not been trying'. An incandescent (and unidentified) West Brom player rejected the claim, suggesting everyone wait to see what happened in the final match of the season – when the top two played each other in the title decider!

His point was a fair one. Liverpool went to Villa Park needing to win, fell behind to Jack Devey's fourth-minute header, then found themselves five goals adrift by half-time. They had been playing into a strong wind, but it was still no excuse: this was another craven capitulation to file alongside the FA Cup collapse. None of which should detract from the manner in which Villa won the title: 18 goals from their last three games in a single week, from a point of no return. 'If we cannot retain the title next season,' said a gracious Devey as he scooped the trophy, 'I hope Liverpool win it.'

But Villa did retain it, winning the first championship of the new century by seeing off another spirited Sheffield United challenge. Liverpool meanwhile went into glorious meltdown. They lost the first eight games of the 1899–1900 campaign amid rumours of Herculean levels of boozing within the squad. Rock bottom of the division, they found themselves five humiliating points behind

Glossop, a small-town project funded by Samuel Hill-Wood, the young Eton-educated son of a Derbyshire mill owner.

Master Hill-Wood had decided that ploughing money into his local team, and seeing how far they could get, would be a wizard wheeze. Calling in a few favours from well-connected Tory pals, he managed to get the club elected to the Second Division in 1898. He enticed some Scottish players down south with big wages and jobs at the mill – the star turn was the splendidly monickered defender James 'Punch' McEwan – and Glossop won immediate promotion, finishing the 1898–99 season just behind Manchester City but ahead of another local rival in Newton Heath.

Glossop's sole season in the sun proved to be a mixed bag. They were whipped 9–0 at Villa Park in their second game in the top flight, but quite deliciously got their revenge over the reigning champions in mid-December, beating them 1–0 at home. A crowd of only 6,000 witnessed that seismic shock, though the attendance sounds a damn sight more impressive when you consider it constituted a third of the town's population. There was clearly some decent talent in the side: Punch McEwan went on to win the FA Cup with Bury, 'Graceful Arthur' Goddard later won the League with Liverpool, and Herbert Burgess became a title-winner with Manchester United and manager of Roma. But over the whole piece it was all too much. The Villa win was one of only four all season, and Glossop found themselves dumped straight back into the Second. Hill-Wood lost interest, and the club eventually slipped out of the League in 1915. Glossop remains the smallest town in the country to have ever hosted top-flight football, while Hill-Wood took control of Arsenal in the late twenties, and would enjoy a much more successful crack at First Division life second time around.

Liverpool finally won a couple of games, clambering above Glossop in November. But they were still in all sorts of trouble, second bottom, come January. The mood was grim, not helped by the death of striker George Allan, who had succumbed to tuberculosis a couple of months earlier. But Watson raised spirits with another wily signing, Sam Raybould from New Brighton Tower. Raybould scored seven times as Liverpool won nine of their last 11 matches, finishing comfortably in mid-table. It was a remarkable turnaround, and Liverpool's restored confidence continued into the 1900–01 season. They won five of their first seven, and then, in an unbeaten sequence that began at Watson's old club Sunderland, nine of their last 12. Liverpool secured their first title after doing what they couldn't do at Villa Park two years earlier: holding their nerve in the final game. Requiring just a draw at West Bromwich Albion to pip Sunderland, they won 1–0, Johnny Walker bundling home after Raybould's long shot had caused all manner of panic.

Watson thus became the first manager to win the title with two clubs. His fourth personal championship victory put him one behind George Ramsay on the roll of honour. Two of the greatest managers of all time, all right. And neither was finished quite yet.

2

Colin and Toffee Bob lead the renaissance (1901–02 to 1908–09)

The Bally Manufacturing Co. of Chicago, Illinois is commonly credited with the invention of multiball, a groundbreaking feature of its 1956 nine-ball pinball table Balls-a-Poppin. But the concept was old hat. Turns out a handful of cynical Victorian soccer players from the north-west of England had beaten the glamorous American leisure specialists to the punch by nearly 60 years.

The 1898 Test Match between Burnley and Stoke was a risible fiasco. At that point in time, the Second Division was only six years old, and the Football League had yet to settle on a sensible method of shuttling clubs between the divisions on merit. There was no automatic promotion and relegation at the end of each campaign: next season's status was instead determined by the outcome of Tests between teams at the bottom of the First and top of the Second. Initially these were simple-to-understand winner-takes-all ties, but the format soon morphed into a mini-league which hadn't been thought through properly. It wasn't quite a round-robin: teams faced the sides from the other division twice, but didn't get to play the club from their own division at all. Lop-sided injustice was inevitable.

The 1898 Tests saw First Division stragglers Blackburn Rovers and Stoke bundled together with Second Division success stories Burnley and Newcastle United. The matches panned out in such a way that Burnley and Stoke went into their final meeting knowing a draw would send Burnley up while maintaining Stoke's top-flight status, and there was nothing Blackburn or Newcastle could do to stop them. The resulting goalless borefest was as grimly predictable as it was lacklustre, though the brazen lack of subtlety on show proved too much even for a partisan crowd fully aware that the pact ensured First Division football for all concerned.

Both sides were clearly 'devoid of interest and energy', according to one spectator account. There were no shots on goal. The players repeatedly hoofed the ball into touch, only interested in letting the clock run down. A couple of so-called passes were deliberately hoicked straight out of the ground. The crowd, having paid precious coin and therefore rather incensed at the abject nonsense unfolding in front of them, fetched the balls back and dispatched them onto the field of play by way of protest. The pattern kept repeating, and at one point, five balls were a-poppin around the pitch. 'It is impossible to ignore the fact that these Test games have proved an utter farce,' ran a hard-hitting editorial in the *Manchester Guardian*. 'A change of some kind is absolutely necessary if the contests are in future to be regarded with any seriousness. We leave the problem to the League with our commiseration.'

After a month-long controversy, the powers-that-be decided to expand the First Division, offering Blackburn and Newcastle instant promotion by way of recompense. It was a decision that would have a lasting impact on the game – partly because the Tests were abolished and a new system of automatic promotion and relegation was put in place, but also because Newcastle, having reached the top flight at last, were now finally able to lock horns with Sunderland. Both clubs would exert a huge influence on the Football League, and each other's destinies, over the next decade.

The rivalry made an instant impact. The very first Tyne and Wear derby, played on Christmas Eve 1898, saw a crowd of 30,000 congregate at Sunderland's new Roker Park. Twenty special trains were chartered to cart Newcastle's support 15 miles south. The visitors, struggling at the foot of the table, earned themselves a priceless 3–2 win. Toon striker Jock Peddie – a cult player at best, if the contemporaneous reports describing him variously as 'highly praised', 'roundly abused' and 'aggravatingly slow' are anything to go by – was the two-goal hero. A buoyed Newcastle ended the season comfortably in mid-table. This allowed them to take their turn in hosting the Christmas party exactly one year later, whereupon they let a 2–1 half-time lead slip, crashing to a 4–2 defeat. But this was only the first rise and dip of the rollercoaster.

Newcastle were getting close to something special by 1901–02. They had the best defence in the country, though goals were sometimes a problem. Sometimes. In the first eight matches of the campaign, they failed to score on five occasions. In the ninth, they beat Notts County 8–0. In the hope of finding a little more consistency, they signed one of the great amateurs of the day from Queen's Park in Scotland. Robert Smyth McColl came to prominence in 1899 after scoring hat-tricks in consecutive matches for Scotland against Wales and Ireland. A year later, wearing the primrose-and-rose hoops of Scottish FA patron Lord Rosebery, who was watching Scotland play for the very first time, McColl scored another hat-trick in a 4–1 rout of the old enemy England. (For the record, he had set up Scotland's other goal that day, and pinged another shot off a post.)

However if there's one sure thing in football, it's that there are no sure things in football. McColl's international scoring record of 13 in 13 was a mite deceptive, as he wasn't an out-and-out goal-getter. In three seasons with Newcastle United, he would only score 20 times. His goals wouldn't be enough to propel the Toon to the 1901–02 title. But in the long run, that wasn't really the point. McColl brought some Scottish suss to Newcastle, passing on all his knowledge, expertise and experience to Colin Veitch, a young local polymath who was all ears.

Veitch was smarter than your average footballer. Steeped in the arts, he has been described variously as a scholar, playwright, theatre impresario, producer, composer and conductor. A local public school asked him to become their headmaster. The Labour Party wondered whether he'd stand as a Member of Parliament. He was buddies with George Bernard Shaw, for goodness sake. This Renaissance man was also a versatile midfielder, and soaked up McColl's teachings like a sponge. His thirst for knowledge would stand Newcastle in good stead over the next few years. But not quite yet: before the trophies started rolling in, McColl returned to Scotland in 1904, first to play for Rangers and Queen's Park, then to set up a sweetie shop bearing his name. 'Toffee Bob', as McColl became known, grew R. S. McColl into one of the biggest newsagent chains in the country.

Sunderland, pipped at the post by Liverpool the previous season, won the 1901–02 title. It was an easy, drama-free success, and their first of the post-Tom Watson era. Only goalkeeper Ned Doig and striker Jimmy Millar remained from the Team of All the Talents. Defender Sandy McAllister was the only ever-present, and was rewarded by grateful fans with a piano. (Promising young local Alf Common didn't last so long: he started the season in Sunderland's forward line, but was sold to Sheffield United early on for £350. He returned to Sunderland before being offloaded to Middlesbrough in 1905 as the world's first-ever £1,000 transfer, the last notable mark he left on the game.)

Sunderland should have retained their title in 1902–1903, but gave it up in excruciating circumstances. In March, they entertained fellow championship challengers The Wednesday at Roker Park. Had they won, they would have gone top, ahead of their guests with three games in hand. But Doig and McAllister were injured and missing, as was Andy McCombie, a third component of a defence that had been by some distance the best in the country. Wednesday scrapped hard and won a tight match by a single Andrew Wilson goal. On the way home, their coach was pelted with stones by incandescent locals. Sunderland were forced to close Roker for a week as punishment, so played their first-ever home League derby against north-east rivals Middlesbrough at – where else? – the ground of Newcastle United.

The match against Boro was Sunderland's penultimate of the season. They won it 2–1, a result which placed them a point behind The Wednesday, who had completed their fixture list. (Neither team had exactly ripped it up during the run-in.) The destiny of the title was in Sunderland's hands, though their last game was, like the one before it, also at St James' Park. Only this time, it was against their bitter rivals Newcastle. Ludicrous rumours flew about, claiming that Newcastle were happy to throw the match to ensure the championship stayed in the north-east. Such innocence! Newcastle put paid to that notion with a battling defensive display against a slightly manic Sunderland. They scored the only goal in the second half, Toffee Bob with a sweet strike that ensured their arch enemies came unstuck.

Sunderland didn't even finish as runners-up. Aston Villa pipped them for second place on goal average with five wins and 15 goals in the last 15 days of their campaign. The final match of that particular snatch-and-grab was a 5–0 triumph over Middlesbrough: another of Sunderland's local rivals adding to their pain. The Wednesday were the champions, though their final points haul of 42 was the lowest winning total by a title-winning side in an 18-team division. There was plenty of media comment suggesting the Owls had entered the pantheon in a rather cheap manner. The new champions responded to the criticism by losing only one of the first 11 games of the 1903–04 campaign, then building on that start by winning nine in 11 between January and March. They retained their title comfortably, three points ahead of Manchester City, this time with a healthy total of 47.

Harry Chapman – whose brother Herbert would have something to say soon enough – was the top marksman in both of Wednesday's championship seasons. But Andrew Wilson was most beloved by the fans, a fact best illustrated by the paranoid panic which gripped Sheffield in early 1904. Wilson had taken a whack to the head against Nottingham Forest, an injury that caused him to miss several matches. A rumour quickly spread that he had died, the situation not helped by one local trader announcing the supposedly tragic news by posting it in his shop window. Wilson was in fact alive and, if not well, then recuperating quickly. He went on to play for the club until 1920, scoring 216 goals in 540 games. Twitter and its concomitant world of unverified nonsense is merely a modern twist on an age-old phenomenon.

Wednesday's real strength, though, had been at the back. In 34 games, they had only let in 28 goals. With the exception of third-placed Everton, similarly parsimonious with just 32 conceded, no team got within 17 goals of that record. On the flip side, their goals-for total was a mere 48.

In a glorious statistical quirk, Liverpool managed to get themselves relegated that same season having scored 49. It was the first major setback in Tom Watson's career, a result of a long-term injury to Sam Raybould and the coldest of cold starts, five losses in a row that could never quite be clawed back. Watson would not take this personal affront lying down.

In late November 1904 Everton travelled south to face the first club from the capital to reach the First Division: Woolwich Arsenal. The recently promoted Londoners were a mid-table concern, though they boasted an above-average defence. Everton blew the misers away with an irresistible display of attacking verve, and were closing in on a 3–1 victory when, with minutes remaining on the clock, the referee inexplicably abandoned the game due to fog. Was the weather a good old-fashioned London pea-souper, or merely a few wisps of mist? It was never fully established. What is certain is that Everton, in total command with the game wrapped up and the clock ticking down, were livid when the whistle blew. Two thoroughly deserved points had been wrested from their grasp.

The repercussions of that abandonment were grim for Everton. Bureaucratic efficiency was still very much a pipe dream in the infant world of professional football, and the fixture could not be replayed until April. It was eventually shoehorned into Everton's hectic end-of-season schedule, 24 hours after a defeat at Manchester City. Arsenal beat an exhausted Everton, who went on to finish the 1904–1905 season one point shy of top spot. The win unfairly snatched away in November couldn't have been more costly. The gods of weather owed Everton a little sunshine.

Spin it another way, though, and Everton had lost two of their last three, hardly the sort of *carpe diem* behaviour that wins titles. Fellow hopefuls Newcastle United, by contrast, were determined not to let their opportunity slip. It initially looked as though they would stutter horribly during the run-in, too. Sunderland – who else? – appeared to have put the kibosh on Newcastle's title bid three matches from the finishing line with a 3–1 win at St James' Park. That left Newcastle having to win their last two games, both away, to have any hope of pipping Everton.

The first was at outgoing champions The Wednesday, and having fell behind early, Newcastle were still a goal down with 11 minutes remaining. But inside-forward Ronald Orr refused to kowtow to fate. After sending in a few speculative long-range efforts to unnerve previously dominant opponents, his relentless pressing led to two Jimmy Howie goals, and he sealed the win himself with a late penalty. Then in the final game of the season at Middlesbrough, Orr whistled home a low shot after five minutes, setting the tone for a 3–0 win that gave Newcastle the 1904–05 title, their first.

They won their second two years later. Their 1906–07 success was a far less stressful affair: they led since January, and virtually sealed the deal at the end of March with a 3–0 win over newly promoted surprise challengers Bristol City, although they made a slap-up meal of gaining the very last point they needed, losing at Notts County before eventually claiming it after a dour goalless draw at home to Sheffield United. Orr, the hero of the first title win, had a poor game, and his every touch was booed. It was nothing personal, though: at the final whistle, the Newcastle crowd, who had hoped to witness a celebratory rout, treated every single member of the freshly crowned champion team to a cavalcade of catcalls. It was the first time Newcastle had failed to win at home all season.

In between times, Liverpool became the first newly promoted side to win the title in 1905–06. They had been relegated two seasons previously, their defence palpably no longer fit for purpose. The jig looked up for the club in more ways than one: founder John Houlding had recently died, and it wasn't totally clear whether those left in charge could be bothered to continue. There were rumours of plans to build houses on Anfield; the very existence of Liverpool was in doubt.

Tom Watson ploughed on, though, providing the necessary boost to morale. He brought in his trusty old pal Ned Doig from Sunderland, and the 37-year-old veteran keeper's experience helped Liverpool rediscover their confidence at the back. In the much easier Second Division, spirit was quickly re-established and spread throughout the team. Liverpool bounced straight back to the top flight at the first attempt, winning 27 of their 34 matches, scoring 93 times and letting in just 25. It was enough to change the mood music around the club, and Liverpool soon found themselves on sound financial footing again.

Not that everything had been immediately fixed with one swish of the Watson wand. Liverpool started the 1905–06 season terribly slowly, losing five of their first eight matches, disturbing shades of their recent relegation season. The run saw them concede four goals at Everton and five at Aston Villa. But this time Watson was able to effect a turnaround. And how. He replaced the quick-fix Doig with the younger Sam Hardy, and gave striker Joe Hewitt a chance up front. A run of nine wins in ten took Liverpool top by Christmas, and though Preston North End kept them honest until April, their title win was rarely in doubt.

This was Watson's last hurrah. Liverpool finished runners-up to Aston Villa in 1909–10, and Watson took the club to a first FA Cup final in 1914, which his team lost to Burnley. He died suddenly a year later, cut down by pneumonia and pleurisy. The faithful Doig, who had won three titles with Watson at Sunderland, and Alex Raisbeck, the undoubted star of the manager's two championship teams on Merseyside, helped carry the coffin to an unmarked grave in Anfield Cemetery. Doig fell victim to the Spanish flu pandemic four years later. He was buried in the same grounds, less than 20 yards from his old boss.

Something had been stirring in Manchester. City had come to prominence in the 1903–04 season, finishing runners-up to The Wednesday while scoring 23 more goals than the champions. Their star player was toothpick-chewing Billy Meredith, a winger of outrageous skill and rapidly increasing fame. He scored the winning goal in that season's FA Cup final, selling Bolton Wanderers keeper Dai Davies an outrageous dummy, shaping to cross only to batter a surprise shot into the top corner from a tight angle. 'You will forgive my natural partiality and excuse me for expressing my satisfaction at Manchester's success,' simpered guest of honour Arthur Balfour, the prime minister and member for the Manchester East constituency, in a post-match speech, before adding with uncharacteristic self-deprecation: 'I can only speak to you as an admiring ignoramus . . . what a gallant fight has been fought!'

A rather less honourable throwing of hands occurred at the end of the following season. City were involved in the 1904–05 title race that eventually saw Newcastle United pip Everton by a point. In with a shout on the final day, they needed to win at Aston Villa to have any sort of chance. Meredith was, for once, a complete bystander as City went down 3–2. As a result, they finished the season third, though another near miss proved to be the least of their worries. The match had ended in robust fashion: Villa captain Alec Leake threw mud at City's Sandy Turnbull, who reacted by waving a stiff two fingers in his opponent's face. The two ended up trading blows and were fortunate not to be sent off. Afterwards, still fuming, Leake claimed that Meredith had offered him a £10 bribe to throw the match. Meredith denied the accusation, but was banned for a year anyway. He then received an additional suspension for asking City to pay him during his ban. The FA, their interest in City's financial affairs piqued, found the club were offering players a host of illegal inducements. At the end of the 1905–06 season, seventeen players – nearly the entire first-team squad – were suspended and fined, while manager Tom Maley received a *sine die* ban. City were forced to put up their squad for auction at the local Queen's Hotel that November.

While City were unravelling, another force was rising across town. Newton Heath joined the new First Division when the Football League and Alliance League merged in 1892–93. They finished bottom in their first campaign but retained their status upon winning a Test Match against Small Heath only to finish bottom again in 1893–94. This time they lost the Test against upwardly mobile Liverpool, and became only the second club, after Darwen, to suffer relegation. Newton Heath found it impossible to bounce back, and by 1901 were in dire financial straits. In a fit of desperation, they decided to stage a fundraising bazaar. The result initially appeared farcical: when the cost of hiring a hall was factored in, barely a bronze centime of profit had been turned.

But there's more than one way to skin a cat. The club captain Harry Stafford had brought his St Bernard dog, Major, along to the bazaar, strapping a collection tin around its neck and letting it mooch around in search of coins. Predictably enough, poor Major got lost, and was eventually found by a friend of local brewing magnate John Davies. His daughter having fallen in love with Major, Davies went off in search of the owner with a view to purchasing the mutt. Sweet serendipity: Davies and Stafford got talking about Newton Heath, sewing a seed in the brewer's mind, and when the club was threatened with a winding-up order a year later, Davies and three friends stumped up the cash to save the club. A rebrand was mooted. According to the *Manchester Evening News*, 'one old supporter suggested that the name of the club should be changed to Manchester United, but this did not meet with much favour'. However after Manchester Celtic and Manchester Central were given short shrift, and with nobody able to come up with anything better, the United suggestion was rubber-stamped in true that'll-do fashion. Major was given a treat for being a good boy.

In 1903 the all-new Manchester United gave their manager's job to Ernest Mangnall, a smooth operator who had kept nearby Burnley afloat during some difficult times. The dapper Mangnall – all clipped moustache and straw boater – set about hauling the club out of the Second Division. His game-changing purchase was Charlie Roberts. An incongruous sight in 1980s-style thigh-high shorts – the authorities tried to force him into contemporaneous knee-covering breeches, to no avail – Roberts was similarly ahead of the game as a ball-playing defender. As captain, he calmly guided United to promotion in 1905–06.

United won their first match in the top flight since the days of Newton Heath, beating a Bristol City side also freshly promoted and destined to finish second behind Newcastle. Manchester City, however, did not start the 1906–07 season quite so impressively. Effectively a team of new recruits in the wake of their close-season punishment, they went down 4–1 at home to Woolwich Arsenal. The result can partly be put down to the extraordinary heatwave burning up the country: the *Manchester Guardian* rather over-excitedly claimed that the thermometer was at '120 degrees Fahrenheit', though it was certainly over 90. City, parched and frazzled, ended the game with just six players left standing, having endured 'toils which would have meant death to ordinary men'. But even the partisan local paper could only stretch the point so far. 'It was clear that City were in poor condition for a professional football side.'

City followed that horror show two days later by crashing 9–1 at Everton. 'The City players were thought to have recovered from Saturday's prostration,' reported the *Manchester Guardian*, 'but the result of the play showed the effects still remained.' The result remains Everton's biggest victory in League history, the weather gods giving them a little something back for the fog-bound farce that cost them the 1904–05 title.

City eventually regrouped and ended the season comfortably clear of the relegation places, though there were still two other huge blows to suffer during that campaign. Billy Meredith, still suspended, crossed town to join United in October 1906. Then a month later, Ernest Mangnall insouciantly sashayed through the foyer of the Queen's Hotel, past other club managers waiting patiently and politely for the official start of the City player auction, and brazenly struck agreements to sign forward Sandy Turnbull, defender Herbert Burgess and winger Jimmy Bannister, before swanning back out into the bracing Mancunian evening.

Meredith, Turnbull, Bannister and Burgess all made their debut on New Year's Day 1907, returning to football after their suspensions. United's Bank Street ground crackled with anticipation. Aston Villa were beaten 1–0, Meredith dribbling at pace down the right before fizzing in a low cross for Turnbull to convert. Before Mangnall's machinations, relegation straight back to the Second had been a very real possibility, but United went on to win ten of their last 15 games, ending their first season back in the top flight in a comfortable top-half position.

The statement of intent rang loud and clear. Mangnall's side flew out of the blocks in 1907–08. Before October was out, they had put four past Aston Villa, Liverpool, Chelsea and Nottingham Forest, five past Blackburn Rovers, and six past the reigning champions Newcastle United on their own turf. A wobble after the New Year culminated in a surreal 7–4 loss at Liverpool, but United responded with a 4–1 win over The Wednesday and eventually sauntered to their first title, nine clear of Aston Villa and a resurgent Manchester City. A *briefly* resurgent Manchester City.

Newcastle won their third title in five years in 1908–09. It was their most dominant display yet. Colin Veitch conducted his team to ten wins in 11 games between January and March; the title was wrapped up when nearest challengers Everton were soundly beaten 3–0 in early April; and the team set a new points record of 53, which could have been a lot more had they not taken their foot off the gas and lost three of their last five matches with the hard yards already covered.

Newcastle being Newcastle, of course, all this exquisite mastery was somewhat offset by the most surreal Tyne–Wear derby yet. Sunderland had travelled to St James' Park in early December; at half-time the score was one apiece. What happened next beggared belief, as Newcastle crumbled in the second period in front of

50,000 mouths agape. George Holley and Billy Hogg both claimed hat-tricks, Arthur Bridgett grabbed a couple more, and the whistle blew on a 9–1 Sunderland victory, still the largest away win in the top flight of English football.

A few miles down the road, the Sunderland and Newcastle reserve teams were taking each other on at Roker Park, where the latest score of the League fixture was being displayed on a board by the touchline. But as the goals started flying in, and the numbers began ticking over at an increasingly surreal rate, the crowd became agitated. Several punters became convinced that the scoreboard operator was in on some sort of joke, playing them for fools. They surrounded the hapless messenger and gave him an advisory shoeing. While it would be difficult to condone such an extreme, unreasonable response, the logic leading to the larruping was sound: to put the 1–9 result in some sort of context, in their previous 15 games, Newcastle had only conceded 13 times.

At least Newcastle's local embarrassment could be played down by the end of an otherwise wildly successful season. Manchester City also embraced haplessness with gusto, but their story had no similarly happy ending. At the start of April, after back-to-back 4–0 wins over The Wednesday and Liverpool, City were safely ensconced in mid-table. Three weeks later, they had lost four out of five games. With several of the teams at the bottom having thrown themselves a lifeline, City toppled down the table and were suddenly in a relegation battle. Still, a point at Bristol City in their final game would be enough to ensure their survival. But with two minutes of a goalless game remaining, Tommy Kelso inexplicably turned Fred Staniforth's cross into his own net. This utterly avoidable defeat took their destiny out of their own hands. Bradford City and Liverpool were still below them, but both could leapfrog the Mancunians with good results in their final fixtures. Bradford were up first. They needed to beat, of all sides, outgoing champions Manchester United. They managed to do so by a single goal. Liverpool were then required to get at least a point away to the new champions Newcastle. They got two, thanks to a last-minute goal from one-time Newcastle title hero Ronald Orr.

A few City eyebrows were raised at Orr's former employers, who clearly had their boots up on the desk, while Manchester United were later fined £250 for fielding weak teams towards the end of the season as they concentrated on winning the FA Cup. But there was no escaping the fact that City, somehow, had managed to get themselves relegated from a position of seeming security. It wouldn't be the last time they were left scratching their heads upon coming a spectacular cropper. In just four years, they had slipped from contending for the title to the Second Division, while their arch rivals established some trophy-winning credentials with a load of their old star players. The 'Typical City' legend started right here, right now.

3

Charlie misses two penalties (1909–10 to 1920–21)

A sequence of 12 wins and three draws towards the business end of the 1909–10 season took Aston Villa well clear at the top. One particularly fecund fortnight saw them slap five goals past The Wednesday and seven past Manchester United. Clockwork striker 'Happy' Harry Hampton knocked in a first-half hat-trick against Middlesbrough on Good Friday, then repeated the feat against Bury 24 hours later. George Ramsay's side finished five points ahead of Liverpool; Tom Watson's men were never seriously in the race. A procession was a fitting end to an imperial phase. Villa had won five titles in seven years during the 1890s; this was their sixth victory in the first 22 seasons of the League. It'd be another 71 years before they'd land number seven.

They shouldn't have had to wait so long: the very next title should have been theirs too. Villa tussled with a rejuvenated Manchester United for much of 1910–11. United's team was much the same as the one which won the title three years earlier. Charlie Roberts was still the linchpin of the defence, Billy Meredith still mangled toothpicks and opposing defences on the wing. The new injection of talent came in the form of striker Enoch 'Knocker' West; the Edwardians had an ear for a good nickname. West knocked them in from all distances and angles.

Villa and United took turns at the top in a tight race, and it looked as though the reigning champions had done enough when they beat their challengers 4–2 at Villa Park in late April.

Happy Harry and his prolific partner Joe Bache both scored for Villa in a match which Roberts missed for United. Meredith was subdued, and Knocker West was dismissed for trading blows with George Hunter. The win put Villa top, with a better goal average and two games left to play, as opposed to United's one. A win at Blackburn Rovers in their penultimate match would effectively secure the title. Late in the second half, Charlie Wallace was upended by Arthur Cowell in the penalty area. He got up to take the spot kick himself, only for Jimmy Ashcroft to save his shot. The match ended goalless.

A win at Liverpool on the final day would still do it, but Villa went down 3–1. Liverpool had done arch rivals Manchester United a solid turn, though Ernest Mangnall's team still needed to win by three clear goals at home to Sunderland. They passed that test in some style. They romped to a 5–1 win, an electric Meredith setting up three of the goals. The new Old Trafford ground erupted. United's players were treated to a day out at the races, by motorcar to Chester, followed by a slap-up feed at the Midland Hotel. A glass was raised to poor Charlie Wallace, whose missed penalty at Blackburn effectively cost Villa the title.

A year later, Manchester City offered United £1,500 for Charlie Roberts. Mangnall was having none of it. But then, a few days later, he accepted an offer from City himself, crossing town to take their secretary's job! It was a sensation right up there with the Billy Meredith switcheroo of 1906, though this time neither club benefited: United fell into a slump that would take the best part of four decades to arrest, while Mangnall won nothing in his time at City. A runners-up slot in 1920–21 was the best he could achieve, although he did leave behind something tangible, having been a prime mover in the construction of Maine Road.

Manchester United did not defend their title well. They ended the 1911–12 season in 13th spot, though relegation looked a serious possibility with three matches left. They had just lost five games out of six, conceding six goals at Aston Villa and Sheffield United, and another three at Middlesbrough. A restorative run of five points from their last three games saved their skin, but they had really tested everyone's nerves. Victory in the nascent Charity Shield was the only consolation from a miserable season: they saw off Southern League champions Swindon Town 8–4, a monumentally absurd scoreline even by the standards of the day. Harold Halse helped himself to a double hat-trick.

The season belonged to Blackburn Rovers, who already had five FA Cups to their name, though all that silver had been gathered in Victorian times. Rovers had subsequently done very little of note in the League – a couple of third-placed finishes apart – but they finally got it together, albeit in unspectacular style. Acclaim was in short supply until they won 3–0 at early pacesetters Aston Villa in mid-February – 'Truly, the Rovers are a great team this season!' trilled the *Mirror* – though other praise was faint. 'I should say this is the most severe defeat the Villa have sustained at home for a long time,' the *Daily Express* harrumphed. 'It shows one of two things: the Rovers have greatly improved or the Villa have deteriorated. I should blend the two.'

The *Manchester Guardian* described Rovers as 'sound rather than brilliant', although did rather grudgingly concede that 'whenever they got near goal they were very dangerous'. Much of this was attributable to the Scottish duo of Wattie Aitkenhead and

George Chapman, the latter – shades of Blackburn's 1995 Premier League winner Chris Sutton – a central defender converted to striker. The manager Robert Middleton also shifted forward Joe Clennell to the wing, where he scored twice in a crucial win over title rivals Everton in April. Clennell then shared the goals with Aitkenhead in the 4–1 win against West Bromwich Albion which clinched the title with a couple of games to spare.

The only real drama of Rovers' run-in came four matches out. Well clear at the top and requiring only a point at Woolwich Arsenal to secure the championship, they conceded two long-range screamers to Pat Flanagan and John Grant just before the interval, then shipped a further three in the second half. The shock 5–1 defeat rattled a few nerves, but Aitkenhead and Clennell settled them against West Brom three days later. As if to illustrate the slightly underwhelming nature of the season, Blackburn's winning total of 49 points was the lowest since a 20-team division had been introduced in 1905.

The 1912–13 campaign would more than make up for all that. Blackburn initially appeared a good bet for back-to-back titles: they topped the table after thrashing Bradford City 5–0 in early December. But injuries at inopportune moments to key players – most notably veteran captain and right-back Bob Crompton, the first professional to captain England – shattered their confidence. They lost five in a row to drop out of contention, although some late-season results – 5–1 against Liverpool, 6–1 at Chelsea and 7–1 over Oldham Athletic – suggested this team's story was not quite finished yet.

Sunderland meanwhile had lost five of their first seven matches, and there was talk of a first relegation for the four-time League champions. Manager Bob Kyle's response was to spend big on Blackpool's Charlie Gladwin, a six-foot-plus, no-nonsense right-back who would deliberately make himself sick before each game to quell his nerves before sauntering out to impose himself on proceedings with a calm force. Completely uninterested in the identity of the opposition, Gladwin routinely set about his defensive tasks in the simple style. At every corner, he would order his teammates out of the penalty area. 'Leave it to me!' It was wise advice. On the occasion captain Charlie Thomson came back to assist, he was caught full in the face by Gladwin's full-blooded clearance. After being brought round with smelling salts, Thomson set about playing for the opposition in a concussed daze.

Gladwin's presence – along with new keeper Joe Butler – calmed Sunderland's defence and gave the attackers confidence to start doing their thing. The team won ten of their next 12, the high point a 7–0 rout of Liverpool at Roker Park, their inside-forward Charlie Buchan, quickly establishing himself as the biggest star in English football, scoring five times. After a Boxing Day defeat at home to fellow challengers The Wednesday, Sunderland lost only one more League match all season, and by mid-April found themselves top of the table and in their first FA Cup final.

Aston Villa stood in the way of both trophies. Ahead of the Cup final, Sunderland inside-left George Holley injured his ankle. Walter Tinsley should have taken his place, but upon seeing the 121,000-strong crowd at the Crystal Palace ground, froze completely. Overcome with pre-match nerves, he was utterly unable to play, and Holley had to hobble through instead. Gladwin conceded a penalty which Charlie Wallace wasted, the first miss from the spot in a Cup final. Wallace's failure from 12 yards at Blackburn had cost Villa the title a couple of years previously, but this error had no serious repercussions, as his side went on to win the Cup regardless.

Sunderland got their revenge four days later in the League at Villa Park. The crowd of 53,000 was a midweek record, but this time Tinsley conquered his nerves, took to the field, and scored the opening goal. Harold Halse, a two-time title-winner with Manchester United, headed an equaliser for Villa, but it wasn't enough for his new side. A draw meant Sunderland required just one win from their last two games, and they wrapped up the title three days later with a 3–1 victory at Bolton Wanderers. Sunderland ended the campaign with 54 points, the highest winning total to date.

Blackburn reclaimed the title in 1913–14, again in an unremarkable season. Rovers continued their stunning late form of the previous campaign by winning their first six matches with a 20-goal salvo. They were momentarily troubled by Manchester United, who won nine of their first ten despite being forced to sell captain Charlie Roberts to Oldham Athletic, the cost of building Old Trafford beginning to bite. But United's wheels came off big time. Just after the New Year, Bolton thumped them 6–1, then Southern League Swindon, who had been trounced 8–4 in the Charity Shield two seasons earlier, knocked them out of the FA Cup. The results were the catalyst for ten losses in the next dozen games, and they plummeted down the table.

Rovers, by contrast, kept going, and sauntered their way to their second championship. World-record signing Danny Shea, a £2,000 buy from West Ham towards the tail end of 1912–13, top-scored with 27, while the diminutive Eddie Latheron, a wily and popular playmaker, pitched in with 13. Another drama-lite title was secured, somewhat appropriately, by a goalless draw at Newcastle. Villa, seven points adrift, finished runners-up for the third time in four seasons. The astonishing George Ramsay had one more trophy left in him – the 1920 FA Cup – but this distant second place marked the end of Aston Villa as regular title challengers.

Oldham Athletic joined the Second Division in 1907 and got to work quickly. Under the management of David Ashworth – destined to win a title with Liverpool in the 1920s – the Latics won promotion within three seasons, and quickly consolidated their status in the top flight. After a run to the FA Cup semis in 1913, they took advantage of Manchester United's descent into penury by making off with Charlie Roberts. The superstar defender lifted Oldham to fourth in the table in 1913–14. Ashworth left for Stockport County, but under new manager Herbert Bamlett, the team took a serious shy at the 1914–15 title.

Ten victories from the first 14 matches propelled Oldham to the top by November. Though that relentless form proved impossible to maintain, they were still in charge come the business end of the season. After a 4–3 win at title rivals Everton in March, they had points and games in hand. But an injury to influential winger Joe Donnachie coincided with the wheels flying off. Oldham lost three of their next four, and the final game of that sorry sequence, an Easter thrashing at Middlesbrough, had serious consequences.

Oldham's defence, usually so reliable with Roberts *in situ*, shipped three goals in the first 20 minutes. With their title dream beginning to dissipate, desperation set in. They began the second half in a collective panic, putting in several rash tackles. It wasn't long before the match boiled over. Left-back Billy Cook conceded a penalty by hacking down Jackie Carr; Boro converted to make it four. Minutes later, depending on whose report you believe, either Cook fouled Carr again, or one of his teammates did. Whatever the reality, Cook got the blame, and was ordered off. Claiming mistaken identity, he refused to walk. His captain Roberts tried to convince him to accept the decision, but in vain. The referee whipped his timepiece out, giving the player exactly 60 seconds to leave. When the time elapsed, Cook was still there, hands on hips, standing his ground. The referee abandoned the match on 55 minutes. But Boro's victory stood. Cook was banned for a year.

Oldham regrouped with wins over Manchester United and Sheffield United, and required just two points from their final two games to clinch the title. But without the suspended Cook, their defence had become unsure. Both of their remaining matches were at home, yet both ended in meek surrender: 2–1 to Burnley, 2–0 to Liverpool. By defeating Oldham, Liverpool gifted the title to neighbours Everton, who had put together a strong late sequence of four wins to grab top spot.

It's impossible not to feel desperately sorry for the Latics, who have never come so close again. Yet it's also difficult to argue against Everton deserving their second title: Bobby Parker rattled up 36 goals in just 35 games, while former Blackburn title-winner Joe Clennell chipped in with another 14. By contrast, for Oldham, only Gilbert Kemp, with 16, had made it into double figures.

It was certainly a painful end to the season for Liverpool. On top of delivering the title to their Merseyside rivals, their beloved manager Tom Watson passed away, and the club became embroiled in a match-fixing scandal. News slowly leaked that their Good Friday defeat at Manchester United had been one huge grift. Large sums had been placed on the 2–0 scoreline with local bookmakers. Striker Fred Pagnam, not in on the caper, was given a hearty dressing down by a couple of less innocent teammates for having the temerity to go for goal. Eight players, four from each side, including championship winners Knocker West and Sandy Turnbull, were eventually banned indefinitely.

But even this outrage was kept in proper perspective by the Great War now raging, and at the Football League's annual meeting in July 1915 the decision was made to suspend competition indefinitely. Hundreds of top players – Happy Harry Hampton, Charlie Buchan, Colin Veitch, Bobby Parker – trooped off to fight the good fight. They were all following the lead of Bradford Park Avenue midfielder Donald Bell, who had helped the small Yorkshire club to the top flight in 1914 only to ask to be released from his contract the minute the conflict began. Bell was eventually killed in the Battle of the Somme. He was posthumously awarded the Victoria Cross for rushing across open land under heavy fire and taking out a machine-gunner with his revolver, a 'very brave' act which 'saved many lives and ensured the success of the attack'. Former title-winners Sandy Turnbull and Eddie Latheron were just two other heroes who didn't come back. Turnbull had salvaged his reputation in the most tragic manner imaginable.

The 1912 FA Cup final had been thoroughly dire. West Bromwich Albion and Barnsley shared 120 goalless minutes at Crystal Palace, then another 117 in the replay at Bramall Lane. All of a sudden, Barnsley winger George Utley slipped a ball forward to Harry Tufnell, who sprinted clear from the halfway line. The Albion's popular left-back, 'Peerless' Jesse Pennington, had an opportunity to cynically send Tufnell crashing to the floor. But he opted against the trip, allowing the Barnsley man to glide forward and win the Cup. Pennington never regretted his sportsmanship, though he did wonder if he'd passed up his only chance of a medal.

Pennington was 36 in August 1919, when League football began again in the wake of the First World War. Few name-checked his team in the pre-season previews. The *Mirror* rattled through a list of 'strong sides' whose 'astute managers have been busy team building ever since the armistice . . . Everton, Liverpool, Newcastle, the Villa, Sunderland, the Sheffield, Manchester and Nottingham clubs, Chelsea, the Arsenal . . . to mention only a few!' The paper did however admit that making predictions after four years of downtime was 'like taking a jump in the dark'. As if to illustrate this, the *Express* suggested that First Division new boys Arsenal would see off Newcastle on the opening day, but Chelsea wouldn't have enough for Everton, still officially reigning champions and the recent winners of a wartime Lancashire competition. Sure enough, Chelsea won 3–2 while Newcastle triumphed at Arsenal. Jumps in the dark.

That Arsenal were in the First Division at all – they had finished fifth in the 1914–15 Second Division – was down to the slick wheeler-dealering of their chairman, the Conservative Party grandee Sir Henry Norris. It had been agreed to expand the First Division to 22 teams for the restart, and it was expected that the previous season's two relegated clubs, Chelsea and Tottenham Hotspur, would be granted a reprieve. But Norris proselytised for a different approach, manipulating the 1915 Manchester United–Liverpool Good Friday fix to his advantage.

He laid out a plan of Byzantine logic. Chelsea were only in the relegation places because of Manchester United's dodgy win, he argued, so therefore had to be saved. Spurs would have gone down anyway, so it was only right for them to suffer the consequences. Instead, the League's members should vote for one other Second Division side to join the two already being promoted as usual. By not pushing for Manchester United or Liverpool to be punished with demotion, Norris curried favour with representatives of the big clubs, who repaid him by voting for Arsenal to join the First Division party. Barnsley and Wolverhampton Wanderers, who had both finished above Arsenal in 1914–15, have never forgotten it. Demoted rivals Spurs have never forgiven it. Arsenal ended the

1919–20 season comfortably in mid-table, with a cigar on. Meanwhile reprieved Chelsea – fuelled by the goals of handsome and charismatic Jack Cock, footballer by day, music-hall tenor by night – finished an impressive third.

Neither team got anywhere near West Brom, who from nowhere strung together one of the great campaigns. They fell behind on the opening day to 1914–15 runners-up Oldham, but Fred Morris levelled things up with a belt from distance before scoring again in a 3–1 win. A fortnight later, champions Everton were hammered in back-to-back fixtures, 4–3 at the Hawthorns, 5–2 at Goodison. Albion hit the top and stayed there for the duration. Peerless Pennington marshalled a dependable defence which conceded just 47 goals, only eight more than divisional misers Newcastle United. But while Newcastle only scored 44 times, West Brom found the net on 104 occasions. Morris claimed 37 of them.

West Brom clinched the title by beating Bradford Park Avenue with four games to go. Pennington and Morris were away on England duty, besting Scotland in a daft 5–4 victory at Hillsborough. Morris, naturally, scored one of England's goals. But in the League, they had missed the money shot. Not that it mattered too much, as they were back in the side for Albion's valedictory final-day 4–0 win over Chelsea. Morris was chaired off the field; Pennington finally had his medal. Two weeks later, West Brom won the (then end-of-season) Charity Shield, beating Tottenham Hotspur, who had won the Second Division having refused to succumb to the machinations of Henry Morris.

John Haworth, like George Ramsay and Tom Watson before him, is one of the great forgotten managers. His run of success with Burnley was nothing short of exceptional. He took the Clarets into the First Division in 1913, won the FA Cup in 1914, then finished third in the League before the Great War paused momentum. But Haworth was not to be denied. His new, improved, post-war team, built around inspirational midfielder Tommy Boyle and striker Bob Kelly, finished second behind West Brom in the first season after the restart. They went one better in 1920–21.

Burnley's title win took a gloriously loopy form: a 4–1 home capitulation to a very average Bradford City in their opening game, followed by two more losses; a 30-game unbeaten run, a sequence which included seven-goal thumpings of Oldham, Leicester and Aston Villa, and which effectively sealed the title; and no wins in their last six matches, the work already completed. The unbeaten run stood as a League record until Leeds United bettered it over two seasons during 1968 and 1969. One of Burnley's biggest fans was Sunderland's Charlie Buchan, who cooed, 'They owed nothing to physique for they were one of the smallest teams that ever performed such great deeds . . . it was all done by teamwork and skill!'

Burnley continued their own epic journey under Haworth with a third-place finish in 1921–22, the manager's last notable achievement. He passed away in 1924, aged just 48, a victim of pneumonia. He was the second Burnley boss in succession to die in office, his predecessor Spen Whittaker mysteriously falling from a moving train in 1910 while travelling to London on transfer business.

Midway through Burnley's wonder run, the all-female works team of Preston-based munitions factory Dick, Kerr & Co. played a Boxing Day charity match at Goodison Park. Dick, Kerr's were one of the most skilful sides in the country – winger Lily Parr also possessed a shot venomous enough to have once broken a mouthy male goalkeeper's arm – and they had been pulling in huge crowds for some time. They rammed Everton's ground with 53,000 paying punters – 14,000 unlucky fans were locked out – and beat St Helens 4–0, raising £3,000 for disabled and unemployed soldiers and sailors.

The women's game had increased in popularity during the war, with so many young male players fighting overseas. That state of affairs was quietly tolerated by the patriarchy, but when attendances stayed buoyant after the restart of the Football League, the old-boy network became overwhelmed by a sense of panic. Exactly what they were worried about is unclear: crowds for the lads elsewhere on Boxing Day were as healthy as ever: 50,000-plus at Sheffield United, Tottenham Hotspur and Liverpool, over 40,000 at Birmingham City, Cardiff City and Arsenal. But the gentlemen had been well and truly rattled. Several hot-faced club directors worried that the women's game could eventually eclipse the Football League. Midway through 1921 Newcastle refused to let their local women's side book St James' Park, despite having let the venue to them in 1919 for a game that raised thousands for war charities. Dick, Kerr had also become politicised, playing a series of matches to raise cash for miners who had lost their jobs when pits were returned to private ownership. Most crucially, all the charity work had lifted a lid on how much cash could be generated by football. Something, the moneymen reasoned, their cover blown, had to be done!

Extremely spurious medical evidence was cited. 'I do not believe women are fitted for violent leg strain!' one doctor quacked in the *Lancashire Daily Post*. Meanwhile unfounded accusations of financial impropriety were loudly made. The FA responded by slapping a ban on the women's game and, astonishingly, left it there until 1971. It was a masterclass in sophistry and political chicanery. Sir Henry, one suspects, would have been impressed.

4

Billy and Frank blow everyone's mind (1921–22 to 1925–26)

Saturday 28 April 1923. Just three weeks after the last patch of concrete had dried at the brand new Empire Stadium in Wembley, the FA staged the first-ever fixture at its freshly built pleasure dome in the 'burbs. They hadn't bothered to make the Cup final between Bolton Wanderers and West Ham all-ticket, working on the assumption that the mega-arena's cavernous capacity of 127,000 would be more than sufficient to satisfy demand. Over 200,000 spectators rushed turnstiles, scaled walls and vaulted barriers, though they still queued up politely at the refreshment bars. This is Britain! The vast crowd spilled onto the pitch. A grey charger – who appeared white in over-exposed photos taken on an overcast day – restored order. Bolton won the match.

'In any foreign capital, the afternoon would hardly have passed without the throwing of stones, the flashing of steel and the snap of revolver shots,' ran a frenzied report in the *Mirror*. 'But then is there any foreign police force or gendarmerie that could have kept its head and temper so well as the Metropolitan Police did throughout this ordeal? I think not!' There were, mercifully, no deaths. But there had been over a thousand injured in the crush. The authorities had got away with one. The day passed into instant legend, one of the most memorable in the entire history of football.

Or was it? That viewpoint very much depended on which game you attended. The antics at the Cup final masked a worrying underlying trend: attendances were dropping because, more often than not, the sport wasn't much fun any more. The classified check for the full programme of First Division Football League fixtures taking place elsewhere that day is quite something:

Arsenal 2–0 Sheffield United
Birmingham City 1–0 Burnley
Blackburn Rovers 0–0 Chelsea
Cardiff City 2–0 Oldham Athletic
Everton 1–0 Preston North End
Huddersfield 1–0 Tottenham Hotspur
Manchester City 0–0 Newcastle United
Stoke City 0–0 Liverpool
Sunderland 2–0 Aston Villa
West Bromwich Albion 1–0 Middlesbrough

Ten matches, ten goals, the First Division card as barren tundra. This near-binary set of scorelines reflected the most hapless day of goal-getting in top-flight history, and being one match shy of a full fixture list due to the Cup final wasn't much of an excuse. Something would surely have to give, sooner rather than later.

Liverpool had already claimed the 1922–23 League championship, holding on to the title they'd won in 1921–22. They'd kept their title defence on track despite manager David Ashworth sensationally upping sticks midway through the run-in for a higher wage at his alma mater, relegation-bound Oldham Athletic. Nobody had won back-to-back championships since The Wednesday in 1904, but otherwise it was hardly the stuff of

legend. The stars of Liverpool's title sides were all defensive opera-
tors: captain and left-back Donald McKinlay; the England
full-back Ephraim Longworth; and the wildly popular goalkeeper
Elisha Scott, whose bond with the Kop ('I speak to these people!')
predates Bill Shankly's populism by nearly 40 years. Liverpool
won the 1921–22 title by scoring 63 goals; they won the 1922–23
version with 70. Given how West Bromwich Albion had rattled in
104 during their championship season just after the war, this
marked a precipitous decline in fun.

The main problem, and source of great irritation, was the
offside law. Under the rule, which had been enshrined in the laws
of the game since 1867, three men had to be between attacker and
goal before the ball was passed to him, to avoid the flag going up.
This generosity towards defenders was increasingly exploited by
the smarter buggers. Billy McCracken and Frank Hudspeth of
Newcastle United had it down to a fine art. The two full-backs –
along with the keeper, nominally the last line of defence in a
2–3–5 formation – would push up to the halfway line. One of
them would then nip into the opposition's half, just before the
attacking side played a pass forward. With only one full-back and
the keeper left in their own half, the attackers were invariably
caught offside, and games often became compressed into the
middle third of the pitch, regularly degenerating into numbing
stoppage-strewn fiascos. In 1922–23 Newcastle scored just 45
times, the joint third-worst total in the division. But their
dependable defence conceded just 37, and they finished fourth.
This was getting out of hand.

Not that the League was totally without excitement during this
otherwise dire era. In 1923–24, Herbert Chapman's Huddersfield
Town pipped Cardiff City to the most extraordinary championship
yet. The bare numbers suggest more of the same: well-drilled

Huddersfield conceded just 33 goals on their way to the title, while scoring a relatively modest 60, shared entirely between their front five of Charlie Wilson, Clem Stephenson, George Brown, George Cook and Billy Smith. But that wasn't the half of the story, as Cardiff missed out on the title by the smallest of margins.

The Welsh side had only joined the League four years earlier, but propelled by the goals of Len Davies, quickly made themselves comfortable. They won immediate promotion from the Second Division, and set about the First in a determined hwyl, finishing fourth in 1921–22 and ninth a season later. They topped the table for most of 1923–24, and with one game remaining led Huddersfield by a point. Chapman's side had two fixtures left, but let that advantage slip, going down 3–1 at Aston Villa in the first of them. Destiny was in the hands of Cardiff. 'After that we got to work with pencil and paper, working out goal averages,' reminisced Huddersfield captain Sam Wadsworth. 'I think most of us gave ourselves headaches. We were unable to agree on the figures.' Chapman stepped in to explain: if Cardiff won their last game at Birmingham City, they were champions. But if they drew, Huddersfield could still nab the title if they beat lowly Nottingham Forest at home by three goals. Wadsworth, after pensively chewing awhile on the end of his pencil, dryly concluded that they were 'cutting it a bit fine'.

Huddersfield started out so nervously against Forest that, according to the *Manchester Guardian*, 'they appeared to be throwing their chance away'. Wadsworth later confessed that 'our football has often reached a higher standard, but we made up for lack of science by super-energy'. They pulled themselves together to establish a jittery half-time lead, George Cook capitalising after Forest keeper Alf Bennett – born, deliciously, in a Derbyshire village called Clowne – spilled a George Brown shot. News that

Birmingham and Cardiff was goalless gave Huddersfield further succour. 'We pulled our belts a bit tighter,' reminisced Wadsworth, 'rolled back our sleeves, and restarted on the business of getting those other two goals.' The Terriers were much improved in the second half, despite the pitch turning heavy in torrential rain. On 57 minutes Cook converted Billy Smith's cross with a fine header. Bedlam at Leeds Road. On the touchline, Chapman hopped around in the vigorous style, imploring his side to push for the decisive third.

But at that exact moment, over at Birmingham City, a goalbound Cardiff shot was handled on the line by Percy Barton. Penalty! But one carrying unimaginable pressure: if scored, it would almost certainly secure the title for Cardiff. None of their more experienced heads fancied it, so the task fell to Len Davies, five days after his 25th birthday. Despite being Cardiff's main striker, Davies had never taken a spot kick before. His uncertain effort flew too close to Birmingham keeper Dan Tremelling, who parried clear. Ten minutes later, back at Leeds Road, Ted Richardson embarked on a long dribble and set up George Brown for Huddersfield's decisive third. After the final whistle, Chapman spent an agonising few minutes waiting by the phone for news from St Andrew's. The call came through: Birmingham and Cardiff had ended 0–0. Huddersfield had done it, in the nick of time, by 0.024 of a goal!

Excitement! Drama! Thrills! But this denouement was the exception that proved the rule. Huddersfield retained their title in 1924–25, conceding just 28 goals in 42 matches, an average of 0.666 goals per game. Attacking devilment was still, on the whole, sadly lacking.

Across the League, attendances continued to fall, so the FA reluctantly began experimenting with the troublesome offside law. In January 1925 their apparatchiks gathered for a fact-finding mission at Norwich City's atmospheric Nest ground. Wedged into an old quarry, this singular arena's signature architectural feature was a 50-foot-high concrete containing wall running along a section of touchline; the wall held back a cliff with a ramshackle terrace teetering precariously on top. The Canaries took on Cambridge University in a friendly, players remaining onside with just two players in front of them rather than the usual three. The game was a free-scoring success, with City winning 5–2. It went down well with the crowd: after all, if spectators were expected to take absurd risks with their lives, the footballers should at least be a little more adventurous when playing the game.

Another fact-finding mission was held at Highbury a couple of months later. In the first half of a game between teams of Amateurs and Professionals, a proposal requiring two lines to be painted across the pitch, 40 yards from each goal, was given a trial run. Under this crackpot scheme, the current offside law would remain the same but would only be implemented within the new segments. But it changed little. 'The extra markings are simply a fresco dedication to Billy McCracken,' quipped the *Mirror*. 'Forwards who cannot beat two backs in 60 yards will never do it in 40.' The two-defenders motion was trialled again in the second half, and resulted in a flowing 45 minutes of football. The Amateurs won 3–1, and the new offside rule was written into the laws in time for the 1925–26 season.

The 'revolutionised' game delivered on its promise with immediate effect. Matches that used to be halted 30 times or more by the linesman's flag and referee's whistle instantly became liquid affairs. 'The game in which the whistle went more than half a dozen times was an exception,' trilled *The Times*. The opening day of 1925–26 was a cavalcade of comic confusion witnessed by 775,000 disbelieving fans across the four divisions: Middlesbrough scored five, while Bradford Park Avenue, Rochdale and Plymouth Argyle all hit six. On an afternoon of high scoring in the First Division – where there was an average 3.9 goals per game, a mighty leap from the previous season's weekly average of 2.58 – it was going to take something outrageous to catch the attention. Aston Villa provided the necessary.

Having finished the previous campaign in 15th place, and with the club in severe financial trouble, Villa weren't expected to do anything of note. So much for punditry! Len Capewell scored five, strolling through the wide-open spaces of Villa Park as the home side drubbed Burnley 10–0. Burnley could claim in mitigation a deep cut over Jack Hill's eye, which caused their half-back to miss large swathes of the match, but playing with ten is no excuse for conceding ten. They didn't push the point too hard.

Previously parsimonious Newcastle meanwhile conceded a couple of harbingers in a 2–2 draw at Bolton. A week later they beat Notts County – themselves no slouches at the old offside caper during the early 1920s – by a fairly comprehensive 6–3 scoreline. Another four days on, they shipped seven at home to Blackburn, Ted Harper putting five past Willie Wilson, who was making quite the debut in goal. This was uncharacteristic bordering on psychedelic: having conceded just 42 times the previous season, Newcastle were on their way to shipping 75 this time round.

The *Manchester Guardian* started placing arch quotation marks around the word 'form'. Four weeks into the season, the chap from *The Times* fell victim to wild palpitations. 'The new football is producing freak results!' he sobbed, as that Saturday's card averaged 5.1 goals per game. Manchester City and Everton shared eight goals in a 4–4 thriller; Tottenham Hotspur came from behind to draw 5–5 with Huddersfield. Any disappointment felt by the reigning champions was offset by the performance of their new £5,000 club-record signing from Aberdeen, Alex Jackson, who weighed in with a hat-trick from the right wing. But still: they'd only conceded 28 in 42 games the previous season. They'd just let in nearly 20 per cent of that total in 90 minutes.

Defences around the country were suffering thundering breakdowns. A further week on, and the weekly goals-per-game average hit 5.36. Blackburn beat Cardiff 6–3, Manchester United saw off Burnley 6–1, Bury tonked Sheffield United 7–4. A total of 194 goals were scored across the entire League that particular afternoon. It's fair to say that not too many players had a firm handle on the new law. Of course, there's always an exception to prove the rule. One team in the country were seemingly unfazed by change: Second Division Hull City, who didn't concede a single goal in their first five games of the season. Their manager? The man directly responsible for all this chaos, the recently retired offside manipulator par excellence, Bill McCracken. It had to be.

Trying to make sense of it all appeared a futile task. But somebody had to give it a go. Arsenal had endured a slightly slow start under new manager Herbert Chapman, freshly enticed from the champs Huddersfield. An opening-day defeat at home to Tottenham Hotspur caused obvious irritation, though that was nothing compared to the 7–0 shellacking they suffered at beyond-inconsistent Newcastle at the start of October. The headline in the *Mirror* painted a quaint picture of bucolic plenty in Albion: LEAGUE GOALS AS PLENTIFUL AS BLACKBERRIES! But the autumnal serenity was shattered by the copy beneath, which spoke of an apocalyptic, dystopian 'epidemic of scoring' that desperately required 'an effective antidote'. It was, claimed the paper, now fully worked up into an end-of-days froth, 'long overdue. What genius will discover it?'

As it happened, the genius was standing on the southbound platform at Newcastle railway station, his face like thunder and arms tightly folded, refusing to catch the train back to London with the abject shower he had recently joined. Herbert Chapman had persuaded Charlie Buchan to move from Sunderland to Arsenal in the summer, a tortuous process which involved compensating the 33-year-old forward for loss of earnings from his north-east sports outfitter, and striking a convoluted and highly unusual deal which promised Sunderland an extra £100 for every goal he scored during his first season at Highbury.

The penny had dropped with Buchan before the season had even begun: an extra man was needed to help the two full-backs deal with attacks. Chapman – rather strangely, given he'd used centre-half Tom Wilson in an unfashionably deep role while at Huddersfield – wasn't of a mind to listen. But the humiliation at Newcastle gave Buchan leverage. He announced that he would rather retire than waste his time getting thrashed every other week. 'I'm not of much use to Arsenal,' he announced, mid-flounce. 'I would like to go back to Sunderland. I still have my shop there.'

A flustered Chapman called a snap meeting at Newcastle's nearby Royal Station Hotel, allowing Buchan to state his case. The player pointed out that Newcastle centre-half Charlie Spencer had dropped deep to create a back three, instead of performing his usual positional duties of shuttling between defence and attack. Spencer had then snuffed out pretty much every Arsenal attack at source, Newcastle enjoying the lion's share of possession as a result. Jack Butler, Buchan argued, could – indeed must – do the same thing for Arsenal. Chapman agreed, the pair thrashing out a scheme which also involved promoting the 'slow as the post' reserve-teamer Andy Neil to take over the traditional playmaking responsibilities Butler would be relinquishing. And so Buchan skipped onto the train back to London. Two days later, he scored twice at West Ham in a comfortable 4–0 victory. Good news for Arsenal, who were at least beginning to come to terms with the new rule (and not a bad result for Sunderland either, another £200 richer).

However a data-set consisting of 90 minutes at bang-average West Ham proved insufficient, and it soon became clear that, when put into practice amid the mayhem, the new theory still needed quite some work. Arsenal lost two of their next three, one of those a four-goal thumping at Sheffield United. A semblance of order was subsequently restored and the team finished the season in second place – they only conceded 15 goals in their last 14 games, impressive stuff given the climate – but even then the trend was misleading. Arsenal finished mid-table the following year after 86 goals whistled into their net; only four teams were more porous. But at least they had a blueprint to work with, and they'd get the balance right in spectacular style soon enough.

Elsewhere, the wild scoring was not by any means over. On one Saturday afternoon towards the end of October, Manchester City obliterated poor hapless Burnley (a team 'at loggerheads with luck' according to the *Manchester Guardian*) 8–3. Two days later, City went down 8–3 themselves at struggling Sheffield United. What were the odds? Absurd juxtapositions were also becoming a way of life for Newcastle, who still hadn't quite got the hang of the three-at-the-back containing tactic showcased so successfully against Arsenal. Hughie Gallacher was prised from Airdrieonians after the United board had run out of patience with six months' worth of stalling, and stormed the Scottish club's weekly board meeting, slapping on the table a record sum of between six and nine grand (rumours wildly varied, depending on which cigar-puffing Airdrie director the papers talked to). Gallacher scored twice and set another up on his December debut against Everton, though he was denied a win by a hat-trick from Everton's own new striking star, William Dean. (Newcastle had unsuccessfully tried to sign Dixie from Tranmere Rovers in the summer, a fantasy front pairing of Dean and Gallacher lost for ever.) The Magpies then went down 6–3 at Liverpool on Christmas Day, before beating the same opponents 3–0 at home 24 hours later.

On New Year's Day, Sheffield United annihilated Cardiff City 11–2. This was quite a result, even by the season's standards, given the previous year's FA Cup final between the pair had ended 1–0 to United. Another example of the lop-sided havoc caused by the new laws? Or a fabled warning of the dangers of festive eggnog? It's a moot point, though if you factored out those 11 goals, Cardiff would have ended the season with the fourth-best defensive record in the land. They also avenged this humiliation in April, winning the return at Ninian Park 1–0. The moral? Beware dairy products laced with rum on Hogmanay.

There was simply no second-guessing any of it. Manchester City, in addition to those back-to-back 8–3s, picked up the habit of registering scorelines that more closely resembled racing odds: they went down 6–5 at Bury on Christmas Day, won 6–1 at neighbours United, and beat Crystal Palace 11–4 in the FA Cup. Bury's festive jamboree was part of a mid-season eight-game winning stretch, the high-point being an 8–1 win over Burnley. A club-best fourth-place finish was their reward, despite 77 goals nestling in their net.

It would be understandable to assume Burnley were ignominiously relegated. In addition to conceding ten at Villa on the opening day, and letting Manchester City and Bury score eight, they gave up six to Sheffield United, Manchester United and hated mill-town rivals Blackburn. By the season's end, their defence, such as it was, had been breached 108 times.

Yet there were high points too. They responded to their opening-day humiliation by thrashing Leicester City 4–0 the very next week. And they took the opportunity to fill their boots on other occasions: a 6–3 Boxing Day win over Leeds, a 5–2 victory against Sunderland, a 7–1 win at Birmingham, and the final-day result that saved them, a 4–1 stuffing of Cardiff. They escaped relegation by a point, leapfrogging Manchester City, who went down after losing 3–2 at Newcastle on a day Hughie Gallacher scored a hat-trick. Gallacher's third was the 100th goal conceded by City during the season. It wouldn't have mattered had City and England outside-right Billy Austin converted a second-half penalty. But it was heroically saved by Willie Wilson, those seven goals conceded on his debut suddenly a distant memory.

City's utterly avoidable relegation was filed alongside their similarly farcical demise of 1909. A week before Austin's missed penalty condemned the club to Second Division football, City suffered defeat in the 1926 FA Cup final against Bolton. They became the first FA Cup finalists to go down in the same season, a fate that wouldn't befall anyone again until Leicester City in 1969.

So Burnley were saved, City gone. Bottom-placed Notts County were already out of it by that tumultuous final day. They ended the season conceding 34 fewer goals than Burnley, but the Clarets had scored 31 more, an apt outcome to a campaign which had seen the rules tweaked, and minds scrambled, for the sake of a more attacking, enterprising, entertaining product. County at least had the pleasure of a valedictory win on the final day: 4–2 over Huddersfield who, fuelled by the jinking genius of Alex Jackson and 35 goals from George 'Bomber' Brown, had long secured their third title in a row. They had never been seriously challenged. Their title hat-trick was the first in Football League history: two-thirds of it secured by Herbert Chapman, the job completed under the yoke of Cecil Potter. But so much for empire building: they haven't won a major prize since.

5

Hughie shoves a referee into the bath (1926–27 and 1927–28)

Après le déluge . . . déluge part deux. The leading First Division marksman during the offside mayhem of 1925–26 had been Ted Harper of Blackburn Rovers. He wasn't the most graceful of players, but he knew how to force the ball into the net, converting plenty of the crosses repetitively flung at him by wingers Joe Hulme and Arthur Rigby, and chasing the constant stream of defence-splitting passes made by wily strike partner Syd Puddefoot (who had briefly been the most expensive player in the world while at – different times – Falkirk). Blackburn were otherwise a mid-table irrelevance, but Harper ended the season with a personal tally of 43 in 37, easily beating the previous top-flight record of 38 set by Everton's Bert Freeman in 1909 and matched by Joe Smith of Bolton Wanderers a dozen years later.

In the fancy new Third Division (North) – the ever-expanding League's popularity knew no bounds – James Cookson of Chesterfield went one better than Harper, scoring 44 in 38 matches to set a new all-division record. Newcastle United's Hughie Gallacher, though, was arguably even more prodigious than the pair of them. He only came down from Scotland in

December 1925, yet ended his first half-season in the Football League with 25 from 22, a rate which would have nudged the half-century were he *in situ* for the whole piece. United rewarded Gallacher in the provocative style, relieving defensive guru Frank Hudspeth of the captain's armband and presenting it to their new star. Not everyone was convinced the move was a wise one. 'I have heard a whisper that some supporters are not pleased at the skipper's mantle being transferred from Hudspeth's shoulders,' whispered Reflector, conspiratorially, in the *Mirror* just before the big 1926–27 kick-off.

The same paper did, to be fair, give credit where it was due a couple of days later, with a U-turning headline that redefined unequivocal praise: CAPTAIN GALLACHER OF NEWCASTLE: SCOTTISH LEADER DOES EVERYTHING RIGHT. Everything right? Well, pretty much: Gallacher scored all of Newcastle's goals in a 4–0 rout of Aston Villa. The last, a 60-yard rococo dribble and drive in the final minute, was missed by most of the St James' Park faithful, who were already streaming out of the exits. Trying to beat the rush is not a solely modern phenomenon.

The supporters soon got on board as Gallacher's genius – at times borderline unplayable – propelled his team into the title race. Huddersfield were chasing a fourth title in succession, and led the division going into March. But they had recently failed to beat a struggling Everton side. Newcastle showed them how it was done by crushing the same opponents 7–3, Gallacher claiming a hat-trick, one of his goals coming at the end of a mesmerising 30-yard solo run. Newcastle took over at the top, whereupon their captain turned the screw. Gallacher scored the only goal against the old enemy Sunderland, who also harboured championship pretensions, then outjumped Huddersfield centre-half Tom Wilson – five foot five beating a six-footer – to register the winner in another title showdown. Another hat-trick was notched in a 6–1 hammering of Arsenal.

The winger Stan Seymour – a local hero destined to serve as manager then chairman of the club – had the pleasure of scoring the goal that secured the title, at West Ham on the same afternoon Cardiff City took the FA Cup out of England. The captain made do with a tally of 36 strikes from just 38 matches. Not quite as high as Ted Harper's mark, maybe, but then Harper hadn't inspired his team to the championship.

Hughie Gallacher wasn't the only striker to have ripped it up in the north-east. Down in the Second Division, George Camsell, a 22-year-old Middlesbrough reserve filling in for injured first-choice forward Jimmy McClelland, embarked on a crazed spree. During October and January, he scored in 12 consecutive matches, a 29-goal rampage which included one brace, a hat-trick, three four-goal hauls and a five-goal romp.

The five came in a 5–3 Christmas Day win at Manchester City. 'A forward of considerable speed and splendid ball control, a marksman to be feared from any reasonable range!' simpered the *Manchester Guardian*. 'He scored five but did little else,' harrumphed the slightly calmer *North-Eastern Daily Gazette*, who if nothing else were clearly determined to hold the local lads to the highest of standards.

When Camsell scored twice at Notts County in February – his 44th and 45th goals of the season – he broke the Football League scoring record set by Cookson of Chesterfield a mere nine months earlier. Poor Cookson! His greatest achievement struck from the history books within a year. And there were still two-and-a-half months of the season remaining. Plenty more time for plenty more goals, and 14 were added to the grand total, despite Camsell suffering a broken thumb and supplier-in-chief Willie Pease missing most of the run-in due to a busted collarbone. Boro were promoted as champions; Camsell ended the season with a scarcely believable tally of 59. His record, opined the *Manchester Guardian*, 'may stand for all time'.

Newcastle's title defence was looking good for a while. On the opening day of the 1927–28 campaign, Gallacher scored a hat-trick in a 3–1 win at fellow title hopefuls Huddersfield. Tottenham were swept aside 4–1. Manchester United received a 7–1 trouncing at Old Trafford, their biggest home defeat since the war. Newcastle kept it going until November, at which point they toppled from the top of the table in dramatic style, embarking on a winless 11-game streak that stretched all the way into January. The nadir came on a bitter New Year's Eve, at a frozen St James' Park against Huddersfield. The visitors led a tempestuous match twice; Gallacher equalised twice. Towards the end, Alex Jackson scored what would prove to be Huddersfield's winner from the penalty spot. Newcastle claimed a penalty themselves for hands but were denied the chance to equalise for a third time by referee Bert Fogg, who was having none of it. Ice and Fogg: a meteorological trifecta was completed as Gallacher, notoriously quick to temper, fell into a rage which burned with the ferocity of a thousand suns. He was cautioned for riffing on the official's surname: 'You've been in a Fogg all afternoon!' Then, having been persuaded by his teammates to go and apologise after the match, he entered the referee's room to find the official standing precariously by the side of a freshly drawn bath. No prizes for guessing.

Gallacher found himself splashed all over the papers when he received a whopping two-month ban for dunking the ref. He skulked off back to Scotland to catch up with old friends, write a few newspaper columns, booze quite a lot, sulk, seethe, and

71

contemplate a permanent return to his homeland. By the time he was available for selection again, Newcastle were well out of the title race. He scored on his comeback, but Newcastle lost 3–2 at home to Bury. A week later they got thumped 5–1 at Burnley, though Gallacher was missing again, albeit at Wembley, causing all manner of havoc as the wizards of Scotland famously beat England 5–1.

Gallacher ended the season with 21 goals as the outgoing champions finished ninth, a decent enough return for the 32 matches he was permitted to participate in. But he was never quite the same for Newcastle again, and was sold to Chelsea in 1930 having fallen out with manager Andy Cunningham, who took a dim view of Gallacher's refuelling habits. Wor Hughie was often caught brawling on the streets of the city, bare-knuckle and half-cut. He also habitually enjoyed a few pints of heavy before matches, supplemented by the occasional half-time Scotch – always, in fairness, diluted with a healthy splash of water.

George Camsell meanwhile suffered undulations in form upon his elevation to the big time. English football's new shooting star disappointed on his First Division debut as Middlesbrough went down 3–0 at Manchester United. He had a glorious chance to make an imprint near the end; a calm sidefoot would have sufficed, but he opted to wildly thrash at the ball instead, with depressing consequences. He notched his first of the season in Boro's second game against Tottenham, then scored two in the first eight minutes against Everton, and another two in the same match after the Toffees had fought their way back to fleeting parity. Another sensational four-goal haul! William Dean, let the record state, helped himself to one of Everton's consolations in Boro's 4–2 win.

Was another season-long spree on the cards for Camsell? No, not quite. He suffered a minor scoring slump, and spoke revealingly of an inferiority complex over 'players who beat me' at the top level. In mid-October he missed a couple of golden chances in a home defeat by Burnley, causing the *Manchester Guardian* to speculate: 'It will not be surprising to learn that the record scorer of last season has been deposed in favour of his predecessor McClelland.' In fact, Camsell managed to hold onto his place, and finished the season with an extremely respectable 33 goals. But he scored only once in the last five games of the season, and a dismal winless run saw Boro fall from the relative safety of 17th to 22nd and rock bottom. Camsell could hardly be fingered for his team's relegation, seeing he'd contributed 92 goals in two seasons, though three gilt-edged opportunities missed on the penultimate Saturday during a 2–1 defeat at Derby County, when the old inferiority complex kicked in and hesitation took hold, proved ever so costly.

Middlesbrough's demise was confirmed on the final day in bitter circumstances: a 3–0 home defeat against equally imperilled neighbours Sunderland, who (as things turned out) would have lost their own top-flight status had the result gone the other way. But the previous year's Second Division champions were immediately heading back whence they came. And it wasn't the only kick in the teeth Camsell suffered that fateful afternoon.

William Dean – but let's not stand on ceremony, it's Bill to his friends and Dixie to the punters – was a star from the get-go. Everton beat cash-rich Newcastle United to his signature in the summer of 1925, after the 17-year-old scored 27 goals in 30 appearances for third-tier Tranmere Rovers. Dixie started whistling them in for his new employers, too, scoring 32 times in his first season at Goodison. That was some achievement by the teenage top-flight debutant: his total was just 11 goals shy of Ted Harper's contemporaneous First Division record, and he'd scored 24 more than anyone else at his club.

Then in June 1926, Dean crashed his motorcycle while on a jaunt with his girlfriend in North Wales, fracturing his skull, breaking his jaw and suffering severe concussion. In the immediate aftermath of the accident, as he lay unconscious in hospital, mere survival seemed touch and go. And for a while after he came round, playing professional football again seemed little more than a pipe dream. But within four months he was planting a power-header past the keeper in a reserve match against Huddersfield. He was ready to go again.

Not before time. Everton had lost seven of their first eight matches in 1926–27, winning just one of their first 13, and were flailing around at the bottom of the table. Dean's reappearance invigorated an insipid attack. He scored on his return in a victory at Leeds, and again a week later at Goodison to see off Arsenal. He plundered four goals on Christmas Day in a 5–4 win over Sunderland. Everton could only scrape survival that year, a legacy of their dismal start, but the antics of their energetic, determined, seemingly indestructible 19-year-old striker – 21 goals, plus another three in the FA Cup, at a rate of almost a goal a game – promised much more.

Everton opened the 1927–28 season with a four-goal home rout over Sheffield Wednesday, their young striker chipping in with one. He then grabbed a consolation in that 4–2 defeat at Middlesbrough – Camsell's aforementioned early flurry – and another in a draw at Bolton. A steady rate of goals became an incessant flow: a couple against Birmingham, another against Bolton, two in matches with Huddersfield, Newcastle and Spurs. Dean's hot streak culminated when he scored all of Everton's goals in a 5–2 win over Manchester United.

West Ham United had been early leaders of the division. Not that they had impressed overly. The match that took the

Hammers top, a workmanlike 2–0 victory over Burnley in early October, was proclaimed by the *Express* to be THE WORST GAME OF THE SEASON. In case the bit in large print didn't belabour the point enough, their scribe Broadcaster, cast adrift on waves of melancholy, announced that 'there is nothing but disappointment in this world'. The 90 minutes, he opined, were 'not bad enough to be funny, just bad enough to be exasperating . . . it was the worst game I have seen for a long time . . . for long stretches nothing happened . . . there was a long stretch of futility . . . it was too dreary for words.'

Oh Broadcaster! Was he OK? Thankfully, he had cheered up no end a fortnight later when West Ham went to Goodison and were thoroughly put in their place. Everton were without Dean, who had scored 17 of their 27 goals by this point, and was away losing in Ireland with England. Back home, his club were expected to struggle. They won 7–0. It wasn't difficult to discern Broadcaster's glee. 'Towards the end the Everton players were winning standing still. Without running at all they would pass to each other, and do it slowly, so as to let West Ham see how it was done, while the Hammers chased round in circles in vain attempts to gain possession. The onlookers were amused!'

A Dean hat-trick against Portsmouth took Everton to the top. (West Ham, for the record, were busy losing seven in eight as they plummeted towards obscurity. Broadcaster's breathing patterns became more regulated.) The Toffees consolidated their position with a 7–1 win over Leicester, Dixie scoring three more. By the turn of the year, when Dean claimed two in a victory at Sheffield Wednesday, he had scored 35 of his team's 63 goals. Everton were four points clear of Huddersfield Town in the race for the title.

Time for a mini-collapse. Everton stumbled their way through a nine-game winless run, even though Dean managed to keep his head during it: a hat-trick at Anfield, of all places, saw him equal Ted Harper's top-flight scoring record of 43. It was still only February, so breezing past Harper's mark was a given, and there was still plenty of time left to line up Camsell's Football League record in the viewfinder. A bronze centime for Dean's thoughts, then, when stuttering Everton failed to find the net in the next four matches. Leaders at the start of March, they ended the month three points behind Huddersfield having played two games more.

Dean eventually rediscovered his shooting boots, with ten in the next seven games. (It should have been 11; a penalty against Bury was struck so pitifully that the keeper was able to jog across and kick the ball away.) Meanwhile it was Huddersfield's turn to crumble. They were chasing a League and Cup Double, but a victorious three-game semi-final epic against Sheffield United drained their energy reserves. Over four days at Easter Liverpool and Middlesbrough both visited Leeds Road and stuck four past the title hopefuls. Huddersfield then lost the Cup final to Blackburn, never recovering from the concession of a first-minute goal, the result of keeper Billy Mercer hesitating under a high ball. The team were nevertheless cheered home by a 10,000-strong crowd lining the streets between Huddersfield railway station and the town hall. Mercer received a particularly loud ovation from a loyal support.

But it wasn't enough to reawaken his spirit. In their next home game, Mercer was nearly bundled into the net early doors by Burnley striker George Beel, and the visitors, employing unashamedly robust tactics against more talented opponents, stuck a couple past the increasingly nervous keeper. That was three home defeats in four matches, and the following week it became four in five as Sheffield United once again launched a spanner into the works, this time by prevailing with ten men. Defeat to the Blades cut deep. Before it, Huddersfield were in charge of their own destiny. Now they trailed resurgent Everton by three points with just two games left. They went down 3–0 at Aston Villa in their penultimate fixture, and the championship went to Goodison for the third time.

Winning the title with a game to spare allowed Dixie to take centre stage in the last match, at home to Arsenal. He had scored four times in Everton's second-last game of the season at Burnley, an improbable haul which had dragged his season's total up to 57. All of a sudden, Camsell's 12-month-old record was a realistic get. Dean scored twice in the first half against the Gunners, a header and then a penalty which drew him level with Camsell. But the record-breaker took a long time in coming. With eight minutes to go, Alec Troup looped a cross into the Arsenal box. Dean rose and battered a header into the top right: his 40th headed goal of the season, and 60th goal overall. Cue bedlam, which couldn't be dampened by James Shaw equalising late to cap a giddy 3–3 draw. 'That's enough,' Dean told the ref in matter-of-fact fashion. 'I'm going off.' He left to a standing ovation before the final whistle sounded.

That wasn't the only grand departure of the afternoon. After the game the legendary Charlie Buchan, playing his last professional match for Arsenal, was presented with a gold-plated fountain pen and pencil as a token of his efforts over the years. But the celebrations were really all about Dean. George Camsell's record of 59, the one they thought 'may stand for all time', stood for just one season. Poor Camsell! Now he knew how James Cookson felt. And relegated on the same day, too. If only he hadn't stopped taking penalties after missing one against Millwall in February 1927. Middlesbrough were awarded another six after that. A target of 65 would surely have left everyone else – even a player as accomplished as Dean – whistling Dixie.

6

Norman releases a novelty record (1928–29 to 1930–31)

When Leicester City won the Premier League in 2016 commentators scrabbled around to find historical precedent for an astonishing heist. Most settled for one of two: wily Ipswich Town's softly-softly steal of 1962, or Nottingham Forest's strident 1978 smash-and-grab. Both comparisons had their merits. All three clubs were of modest size compared to the usual League-winning behemoths. All three teams were proper functioning organisms greater than the sum of their parts, pieced together using discarded or undiscovered talent. And all three had effectively arrived from nowhere, unexpected, unheralded and unannounced, to swipe the biggest prize in English football.

Yet Leicester's title shenanigans are probably more of a piece, rhythmically speaking, with The Wednesday in the late twenties. Consider. Leicester's great escape of the 2014–15 Premier League season was, in its own way, as jaw-dropping as what followed. Having suffered a run of 17 defeats in 23 games, the Foxes were bottom of the table and seven points adrift of safety with only nine matches to go. But seven wins from that final batch of games hauled them to the comfort of 14th place. Precious momentum which served them well the following season, and an integral part of the legend.

As for The Wednesday? They found themselves in a similar bind back in 1927–28, too, rooted to the foot of the First Division at the end of March, seven points adrift of second-bottom Portsmouth. They had won just two of their previous 15 games. 'It is all but impossible for them to overcome such heavy arrears,' sighed the *Manchester Guardian*. The jig looked up. And then a tale of revenge, served cold, was told. It would throw Wednesday a lifeline, and inspire a spectacular change in fortunes.

Wednesday signed inside forward Jimmy Seed from Tottenham Hotspur in the summer of 1927. Seed, an FA Cup winner with Spurs in 1921, had lost his place to Taffy 'Boy Wonder' O'Callaghan and, while brooding in the reserves, had his £8-a-week wage pettily reduced by a pound. Gripped by righteous funk, the 30-year-old Seed decided to hang up his boots and start out in management at Aldershot. But his plans were scuppered. Seed had been on the radar of Wednesday boss Bob Brown for some time, and Spurs decided to parlay that interest into hard cash: they refused to release their player to Aldershot, and sent him up north instead.

For a while, Seed played as though he'd left his heart somewhere in a field in Hampshire. He was unsuccessfully tried out in several different positions as Wednesday struggled awfully. But the planets eventually aligned. Seed's veteran status ensured he was handed the captaincy when long-serving defender Fred Kean lost his place in late February 1928. Then at Easter he took centre stage for the season's pivotal act: two games against his old club Tottenham over the holidays.

Spurs were a very capable side on their day. In February they had beaten champions-elect Everton 5–2 at Goodison. Seed's replacement, the Boy Wonder, upstaged Dixie Dean by scoring four.

In the top half of the table with six games to go, Spurs collectively decided that all the hard work for the season had been completed. Big mistake. On Good Friday, Seed scored in his new club's victory at White Hart Lane, then four days later, on Easter Tuesday, found the net again as Wednesday won the return at Hillsborough. The four points were precious for Wednesday in their desperate scramble for survival; the two defeats proved cataclysmic for Spurs.

Wednesday were still bottom; Tottenham were still ninth. But the entire division was the dictionary definition of nip and tuck: only ten points separated Wednesday from Derby County in fourth! Late-season form would come at a particular premium. Spurs wrapped up their programme a week before most other teams, sloppily losing three of their last four before nipping off for a post-season jaunt around Holland. Despite their late collapse, they were still four places above the relegation zone as they boarded the ferry.

But there was only a couple of points in it. Sure enough, Spurs found themselves watching with impotent horror from afar, as four of the five teams below them ground out the results they required. Sheffield United won at title-chasing Huddersfield. Manchester United thrashed rivals Liverpool 6–1. Sunderland beat neighbours Middlesbrough to send George Camsell back down to the Second. And it was Spurs who went down along with the Boro, because Wednesday completed their great escape, and a run of five wins in the last six, with a Seed-inspired victory over Aston Villa.

The final table was compact, bordering on bijou. Now only seven points separated fourth-placed Derby with the bottom spot. Had basement-dwelling Boro managed to find just four more points along their 42-game journey, they'd have ended up in the top half. The Wednesday had avoided the drop by just one point and yet – exactly like Leicester, 87 years later – found themselves safe and sound in 14th. And like Leicester 88 years on, they didn't spurn a single joule of that precious upwards momentum.

The Wednesday won the 1928–29 title by a point from – and this will please fans of basic narrative arcs – Leicester. The only significant change to their Great Escape team was the shifting in from the wing of Jack Allen to centre-forward. Allen's first game in his new position saw him find the net in a 3–2 defeat at Portsmouth. In his second, he scored all three in a win over Birmingham. In his third, he claimed all four in victory at Bury. The position most emphatically now his, he ended the season with 33 goals, a total he matched the season after as the club – now rebadged as Sheffield Wednesday – retained their title with ease. They finished ten points clear of second-placed Derby County, having scored 105 goals.

Some season for Allen, though his most famous 'goal' was one that was controversially disallowed: a last-minute would-be equaliser in the 1930 FA Cup semi-final against Huddersfield, the referee blowing for full time just before the shot crossed the line. The Terriers progressed instead, and faced Arsenal in the final.

The 1930 FA Cup final was played under the shadow of the Graf Zeppelin. The German airship hovered ominously over Wembley that afternoon, showing off, a heady mix of methane and metaphor. Arsenal won their first trophy against manager Herbert Chapman's former club. Airship apart, it wasn't the most memorable match. Alex James scored one and set up the other in a 2–0 win; his Scotland teammate Alex Jackson was uncharacteristically quiet for Huddersfield. The Graf Zeppelin also stopped off at Victoria Park, where over a thousand London workers took part in the first Red Sports Day. German athlete Otto Schippke gave a 'magnificent display', according to the *Daily Worker*. 'There was something symbolic in the fact that, as the British workers roared

Comrade Schippke home in his heat in the 220 yards, the huge
Graf Zeppelin swung into view over the trees. Up in the air, a
reminder of the imperialist shambles of 1914–18 . . . and on the
ground a German worker cementing the solidarity of the international working class.' What a decade stretched out before them.

The Cup final certainly wasn't a patch on Arsenal's previous
game, a 6–6 mid-table romp at Leicester's Filbert Street five days
earlier, the highest-scoring draw in First Division history. 'Queer
football,' according to the *Manchester Guardian*, working from an
older edition of their style guide. Arsenal had been 3–1 down at
half-time, scored three in eight minutes after the restart, but
couldn't close out a 6–4 lead. Dave Halliday scored four of Arsenal's
goals, but was nevertheless dropped for the final in favour of Jack
Lambert. Chapman set a high bar all right, and, in fairness,
Lambert did score at Wembley.

Alex James had paid back Arsenal's latest bold investment. The
Scottish winger was Arsenal's showpiece signing of the 1929–30
season, a £8,750 purchase from Preston North End. Manchester
City, Aston Villa and Liverpool were also interested, but a
supplementary £250-a-year job at Selfridge's department store,
where he casually demonstrated sports equipment with a fag on,
enticed him south.

There were no similarly high-profile deals ahead of Arsenal's
1930–31 campaign. This wasn't for the want of trying. Chapman
hoped to sign top-rated Austrian goalkeeper Rudi Hiden, 21 and
already an international with the famous Wunderteam. Hiden, a
baker by trade, was lined up with wage-boosting supplementary
work at a London catering firm, and sailed over with a view to
signing for the Gunners professionally once *in situ*. However, he
was stopped getting off the ferry at Dover and refused entry to the
country as an 'alien', the result of a protectionist diktat cooked up

between Ministry of Labour apparatchiks, the players' union and the FA. Burnley chairman Charles Sutcliffe was particularly vocal, calling the introduction of foreign players 'repulsive' and a 'fundamental sign of weakness in the management of a club'. Sutcliffe was sounding off in the small-minded style, and with industrial quantities of brazen chutzpah to boot: his club had just been relegated, and would spend the entirety of the thirties scrabbling around in the Second Division. 'Repulsively weak' Arsenal, by contrast, were about to experience the greatest decade of their entire existence.

Chapman, in a fit of stubborn pique, turned to Dutch keeper Gerry Keyser, who was already a UK resident. Keyser was a fruiterer by day: had he and Hiden ended up in the same squad the aroma of artisan pastries would have wafted down Islington High Street a good 70 years before hipster foodies arrived on the scene. As a result, he was being signed on amateur terms, so there was nothing the uptight suits could do about it. He wouldn't last the season in Arsenal's goal, eventually replaced by Bill Harper and then Charlie Preedy, but that wasn't the point. Chapman was engaged in a running battle with The Man, having also been ordered by the FA to desist with shirt numbering and remove a 45-minute countdown chronograph at Highbury. He pointedly made sure Arsenal reserves continued to wear numbers, and replaced his bespoke timepiece with a common-or-garden 12-hour, 60-minute clock (which soon enough became one of the great icons of English football).

This was just another scrape in an increasingly comical dust-up between traditionalists and modernisers. Not long after the Hiden farce, Arsenal and their close pals from Glasgow, the Rangers, were barred from staging floodlit exhibition matches at Wembley. FA secretary Sir Frederick Wall railed about 'this commercialisation of a great game'; *Sunday Express* columnist Man in the Corner responded with a righteous blast of steam in defence of 'the most progressive and enterprising club in the country'. Arsenal had been, in his opinion, stitched up left, right and centre by the FA and the dusty moralisers of the Preston-based Football League. 'Someone has evidently made up his mind that they are moving too fast, or at any rate at a pace which others cannot follow, and has decided to put on the brake. But Chapman, best-hated and most feared manager in the game, will beat them all. Is it due to northern jealousy? Lancashire, with its many officials in high places, has always looked down on London. If the Arsenal only concentrated on winning the League championship, as they did the Cup, they would go some way towards squaring the balance between north and south.' With exquisite timing, Chapman set about doing exactly that.

Chelsea's preparations for the 1930–31 season were the polar opposite of uncharacteristically parsimonious Arsenal. Newly promoted, the Pensioners embarked on a luxury spree. They splashed £6,000 on Aberdeen striker Alec Cheyne, best known for scoring an 88th-minute winner in a Scotland–England match direct from a corner, the resulting bunnets-off celebration being the genesis of the famous Hampden Roar. Another £10,000 – some breathless reports claimed a world-record £12,000 – was spent on Hughie Gallacher, who by now had fallen out with Andy Cunningham at Newcastle. Then in mid-September, Alex Jackson joined from Huddersfield for £8,500. Yet all-star Chelsea only won two of their first eight games. Gallacher's high point of the season came early, with the reception he received from Newcastle fans on his return to St James' Park. The low point was a dismissal against Grimsby just after Christmas for another full and frank exchange of views with a referee. His colourful Anglo-Saxon polemic led to front-page headlines and leader-column pontificating. 'Effective training will have in future to include a course of conversational manners!' opined the *Daily Mirror*. Gallacher was hit with another two-month ban.

The margins are fine when attempting to build a dynasty from scratch. Arsenal's large investments were starting to pay shiny silver dividends; but for one reason or another, Chelsea's team of costly talent never quite gelled. Chelsea finished 12th in their first season back in the First. They started the following campaign in dismal fashion, and were rooted to the bottom of the league after losing five of their first six. Jackson was his usual mesmerising self: at home against Aston Villa he laid on the opening goal with a skitter of weaving brilliance then scored two of his own. But Chelsea still lost 6–3, and most neutral observers agreed Villa were unlucky not to have hit double figures. Tom 'Pongo' Waring scored four for Villa that day. Dixie Dean put five into Chelsea's net at Goodison a couple of months later. Thanks to a mid-season burst, Chelsea recovered to another 12th-placed finish, but it was far from a happy end to the season. In the wake of their penultimate away match, at Manchester City, news leaked that Alex Jackson would be placed on the transfer list. The player's reputation as one of the most skilful in the world was enough to make the decision front-page news. CHELSEA FOOTBALL BOMBSHELL! screamed the *Mirror*. No official decision was given, but it was confirmed that Jackson 'would not be re-engaged in any circumstances'. Jackson responded that he was 'relived the break has come' as he was 'not happy' at Chelsea, but 'the way in which it has come is not pleasant'.

It transpired Jackson, by his own admission, was carpeted for ordering a round of drinks for his teammates – 'enough for one drink per man after we already had a drink each' – in a Manchester hotel the night before the game with City, which ended in a 1–1 draw. Jackson scored – a tap-in – but otherwise Chelsea's forward line had a stinker in a match they should have won easily. Whether this boozy episode was the real motivation behind Chelsea's decision is debatable. Jackson revealed that he had been asked to extend his contract with the club a couple of days before the City game, but refused to accept, his head turned by Nîmes in France, who were offering significantly better terms. Jackson lost the game of hardball. Chelsea refused to pay up, and initially demanded £10,000 for his registration. No club in England was willing to meet the price. Jackson ended up playing non-league football, then spent an unfulfilling spell in France, before effectively retiring at 28.

Chelsea spent the next couple of years battling relegation. Alec Cheyne picked up injuries, lost form, and chipped off to France. It was down to Gallacher to keep the team afloat. This was despite his usual intemperate travails. He found himself up in front of the beak after a free-for-all in a café on Fulham Broadway with a gang of abusive local fans. Another evening ended with a swift, airborne dispatch from a hostelry on the King's Road. A couple of Leeds United players, coincidentally taking an evening constitutional along the famous thoroughfare before the next day's match at Stamford Bridge, watched in disbelief as the tired and emotional forward came crashing through the saloon doors, across the pavement and into the gutter. The next day, Chelsea beat Leeds 6–0. Gallacher was the star man, scoring one and setting up two more.

Gallacher ran out of money and agitated for a move in order to trouser a signing-on fee large enough to clear some eye-watering debts. Everton and Manchester United showed an interest, but Chelsea opted to sell him to Derby County. He first heard of the deal when he turned up for training one morning at ten o'clock; when the guard blew the whistle for the 6.25 to Derby, he was packed and on the train. So a mere three years into the project, all of Chelsea's big-money signings were gone. A glitzy period in Chelsea's young history – the club was less than 30 years old at the time – ended without reward. The only tangible artefact left behind from the era was the B-side of 1933 Colombia Records release DB1287 by BBC radio comic Norman 'A song, a smile, a piano!' Long. The lead track, a ballad of satirical whimsy called 'Ten Pahnds Dahn', told the tale of a family moving from Hackney to one of the new suburban estates.

> Now I pay instalments 'til the house belongs to me
> I've done a bit of reckoning and as far as I can see
> It's going to be mine for keeps in 1983
> And I'm only payin' ten pahnds da-aaa-aaahn

Similar contemporary social themes were explored on a flip-side that would continue to have cultural cachet for another 37 years: 'On the Day that Chelsea Went and Won the Cup'

> Landlords called round and begged to do repairs galore
> But their tenants said this wasn't fair unless the rents were more
> And a film star had the self-same wife he had the day before
> On the day that Chelsea went and won the Cup

How well the Chelsea barbs played in the theatres up north can only be guessed, because audiences in those parts had their own reference points. Hard to imagine now, but during the early thirties Manchester United were little more than a music-hall joke themselves. The lowest point in their history, in stark statistical terms, came on 5 May 1934. At the dawn of the day, with one game of the Second Division campaign remaining, they sat in the relegation places, visits to Gateshead, Accrington Stanley and

New Brighton awaiting them next season. By sunset, they had won 2–0 at Millwall to send the south Londoners down instead. United's 20th-place finish remains the worst in their entire history.

A sorry state to be in, yet that episode had its plus points: the thrill of escape, for starters, and the relief that comes with the sense of having bottomed out. By contrast, United's 1930–31 First Division campaign had nothing going for it at all. Herbert Bamlett, who had nearly led Oldham to the title in 1915, was the manager, and it was clear he had long lost his mojo. His side had lost the last two matches of the previous season – the final game had been a desperate 5–1 home defeat by Sheffield United, who would have been relegated without the win – and the humiliations continued apace come the new season. They played well enough on the opening day to earn a point at Old Trafford against a lively Aston Villa side. But they didn't get it, goalkeeper Alf Steward fumbling a last-minute Jack Wilson backpass to let Tom 'Pongo' Waring sniff out the winner in a 4–3 romp.

The tone was set. Another 11 consecutive defeats followed. The run included 3–0 losses at Huddersfield and Sheffield Wednesday, a 4–1 derby defeat at Manchester City, another 4–1 defeat at Portsmouth, a 5–1 thrashing at West Ham, a 6–2 stuffing at Chelsea, a 6–0 shellacking by Huddersfield and a 7–4 whipping by Newcastle. Thoroughly average Grimsby Town team came to Manchester and won 2–0 at a canter. The local *Guardian* newspaper noted how Town displayed 'teamwork and understanding resulting in objective passing, instead of the kicking at random and trusting to luck that constituted the "policy" of their opponents'.

Around 3,000 supporters called a public meeting at Hulme Town Hall, passing a vote of no confidence in the management. They decided to boycott the upcoming visit of Arsenal 'as a protest against the inactivity of the directors in regard to strengthening the team'. The symbolic stay-away proved an utter fiasco, as Old Trafford welcomed a 30,000-strong crowd, easily their best of the season. United played well, though Arsenal went home with a 2–1 victory.

The 13th game of the season proved lucky for United, who finally picked up some points by beating Birmingham City on a waterlogged Old Trafford pitch by lumping passes high and hard up the middle of the field in the basic manner. The sodden ball wasn't the only thing in the air that day: excitement was rife, as a grand total of 201 goals were scored in all Football League fixtures, the first time the double-hundred mark had ever been passed. Grimsby stuck eight past Leicester City. A freshly upbeat United travelled to reeling Leicester the following week, and predictably lost 5–4.

Nothing had changed. Middlesbrough manager Peter McWilliam felt it necessary to throw Bamlett a professional lifeline. He publicly called for 'all sportsmen, especially the followers of Manchester United, in the present tragic state of this famous club, to rally to their aid'. If that seems strange now, it would have seemed positively trippy back then, given Boro had themselves lost 7–0 the previous week. That McWilliam was speaking from a position of relative strength to Bamlett spoke volumes about United's plight.

United went to Villa just after Christmas and shipped seven, the home side threatening double figures despite barely breaking a sweat. Goalkeeper Steward, it was wryly noted, had a magnificent game. United enjoyed the Easter holidays a bit more: they won away for the first time in the season at Sunderland, then thumped local rivals Liverpool 4–1. But by then it was already far too late. The hapless Bamlett was bounced out of office, his trademark bowler hat whistling after him, secretary Walter Crickmer stepping up as manager. Crickmer was unable to coerce United into finishing with much of a flourish. United concluded their card meekly, going down 6–1 at Derby, then letting George Camsell score four for McWilliam and Middlesbrough at Old Trafford. Only 3,000 spectators witnessed Camsell's haul, as United quietly slipped out of the big time after the most underwhelming 4–4 draw in League history. The following morning, a gentle earthquake caused by a rock fault in the Irwell Valley shook Old Trafford for ten seconds.

The new offside law was still causing havoc. Manchester United were relegated in 22nd place having let in a whopping 115 goals during 1930–31. Blackpool managed to trump that gargantuan tally, their final goals-against total of 125 a top-flight record that stands to this day. But they avoided the drop, a point ahead of Leeds United, who had an almost identical goals-for record to the Seasiders but conceded on 44 fewer occasions. Leeds also went to Blackpool and won 7–3. But life's not meant to be fair.

Still, one person's defensive calamity is another's goalfest. Towards the top of the table, teams were filling their boots to the brim. Despite scoring 102 goals, a figure that would normally guarantee the title, Sheffield Wednesday couldn't match Huddersfield's feat of three championships in a row. They came third, wise old talisman Jimmy Seed limping off the stage at 35, his knees finally shot. He left Hillsborough to finally fulfil those managerial ambitions at Clapton Orient.

Wednesday were totally outgunned by Aston Villa and Arsenal. Villa ended up as the top scorers in the division with 128 goals, a top-flight record. The previous high-water mark, Wednesday's 105 just the season before, was overhauled in mid-March with eight games still to play. Pongo Waring found the net 49 times in 31 matches, the second-best First Division haul in history; Eric

Houghton scored 30 from the wing. In mid-March they beat Arsenal 5–1 at Villa Park. After the game, Waring took the opportunity to tease Arsenal's vanquished manager. 'You'd like to get me, wouldn't you, Herbert?'

Chapman certainly would have, though the barb is unlikely to have cut too deep. The problem for Villa was this result had been something of an outlier for Arsenal. The Gunners had been matching free-flowing Villa goal for goal, their well-drilled defence soaking up pressure before the forwards burst away on the quick-break. Arsenal travelled back south to lick their wounds, but they were still seven clear of Villa at the top, with a game in hand. They maintained that lead until the end of the season, despite an inferior goals-for column: just the 127. Ah well, they'd settle for smashing the all-time record number of points: 66.

The title had finally been wrested from the Football League's northern and Midland heartlands. The balance had been squared, just as the Man in the Corner had demanded. Arsenal celebrated their epochal victory with dinner at the Café Royal on Regent Street, quite the dapper dandies. Villa officials were sportingly in attendance to raise a toast. Arsenal swanned off for a close-season tour of Denmark and Sweden. Chapman – egotistical enough to announce this to the Reuters news agency – made a bet with a Swedish journalist that Arsenal would emerge from their Scandinavian sojourn undefeated. The wager was a new hat. The Gunners won six out of seven matches against combinations from Copenhagen, Stockholm and Gothenburg, to an aggregate tune of 27 goals to six. The other match was drawn. Herbert returned to London, a wide grin playing beneath a fetching new homburg.

7

Herbert and George sprinkle some showbiz glitter (1931–32 to 1935–36)

Dixie Dean didn't stop scoring goals. After his record-obliterating antics in 1927–28, he followed up with 26 in 29 appearances during an injury-hit season, then 23 in 25 the one after that. Not bad for a young man dealing with oppressive levels of expectation for both club and country – the *Manchester Guardian* branded him a 'failure' for not instantly replicating his 60-goal season – and getting hoofed from pillar to post in the process.

Yet it was all for nothing. Everton began to collectively misfire. With pretty much the same personnel, their 1928–29 title defence was a shambles. Standing on the periphery of the title race in March, they closed out with eight losses in nine games, finishing a miserable 18th. The trend continued at the start of the following season with only one win in the first seven. Money was invested in striker Tosh Johnson and all-rounder Tommy White, while legend-in-waiting Ted Sagar made his debut in goal as a 19-year-old. But this wasn't their time yet. In early April, fellow strugglers Grimsby Town came to Goodison and won 4–2, Joe Robson their ersatz Dixie with a hat-trick and an assist. It was Everton's sixth straight defeat. Rock bottom and four points adrift of safety with five games to go, it looked all over.

Everton made a game effort at a glorious escape. They were once again without the injured Dean during the run-in, but closed the gap by winning three of the next four and drawing the other (and they should have won that, having been 3–1 up at Manchester United only to nervously fritter away their lead). Going into the final day, they required a win at Goodison against Sunderland to have any hope of staying up. Pressure enough, so they certainly didn't need the anonymous letter sent to Sunderland ahead of the game, with a Liverpool postmark and on a Merseyside bookmaker's headed paper, which alleged that arrangements had been made for a 2–0 home win. Everton chairman Will Cuff furiously denied the accusation. 'It is an outrageous suggestion! Rather than countenance such a thing, we would go into a fourth division! It is plain the anonymous man has a diseased mind!'

Everton ended up winning 4–1, nothing was ever proved, and much good the victory did them anyway, for all the sides above them won too. Founder members of the Football League 42 years earlier, they now slipped out of the top tier for the very first time. 'It is a salutary lesson on the limitations of the power of the purse,' preached the very reverend *Manchester Guardian*. Only Aston Villa and Blackburn Rovers remained as unbroken members of the First Division.

Dixie Dean, as the leading striker in the land and having done his bit, would have been within his rights to chip off. But he was the loyal sort: in the wake of his 60-goal season, he had turned down a generous £25-per-week offer to join the New York Giants in the fledgling US soccer league. So he was always going to stay and help sort the mess out. Everton won the 1930–31 Second Division with a month to spare, scoring 121 goals. Dean claimed 39 of them in 37 appearances. A fine response to adversity, though *The Times* suggested the job was only half done: 'The side will have to be much more consistent than in recent years if it is to take once more a high place in the First Division.'

You want consistency? Back in the big time, Everton strung together a sequence of fixtures between mid-October and the end of November that redefined the word: they routed Sheffield Wednesday 9–3, Newcastle 8–1, Chelsea 7–2 and Leicester 9–2. Four matches, 33 goals, 16 of which were scored by Dean. Everton built a lead big enough to allow a sticky patch mid-season plus home and away losses to reigning champions Arsenal. They became only the second newly promoted team, after neighbours Liverpool in 1905–06, to win the title. Dean helped himself to 45 this time round.

Arsenal won the next three championships. The first in the sequence looks something of a formality on paper: they ended the 1932–33 season four points clear of nearest challengers Aston Villa, having scored 118 goals to their 92, their goal average 1.93 to 1.37. They won 16 of their first 20 games. The final match in that sequence was a festive feast for the Highbury faithful: a 9–2 Christmas Eve win over Sheffield United, Jack Lambert scoring five. The game is described in the club's official history as 'the height of Arsenal's powers in the whole inter-war period'.

It's a long way down, and just three weeks later, Chapman's Arsenal reached their undoubted nadir. The table-topping Gunners were drawn away to Walsall, tenth in the Third Division (North), in the third round of the FA Cup. 'It will be the joke of the day if the League leaders are beaten,' opined the *Manchester Guardian*. The manager made all the right sounds ahead of the David versus Goliath face-off. 'We look upon our tie with Walsall just as seriously as though it were with Aston Villa,' Chapman insisted, before sending his men out for double training sessions and feeding them restorative oysters and tripe.

But talk, like tripe, is a cheap cut. Chapman decided to rest two of his biggest stars in Eddie Hapgood and Joe Hulme, while throwing in two reserves and a couple of first-team debutants. Arsenal went down 2–0. One of the reserves, Tommy Black, disgraced himself by cutting Walsall striker Gilbert Alsop off at the knee, a foul which resulted in a bench-emptying brawl. On the train back to Paddington, Chapman told Black never to darken Highbury's door again, and that his boots would be sent home with some transfer forms to sign. Black was dispatched to Plymouth, which in terms of distance from north London is like being sent to Coventry twice.

Arsenal responded to this national humiliation with a 2–1 home win over Manchester City, though they were far from impressive, Cliff Bastin scoring an undeserved winner three minutes from time. It was a rare victory during an uncharacteristically rocky period between January and March. Chapman, increasingly exasperated, decided to make Arsenal's kit more distinctive, with a view to helping his out-of-form players pick a pass. His idea was a riff on a suggestion by his friend Tom Webster, a cartoonist for the London *Evening Standard*. Webster often played golf wearing colourful tank tops over long-sleeved white shirts. One day, while out with Chelsea boss David Calderhead, he suggested his blue-and-white-sleeved combo might make a good look for the Pensioners. Calderhead, at 68 a Victorian gentleman and thus conservative of taste, demurred. So Webster sketched out some red-and-white designs for Chapman and Arsenal instead. Always a sucker for a new gimmick, Chapman ordered a job lot of red merino-wool sweaters, told his players to yank them over some white cricket flannels, and an iconic look was born.

Not that the sartorial switch worked immediate wonders. On 4 March 1933 Arsenal ran out sporting their new look, and copped cat-calls and dog's abuse from their own support. The Jockeys, as Arsenal were briefly known to terrace wags, lost 1–0 at home to Liverpool. But just as they started to feel the breath of Sheffield Wednesday and Aston Villa on their brand new collars, something clicked. Arsenal thrashed Villa 5–0 and Wednesday 4–2 as part of a well-timed five-game winning burst. A 3–1 win at blue-sleeved Chelsea secured the title for English football's nattiest dressers. They hadn't quite worked out how to stop the colours running in the wash, but they'd sort that out in time.

The shirts proved to be Chapman's last major innovation, the 1932–33 championship his final success. He hadn't stuck around to see the Huddersfield Town side he built complete their hat-trick of titles in 1926; now fate ensured he wouldn't witness his Arsenal making it three in a row either. Chapman saw in 1934 with a chill, but kept working regardless, travelling to Sheffield to run the rule over upcoming opponents Sheffield Wednesday, then going to Guildford City to watch the Arsenal third team in action. Upon making it back home, his temperature racing out of control, he repaired to bed. The doctor diagnosed pneumonia, a killer before penicillin became widely available. Chapman died in the early hours of Saturday 6 January, the day Arsenal were slated to host Wednesday.

There was no postponement. At a solemn Highbury, a bugler played 'The Last Post'. The crowd of 50,000 respectfully removed their hats and caps. Chapman's seat in the dugout was left symbolically empty. Arsenal could only manage a draw. Cliff Bastin was kicked around the park like a rusty tin can; he was eventually carted off on the shoulders of trainer Tom Whittaker towards the end of a game that briefly threatened to boil over.

It was a day of heightened emotion. At Blackpool, a rogue clearance hit a supporter full in the face. The game was stopped for several minutes as the police tried to calm the irate punter down; for a while, he demanded the player responsible be arrested for assault. In the Third Division, Stockport put 13 goals past Halifax Town without reply, a new Football League record. Halifax goalkeeper Steve Milton had been making his debut. Perhaps most outrageous of all were the scenes at Villa Park, where frustrated home favourite Pongo Waring, his side 5–1 down, was ordered off by referee Peter Snape for going in too hard on Tottenham keeper Joe Nicholls. Waring reacted to the decision with theatrical disbelief, shaking his head ostentatiously and refusing to walk. Snape reacted in kind, reaffirming his decision with a mime artist's flourish, gesturing in the direction of the tunnel. It was all too much for the suffering home support. As Waring trudged off, stones, bottles, apples and oranges cascaded onto the pitch. One fan shaped to remonstrate with a linesman, but before he could engage, he was clipped around the lug by a nearby bobby and dispatched back into the stand. A small boy then rushed the field of play, though only to gather the discarded fruit. The little lad filled his pockets, then scampered off for a feast.

In a grim coincidence, Chapman was not the only sporting legend to pass away that day, destined to miss the fruits of his genius: Alister MacKenzie, the renowned golf-course architect who had just completed the layout of Augusta National, died two months before the first drive was hit at the inaugural Masters Tournament. A thoroughly miserable period concluded when Arsenal director H. Langham Reed suffered a fatal seizure while dressing to attend Chapman's funeral.

Another director of the club, George Allison, took over temporary control of the team, though he was very much a *laissez-faire* figurehead, the public face of a triumvirate made up by trainer Tom Whittaker and reserve team manager Joe Shaw. The trio guided Arsenal home in a fairly uneventful title race. Huddersfield and Derby both took brief turns at the top, but were quickly overhauled by a side who were efficient rather than spectacular: the Gunners' goals-for total in 1933–34 was just 75, a whopping 43 fewer than the previous season. A parsimonious defence was the crucial difference this time round.

While Chapman knew a thing or two about generating publicity, Allison was pure showbiz. An early BBC star, he became famous as a radio commentator when the medium took traction in the late twenties, and covered FA Cup finals, England–Scotland matches and the Grand National steeplechase. He also wrote a regular column for the *Daily Express*: George Allison's Broadcast. 'Good morning, everybody!' he would trill. 'This is Allison calling!'

The rumour mill went into overdrive. Would Allison take over as manager permanently? An old hand at playing the media like a flute, he led club officials and journalists on a merry dance designed to make him appear windswept and interesting. After a deliberate period of post-season silence, desperate hacks were eventually tipped off that, according to 'communiqués from New York City', Allison had resigned from a role he held at the London bureau of the W. R. Hearst newspaper organisation. 'I know nothing of his business affairs,' shrugged confused Arsenal chairman Sir Samuel Hill-Wood when asked what on earth was going on. 'I cannot get in touch with Mr Allison as I am told he has gone to Ireland to be present at the draw for the Irish sweep.'

Allison eventually resurfaced, and took over on a bumper contract far in excess of Chapman's £2,000 annual stipend. 'I have had about 32 years experience of professional football and, I believe, some reputation in the football world,' he announced. 'I do not say what kind of reputation! But I wish to say that the

Arsenal will continue to carry on in the best traditions of association football if anything on my part can assure it. We shall continue to secure the finest players available.'

Tottenham Hotspur finished third in 1933–34. They came in a good ten points behind Arsenal, and were never in the title race, but it was a fine performance nevertheless from a newly promoted team. George Hunt was the driving force: the 'Chesterfield Tough' had scored 32 goals during their promotion season, and 32 more upon on his arrival in the First Division. Yet their success was not just down to the exploits of one star, and Spurs were held up as exemplars of a new approach.

'There is evidence that the leading League clubs are abandoning the system whereby team-building is synonymous with the expenditure of thousands of pounds on readymade stars,' began a special report in the *Daily Mirror*. Spurs had 'proved up to the hilt that the nursery system can be made to pay. The Spurs' success on their return to the First Division was a triumph for their declared policy of developing their own talent. Their team was packed with youngsters whom they had discovered themselves. And this team took them to third!'

You can bet your bottom dollar that Manchester City right-half Matt Busby was taking copious notes. But whether the business of football, still in its infancy, was quite ready for such root-and-branch reassessment of player development and transfer policy is a debatable point. Spurs lost experienced defender Arthur Rowe to injury during the following season, and the whole thing fell apart with indecent haste. The youngsters embarked on a 16-game sequence without a win, and finished rock bottom of the 1934–35 table. Tottenham wouldn't get back into the top flight until the fifties, though some things are worth waiting for.

Allison and Arsenal by contrast continued to spend big, landing the tough-tackling Wilf Copping from Leeds and Ted Drake from Southampton, and a third consecutive title was in the bag soon enough. Drake, strong and direct but clever enough to link up when required, was billed by his new manager as 'the best centre-forward in the world'. The hyperbole wasn't totally absurd: he scored 42 times in 1934–35, including seven hat-tricks, as Arsenal returned to free-flowing ways.

Arsenal couldn't make it four in a row, though their consolation prize in the 1935–36 season was the FA Cup. Drake was injured for most of the campaign, yet the two signature moments of the season would still be his. He grabbed the only goal against second-tier Sheffield United in the Cup final, defying instructions to shoot with an injured leg, his knee swathed in bandages the size of a bath-towel. But even that showstopper took second place to his seven-goal haul in the League at Aston Villa in December 1935. It's still the greatest striking performance in English top-flight history.

Drake's seven came from nine shots. For the record, one of the unsuccessful attempts was saved by Villa keeper Harry Morton, the other smacked the crossbar. Nobody's perfect. And spare a thought for poor Allison, who wasn't there to witness his star signing running amok. He was home in bed with a head full of flu, and had to make do with an ever-expanding quilt made from telegrams, each comfy missive informing him of Drake's latest net-busting achievement. Villa took their humiliation in good grace, queuing up at the final whistle to shake Drake by the hand. They later presented Arsenal's seven-up hero with the match ball, signed by all their players.

Villa had got used to making magnanimous gestures. The masters of the Victorian era were rooted to the bottom of the table. It was already the third time they had meekly shipped seven goals at home, and the Christmas bells hadn't even starting ringing yet. The ones for raising alarm, however, were pealing like billy-o. Villa's defence was in a parlous state, partly because record signing Jimmy Allen, a £10,500 stopper bought from Portsmouth a year earlier, was taking an aeon to settle in the Midlands. So in November another centre-back, Tommy Griffiths, was purchased for £5,000 from Middlesbrough, while a new left-back, George 'Icicle' Cummings, arrived in an £8,000 deal from Partick Thistle. Both had barely been brought together before they were ripped apart again by Drake.

Villa, once proud but now simply desperate, coughed up an eye-watering £35,000 on various players between November and January in the hope of reviving their moribund team and swerving relegation. Their penultimate match of the season was at Arsenal, where they regained a little dignity in a narrow one-goal defeat. But it was far too late for Villa. They ended the season second from bottom, having let in 110 goals. Not even a joint-fifth-best scoring tally of 81 could save them. The grand old giants, six-time title winners, Football League founders and the club of Old Mac, were relegated for the first time in their history.

Arsenal's three-year reign at the top was ended by Sunderland, who fair flew out of the blocks in 1935–36. Roker Park was the centre of operations: the north-eastern giants won their first 11 home games of the season, the last of that sequence a mesmerising 5–4 win over the reigning champions. Sunderland's playmaking genius Raich Carter dominated as usual, scoring twice; flying winger Jimmy Connor hit the decisive goal; a late deflection gave the scoreline a flattering sheen for Arsenal. At this point, just after Christmas, Sunderland were already seven points clear at the top,

Carter and Bobby Gurney regularly in the goals, their lead seemingly unassailable.

All that promised a serene procession to the title, but the second half of the season didn't quite pan out like that. The championship chase had been written off in the press as a 'one-horse race', but Sunderland failed to win a game between late February and April, allowing Derby County and Huddersfield Town to stay in the hunt. Their loss of form was eminently understandable. At the start of February, Chelsea came to Roker. Sunderland were leading 2–0 with 20 minutes to go, very much the better side, until a couple of late howlers by 23-year-old goalkeeper Jimmy Thorpe ensured the match ended in a 3–3 draw. The mistakes were sufficiently absurd for a disbelieving home support to give their keeper some trenchant stick. Thorpe was also fingered in the press on Monday morning, that weekend's fall guy for a disappointing result. It was nothing out of the ordinary.

But as the very same papers landed on breakfast tables across the country, Thorpe turned up for work feeling unwell. One of the Sunderland directors, a qualified doctor, found Thorpe had a badly bruised left eye and injuries to the back of his head. It turned out that early in the second half of Saturday's match, before Chelsea launched their comeback, Thorpe had bravely gathered a corner kick only to fall into the middle of a penalty-box mêlée and receive an accidental shoeing. He lay prone for a minute or so, motionless, but eventually hauled himself to his feet and continued playing. Nobody thought anything of it. Now, however, with the clarity of hindsight, it was obvious he had been seriously concussed. The mistakes that followed had been a dazed inevitability. Thorpe was ordered home to rest and take care of himself.

That evening, the young man became delirious and was rushed to hospital. He slipped into a diabetic coma – he had been treated for diabetes a couple of years earlier only to be discharged as 'permanently cured' – and never regained consciousness. 'When Jimmy came home after the match he didn't look well, but he was a boy who would not say much at any time,' sobbed his grief-stricken father, defending Jimmy's honour to the last. 'There is no doubt he was not himself when Chelsea scored their last two goals.'

Farce soon accompanied tragedy in fate's attempt to derail Sunderland's previously serene progress to the title. Towards the end of February, the pinch-faced mediocrities of the Football League decided to scrap all of the remaining published fixtures and reorder them on the hoof in a bid to stop the increasingly popular football pools from doing their trade. The fixture list was a fundamental part of the pools; in fact the whole business model was based around it. The League's decision was fuelled partly by residual Victorian prissiness regarding gambling, but mainly by equally old-fashioned green-eyed jealousy, the pools firms coining it in off the back of the sport.

Ludicrous bedlam was the predictable result of this petty order, as clubs only found out who they were playing, and where, 24 hours before a game. Fans didn't have a clue what was happening, while the railways were unable to arrange trains to meet demand. Gates plummeted. On the front page of the *Mirror*, the nation's biggest-selling paper, a desperate plea to END FOOTBALL POOLS WAR! took precedence over the new King Edward's first broadcast to the nation since his accession, news of which was shunted into a small box down the page. The decision was overturned after two Saturdays of futile nonsense which saw a discombobulated Sunderland lose at Preston and ship a three-goal lead in a home draw with Everton.

Despite it all, Sunderland got their act back together just in time. The wake-up call came at the end of March, with a 6–0 humiliation at local rivals Middlesbrough. Sunderland ended the game with nine men, the occasionally temperamental Carter kicking out in frustration, his partner down the right flank Bert Davis also sent packing for mouthing off at the referee. But Derby and Huddersfield had repeatedly spurned chances to close the gap at the top. Carter returned to his scheming best in the next match, orchestrating a 5–0 home win over Portsmouth. Nine days later, on Easter Monday, he was waving the baton at Birmingham City, where Sunderland secured the prize with three games to spare in a spectacular 7–2 win.

Sunderland's first title since 1913 was their sixth overall, and brought them level on the all-time honours list with freshly relegated Aston Villa, whose demise – coupled with the simultaneous relegation of Blackburn Rovers – meant that none of the 12 originals from 1888 could boast unbroken membership of the First Division. The new champions, who joined the League two years after its formation, were suddenly the only club never to venture outside the top flight. A boast they'd be able to make for another 22 years.

8

Sam gets lost in the fog (1936–37 to 1938–39)

Nutritional science was very much in its infancy during the 1930s. Here's George Allison of the Arsenal, upon being asked what steps a footballer should take to continue playing after the ripe old age of 30: 'I suggest cutting out tea and coffee and drinking milk instead. Or water. It is not easy to give up tea and coffee. There is the same kind of physical or chemical difficulty that one finds in giving up cocaine or any kind of dope. There is for a time low spirits or depression. But in time it passes completely away. One becomes as fond of milk as other men are of beer. Milk drinkers can play in the hottest weather without the least inconvenience.'

In 1934 Allison signed James Marshall from the Glaswegian giants Rangers. A talented inside-right, Marshall had won six Scottish titles and three Scottish Cups, averaging a goal every other game. He was also a qualified doctor who was moving to London in order to further his medical career. Like his new manager, he was well versed in cutting-edge developments in the field of isotonic replenishment. 'Champagne as a producer of energy is the safest of all stimulants,' he opined. 'It acts at once and leaves no harmful effects. It dulls the sense of fatigue so that the player feels refreshed and reinvigorated. The sparkle of the wine and the instinctive belief that it is doing him a power of good work upon his imagination, so that he steps out of the dressing room ready to win any match against any odds!'

Dr Marshall also held trenchant views on the benefits of smoking: 'Is it wise for the man who smokes his 25 or 30 cigarettes a day to give up entirely for two days before an important fixture? I should say that it would most likely be harmful. The man who smokes his modest ten may reduce his allowance to five during the season, and the constitution will very soon get used to it. But I would not advise the heavy smoker who is an athlete to give up his smoking entirely just before a big physical effort. Equally, a cigarette will steady the nerve of many an excited footballer.'

But drugs other than nicotine were considered beyond the pale, and there were constant rumours of clubs doping their players up to the eyeballs. Arsenal themselves had dabbled with amphetamines as far back as 1925, when Herbert Chapman's predecessor Leslie Knighton was approached by a Harley Street quack clutching a small bag of white tablets said to magically boost courage and strength. Knighton sampled the pusherman's wares and was soon off his noggin. Overwhelmed with a desire to dance, prance, sing and shout he momentarily considered tearing down all four walls of his Highbury office with his bare hands, a task he suddenly felt within his capabilities.

Knighton resolved to pass the tablets on to his men. 'There is nothing wrong in giving a team a tonic!' he convinced himself. Such pills were not yet illegal, science outpacing the game's governing bodies, though Knighton kept it quiet as the prim and proper British public were sure to disapprove of anything that could be construed as offering an unfair advantage. The tabs were discreetly dished out ahead of an FA Cup tie at West Ham, only for the match to be called off. Arsenal's lip-smacking players scattered about London in search of liquid refreshment. 'We drank water until I felt that the Thames would dry up,' Knighton panted.

A second dalliance with the pills, when the Cup tie finally went ahead, resulted in up-for-it Arsenal rushing around feverishly. They ran 'like Olympic sprinters' and 'jumped like rockets', according to Knighton. But they could only draw 0–0. The results, admittedly from a small data sample, were inconclusive. But the players disliked the savage thirsts the pills brought – described as 'red-hot and soul destroying' – and so with a defiant yell that 'nearly split the roof', they refused to continue with the experiment. Knackered, they were knocked out of the Cup.

A decade on, Dr Marshall set out a logical argument that doping was nothing to worry about unduly. Punters would be able to cop the signs a mile off, he reasoned, and in any case it would be 'so highly dangerous, in more ways than one, that it is impracticable . . . I think we can safely pooh-pooh the idea that nasty managers are dabbling with dangerous drugs'. With the good doctor having spoken, much of the concerned chatter died down. For a while. But it never faded away completely, and the issue would become a hot potato once more as the decade drew to a close.

During a match at the Valley in early September 1934 Charlton Athletic supporter William Hall collapsed on the terrace and passed away. At the inquest into his death, held four days later, the coroner for south-east London asked a family member whether Hall ever got excited during matches. 'No, not in the slightest,' his stepson replied. The coroner considered the answer before reaching his verdict: 'It must have been the strain of standing.' Charlton had never been the sort to get their fans' hearts a-flutter.

Poor old Mr Hall just missed out on his club's golden era. For the excitement levels at Charlton, under new manager Jimmy Seed, were about to be taken up a notch. After limping away from Sheffield Wednesday in 1931 Seed took over at Clapton Orient, to whom he had been recommended by his friend Herbert Chapman. Arsenal were scheming to use Orient as a nursery club for talent, and Seed was excited to be part of a cutting-edge experiment in player development. But when the FA put a stop to Chapman's expansionism, Seed increasingly saw no future at the club (not least because at one point, in the immediate wake of the FA ruling, Orient were left with no registered players, Chapman having taken everyone back to Highbury).

The Arsenal manager still had a positive role to play in Seed's story, though. He invited the Orient boss to a banquet held in celebration of his team's 1932–33 championship win. Seed of Clapton found himself seated, alphabetically, next to a representative of Charlton, who had just been relegated to the Third but had a few pennies to spend. They were looking for a new manager with new ideas. Seed eagerly threw his hat into the ring, landed the job, and set about injecting some much-needed energy into the club.

On the evening of the inquest into Mr Hall's demise, Charlton won at Torquay, goalkeeper Alex Wright earning plaudits for an inspired performance. The following morning, before the team made their way back to London, Wright went out swimming at Torre Abbey sands. He was preparing to dive from a raft when it was hit by a wave. Wright fell head first into shallow water, cracking his head on a rock and fracturing his spine. His mother and sister raced south overnight from Glasgow and reached him ten minutes before he died.

A tragic week at the Valley, but kinder days lay ahead. Seed signed Brentford striker Ralph Allen, whose 32 goals powered

Charlton to the 1934–35 Third Division (South) title. By the end of the campaign, the void in goal left by Wright had been filled by Sam Bartram, a 20-year-old who had played as a left-half and a centre-forward in the Wearside League, only to be spotted by Seed's brother Anthony while standing in for his team's injured keeper.

Charlton won instant promotion from the Second, becoming the first club to make it from the Third to the First in successive seasons, a feat not to be repeated until Queens Park Rangers did so in 1968. Seed didn't change much, bar laying out a cool £1,000 on Gillingham forward George Tadman while sending Allen to Reading for £828. A whopping net spend of £172. And every penny was well spent, as Tadman ended 1936–37, Charlton's first season in the top flight, as the club's leading scorer. He achieved that feat by scoring just 11 goals – the Dixie *de nos jours* he was most definitely not – but that wasn't really the point. Charlton's game-plan was to keep it steady rather than spectacular, goalscoring winger Harold Hobbis their one nod to aesthetic embellishment. Stay focused at the back and see what transpired.

The plan Seed sowed nearly reaped a spectacular harvest. Charlton kept grinding out one-goal victories, and were top going into March. The critics remained resolutely unimpressed. 'I am glad my future does not depend on adequately filling up an examination paper that would explain the success that has come to the Charlton club, for I simply could not do it,' huffed *Express* columnist Trevor Wignall, utterly perplexed that a team from the Third Division, pretty much, was now on the verge of the English title. 'The forward line is competent but not one of them would cause a rush if they were placed on the transfer list. The defence, good though it is, can be rattled. It seems to me the only things that can be fallen back on are comradeship and splendid team work.'

Faint praise, offered grudgingly. Though to be fair, Wignall's analysis was borne out by events. Subsequent victories over Preston and Manchester United were slight and rather fortunate, and suggested Charlton were beginning to run on fumes. The wheels whistled off the wagon just before Easter, when a 5–0 thrashing at Derby was followed by a 3–0 loss at Chelsea. Comradeship kicked in: Charlton responded bravely with a thumping 4–0 victory over an emerging Wolverhampton Wanderers, followed by four more wins in their last six games. But the resurgence came too late. Arsenal initially took over the leadership, but it was Manchester City, with games in hand and wind in their sails, who made the decisive charge.

Past masters at dropping from mid-table like a stone, City went the other way this time. After a couple of heavy losses in December – a 5–1 mauling by a Sheffield Wednesday side bound for relegation, and a very unmerry 5–3 Christmas Day spanking at Grimsby – they got their act together in style. They didn't lose again in the League, storming up the division as their four-pronged attack of Peter Doherty, Eric Brook, Fred Tilson and Alec Herd clocked up 80 goals between them. The signature performances were a couple of five-goal beatings of Liverpool around Easter, when it became clear City meant business. They scored 36 times in their last ten games to breeze past Arsenal and claim, at long last, their maiden title.

The Gunners gave up second place to Charlton, who deserved something for their gritty heroism. Seed's team finished just three points behind City, despite scoring 49 fewer goals. The following seasons saw them finish third and fourth using the same no-frills blueprint. Arguably the most memorable moment during that period came when they faced Chelsea on Christmas Day 1937, and an old-fashioned London-style pea-souper descended on

Stamford Bridge. With visibility down to inches, never mind feet or yards, the referee was forced to abandon the game. The problem was nobody bothered telling Sam Bartram, who stayed in his goal for a full three minutes after all the other players had departed for the changing rooms. He had simply assumed his teammates were down the other end, piling on the pressure in the thick fog. The power of positive thought, right there.

The initial pattern of 1937–38 was not dissimilar to the previous season: up until Christmas, Man City were bumbling their way to mid-table mediocrity. But instead of an upsurge, confidence betrayed them once again. Six losses and two draws during February and March saw them plummet into the relegation places. A late-season rally looked to have saved their bacon: Eric Brook scored four in a 7–1 win over West Bromwich Albion, Peter Doherty three in a 6–2 evisceration of Leeds United, a win in the penultimate game of the season which took them four places clear of trouble. They were level on points with all the teams below, but blessed with a far superior goal average. A win at fellow strugglers Huddersfield Town would guarantee the champions' safety.

And so with just over a quarter of an hour to go, Alec Herd unleashed a blistering 35-yard drive that had Huddersfield keeper Bob Hesford beaten all ends up. The ball crashed against the bar and back out. Town – who had just lost the FA Cup final to Preston North End in the last 30 seconds of extra-time, and were probably due a bit of luck – went straight up the other end. A long throw caused a kerfuffle in the City box, and Bobby Barclay toe-poked the ball over Frank Swift's prostrate frame and into the net. City responded to falling behind with a few desperate attacks, at one point surrounding the referee when the ball was stopped on the Huddersfield goal-line by what was in effect a rugby scrum.

No goal. No penalty. No more time. The final whistle blew. City then found out that all the teams below them in the table, bar one, had secured precious victories. The champions were relegated, a unique achievement, despite scoring 80 goals.

Anyone for a counterfactual? Had Herd scored with his 35-yarder instead of hitting the woodwork, and City hung on for the win, Huddersfield would have gone down instead. In that scenario, Huddersfield would have become only the second team to lose an FA Cup final and suffer relegation in the same season. The first? Manchester City in 1926. Of *course*.

At 3.40 p.m. on 16 September 1937 the sport of association football crashed through the looking glass. Television turned up. The BBC's fancy new outside broadcast cameras pitched up at Highbury, where Gunners manager and seasoned broadcaster George Allison put his lads through their paces in a 15-minute programme, *Football at the Arsenal*, wedged between a British Movietone news bulletin and the Mickey Mouse cartoon *The Wayward Canary*. The action was pinged back to the Beeb's nearby Alexandra Palace headquarters, where it was instantly transmitted to the couple of thousand of wealthy set owners peppered around north London. Viewers were treated to crisp, clear pictures of a kickabout between Arsenal's first XI and the reserves, as well as some 'football demonstrations' described by ringmaster Allison. 'Clifford Bastin will now show you how a football should and should not be trapped. First, do it badly!' Bastin followed the orders with a couple of theatrically heavy touches. 'Now show how it ought to be done!' Sure enough, Bastin provided viewers with the world's first action replay, the ball accidentally clanking off his foot and flying several yards away. His teammates, sat on the Highbury turf, crumbled with laughter.

'We'll always be happy to see television here at any time!' smiled Allison, as ever sensing the prevailing breeze. The Preston–Huddersfield FA Cup final was shown in part at the end of the 1937–38 season, and the following year's England–Scotland international became the first game to be broadcast live in full. But while it would take a while for the full effects of this experiment to be felt by the Football League – the best part of half a century, in fact – the genie was out of the bottle. Allison signed off the historic broadcast by announcing the upcoming Mickey Mouse cartoon. As the picture faded, one of his players could be heard cracking wise: 'Ah, here's something really worth watching.' Media meta-jokes are nothing new.

Arsenal got back to serious business. As Ted Drake was struggling with injury, they sourced a big-money stand-in: George Hunt, the 'Chesterfield Tough', £7,500 from Spurs. The transfer was a huge surprise, partly because nobody had moved from White Hart Lane to Highbury before, but mainly because the 27-year-old striker's career was rumoured to be as good as over. Hunt denied the allegations vociferously: 'People circulate lying gossip. For example, I was on the razzle every night. But I rarely touch a drink! I suppose this sort of tale started because I'm a sociable type of man who enjoys tinkering on the piano.'

Hunt was good for a sing-song, but he wasn't quite the marksman of old. Sharp enough to have once hit three hat-tricks in six games at Spurs, he was off the pace across town. Too eager to please, anxiety seeping into every pass and shot, he scored just three times in 18 appearances before being moved on to Bolton Wanderers. A refreshed Drake reclaimed his place and ended the season as his club's top scorer again. Even so, Hunt's efforts were enough for a League medal. Arsenal ended the 1937–38 season as champions, securing their fifth title in eight years. But they had to fight like blazes for it.

Brentford had, like Charlton before them, risen from the Third Division (South) to surprise the top-flight *cognoscenti*. In 1929–30 Harry Curtis's side won all 21 of their home games in the third tier, yet somehow failed to win promotion on account of bang-average away form. Three years later, they made it to the Second, and after a season of consolidation went up again. Despite some early hiccups, they finished fifth in 1935–36, their virgin season in the First: the club-record £6,000 signing of goal-a-game David McCulloch from Heart of Midlothian had been the key to their successful acclimatisation. And by 1937–38 they were ready to take a serious tilt at the title.

In mid-October they moved top of the League by eviscerating the famously parsimonious Charlton defence. They won 5–2 in a match which saw wing half-backs Duncan McKenzie and Tally Sneddon switch places with mind-boggling speed and fluidity. 'It would be difficult to overrate the quality of the football Brentford played,' purred the man from *The Times*. 'They were so clever, so adaptable in their ideas. McKenzie and Sneddon looked capable of murdering the Charlton defence.'

Towards the end of January, a 3–0 win over Everton gave Brentford a four-point advantage over Wolverhampton Wanderers. Arsenal at that point looked completely out of it, seven points back. But an eight-game run of six losses and two draws put an abrupt end to the fairytale. McCulloch started to spurn easy chances. Doubts crept in. The defence took on a ragged look. 'Brentford seem to have shot their bolt,' was the blunt assessment of the *Manchester Guardian* after Portsmouth beat them 4–1 in mid-March. They trailed in sixth.

The few late-season successes Brentford did enjoy served mainly to galvanise others into action. A 6–1 rout of rock-bottom Grimsby

Town cleared heads to such an extent that the Mighty Mariners won five of their last seven to escape relegation by a point. Arsenal, meanwhile, were routed 3–0 at Griffin Park on Easter Monday, keeper Joe Crozier knocking Ted Drake spark out when attempting to punch the ball clear. Drake was carted off on a stretcher, eventually re-emerging five stitches later, swathed in bandages, to meander around on the wing. At the end of the game – during which he received dog's abuse from an unsympathetic home crowd – he was carted off half-conscious by trainer Tom Whittaker, a towel covering his head, and sent to hospital. Arsenal's response was to win their final three matches of the season.

Arsenal had made a determined late run, yet it shouldn't have been enough. Wolverhampton Wanderers, led by charismatic and ever-so-slightly scary manager Major Frank Buckley, looked the real deal. Major Buckley had shown immense bravery during the First World War, his lungs taking a severe pounding from shrapnel and poison gas on the Western Front. That put an end to an average playing career, but his stint in the army stood him in good stead when he embarked on life as a manager. He had served in the Football Battalion, made up of amateur and professional players as well as supporters, and the friends he made with knowledgeable football men all around the country eventually served as a ready-made scouting network. Hot talent was on tap! The Major, with a little help from his friends, quickly developed a reputation for sourcing promising players on the cheap, then selling them on for large sums of money.

He was also at the cutting edge of physical conditioning. Trips to the seaside for long runs up and down the beach were refreshingly old-school; fitness camps in army-style barracks were a tad more extreme. Buckley took delivery of an 'electric horse', a moving platform on which players stood, holding onto rubber handles for dear life, as the machine vibrated like a bucking bronco, leg muscles being yanked around in an extremely vibrant manner.

Having joined Wolves in 1927, Buckley sold on more than £100,000 worth of talent during his first decade at the club. Fans began to get irked at what appeared to be the prioritisation of profit over glory. After a home defeat by Chelsea in November 1936, with Wolves struggling at the wrong end of the table, around 100 supporters raced onto the field of play. Initially it was thought they were going for the referee, but it turned out they were desirous of some hot chat with Buckley over transfer policy. Arthur Simmons of the *Daily Express* was aghast at the outpouring of fan frustration: 'It is a pity they cannot be held up to ridicule by being spanked in Wolverhampton market place. I am all for decorum in matters of flesh, but "trousers down, take that, and that, and that!" would be a fitting corrective.'

Buckley pleaded patience, and was justified when Wolves rallied to finish fifth in 1936–37. He now had a team more attractive than their reputation for an overly physical long-ball game suggested, and was ready to make a move for the title in 1937–38. Stan Cullis stood at the heart of the defence; the skilful inside forward Bryn Jones and dependable goalscorer Dennis Westcott were the threats up front. Towards the end of the season, Buckley unearthed another star in 18-year-old Dicky Dorsett, who in only his fourth senior appearance scored four times in a spectacular 10–1 Good Friday win over Leicester City. Westcott also hit four that day. Wolves even contributed Leicester's consolation, Cullis heading into his own net.

There were suggestions that Buckley had deliberately flooded the pitch beforehand, and Leicester hadn't been able to arrange suitable long-studded footwear at short notice. Still, ten goals are ten goals, and it couldn't have been the sole reason for the rout. After all, the same trick didn't pay off 24 hours later when Preston held Wolves 0–0 on another Molineux quagmire. Either way, the hard work appeared complete: a win at Sunderland on the final day of the season would give Wolves their first League title. But they fell behind early doors to a Raich Carter goal, and never looked like getting back into the game. Arsenal, on the other hand, breezed past Bolton 5–0 to take the title by a point, two-goal Cliff Bastin back in his groove, that brief humiliation in front of the BBC cameras having long been lost to the ether.

Wolverhampton's lethargy at the business end of 1937–38 came as something of a surprise because Buckley was notorious for injecting his players with extract from monkey glands, a new scientific wheeze designed to fill the squad with confidence and vigour. The injections were first administered to the team in 1937 by chemist Menzies Sharp, whose 'secret remedy' was influenced by French experiments in which testicles from young animals were grafted onto old knackered ones, causing the senior creatures to magically regain some of their youthful vim. Buckley tested out a dozen injections on himself, enjoyed how he felt, and imposed a course on his squad.

The practice was extremely controversial. 'If players have got to be doped to get results, things must be pretty bad,' blasted Bolton Wanderers captain Harry Goslin. 'It is a selfish policy, and the principle of the thing is wrong.' The FA eventually 'voiced disapproval' of the treatment after holding a summit meeting, though most of the affronted passion that day was reserved for another contentious issue, that of 'showing strongly against the televising of League matches'. Gland treatment was not made illegal.

'Buckley's Babes', as the press semi-affectionately christened them, started 1938–39 slowly, partly depressed by the loss of Bryn Jones to Arsenal in a world-record £14,000 deal. The shy Jones struggled at his new club, while his old pals fared little better. By the end of October, Wolves were a point off the bottom. It subsequently transpired Buckley had taken the team off the glands. They were soon back on them – Buckley confessed as much in the press – and won 19 of their next 23 matches. The signature performance was a 7–0 obliteration of Everton, who had started the season themselves with six wins on the bounce, and had remained at the top pretty much ever since.

Everton's new star striker Tommy Lawton said hello to his England teammate Cullis before kick-off. 'He walked past me with glazed eyes,' Lawton later recalled. 'There's no question they were on these monkey pills, and when they licked us 7–0 I was sure of it. It was heavy going, and they hadn't raised a sweat.' Everton arrived back at Molineux a fortnight later for an FA Cup tie, only to find the pitch little more than a sea of mud. Buckley initially refused to give Everton's trainer the key to the boot room so the visitors could attach longer studs. He eventually relented, and Wolves won the tie 2–0 anyway.

Wolves were now hot favourites for the first Double of the twentieth century. 'They are a law unto themselves, they are magnificent, they are unequalled!' trilled the *News of the World*. But their slow start – and Everton's fast one – came back to haunt them. Wolves' defence buckled in three consecutive away games, shipping three at Birmingham, five at Stoke, and four at Preston. Everton cruised home to claim a title that was thoroughly deserved, not least because in Lawton they had found a more than adequate replacement for Dixie Dean: he had scored 35 goals in 38 appearances. (The old warhorse Dean, before being packed off to Notts County the previous season, had spent hours coaxing brilliance out of young Lawton on the training ground, full in the knowledge that he was hastening his own demise at Goodison. There's taking one for the team.)

Buckley's Babes gained no succour at the Cup final. They were given a stiff lesson by Portsmouth, who sashayed to a 4–1 victory attributed in part to the beneficial power of . . . monkey-gland elixir. Hoist by their own petard. 'Portsmouth easily deserved their win,' sighed a dejected but sportsmanlike Cullis as he trudged away from Wembley. 'Ah well. Perhaps next year.'

9

Stanley and Bob go to war (1946–47)

The 1939–40 season kicked off on 26 August 1939. It was all over eight days later, an exercise in futility from the get-go. Trouble had been brewing for some time and everyone knew exactly the way things would pan out. 'I've not had much of an education, and I know nowt about politics and the like,' the Leeds United full-back Bert Sproston admitted to superstar Stoke City winger Stanley Matthews a year earlier, as the pair sat in a Berlin coffee shop while on tour with England, a motorcade carrying the Führer whistling past the window. 'All I know is football. But the way I see it, that Hitler fellow is an evil little twat.'

The inevitable occurred on the second weekend of the new campaign. Blackpool beat the previous season's runners-up Wolverhampton Wanderers 2–1 at Bloomfield Road. Jock Dodds – at £10,000 from Sheffield United the second most expensive player in history behind Arsenal's Bryn Jones – scored twice. His goals sent the Seasiders to the top of the table, the only club in the division with a 100 per cent record after three games. Elsewhere, goal machine Ted Drake hit four as Arsenal beat Sunderland 5–2 at Highbury; Tommy Lawton notched a couple as champions Everton drew at Blackburn Rovers; Newcastle United put eight goals past Swansea Town in the Second; Bournemouth beat

Northampton 10–0 in the Third; and Neville Chamberlain declared war on Germany.

The expansionist machinations of the Evil Little Twat didn't just put an abrupt break on Blackpool's dreams. Stoke City were on the verge of what appeared to be a golden era. The club were League founder members as Stoke – the City appendage was only added in 1925, after the relatively small borough of Stoke-on-Trent was rewarded with city status for the importance of its pottery industry. But they hadn't achieved much of note during the early years, other than losing their League status twice and going into liquidation once.

But during the 1930s Stoke finally began to get their act together. The local prodigy Matthews made his debut on the right as a 17-year-old in 1932, and soon enough dribbled his way to the very top, the most famous player in the land thanks to a trademark body swerve which regularly laid waste to a trail of defenders. In 1935–36 Stoke came fourth in the League, their best finish yet. Freddie 'Nobby' Steele cut a swathe at the sharp end: he scored 33 in 1936–37, a club record that still stands. The highlight of that season was a five-goal haul in a 10–3 romp against local rivals West Bromwich Albion. Meanwhile a brilliant young defender, Neil Franklin, was waiting in the wings to make his debut. Stoke were on the up, to the extent that an extremely complimentary nickname was coined by the southern press: 'the Arsenal of the North'. Momentum was on their side; what a time for a war.

The conflict also stole from Matthews his peak years: he was a budding 24 when it broke out, but approaching veteran status at 30 when the peace accords were signed. Goodness knows what Stoke would have achieved had the international crisis not escalated when it did. Mind you, they should still have won the title when the League resumed seven years later. Sad to say, their failure to do so is less attributable to Sproston's Twat, more the result of a thoroughly unnecessary (and very modern) clash between a manager and his star player. It was an ego frenzy that proves while the past may be a foreign country, diplomatic channels remain open and there's no border control.

Stoke City were managed by Bob McGrory, a no-nonsense Scottish boss cashiered straight from Central McCasting. McGrory played 511 times as a right-back for Stoke – a club record at the time – and was a close friend of the team's right-winger Bobby Liddle. The emergence of Matthews saw Liddle lose possession of the number seven shirt; it would seem McGrory never forgave the hot new talent for usurping his old pal.

McGrory, old-school to his boots, was also unhappy with the media presence cultivated and maintained by Matthews, who was well aware of the value of visibility. So when the player's contract came up in the summer of 1937 McGory engineered an argument. Stoke's directors tabled a new signing-on fee of £500. Matthews wanted £650, the full amount allowed under regulations. McGrory ordered the board, in no uncertain terms, to block any increase. Matthews eventually backed down after negotiating a marginally better offer for himself, plus benefits for Stoke's other top players, though he made sure to publicly register his 'unhappiness' with the way talks had panned out.

Resentment festered and grew. In early 1938 Matthews – valued at £10,000 and the subject of interest from Everton, Wolves, Newcastle, Leicester and Derby – officially asked to leave the club. Pottery workers in Stoke-on-Trent were reported to be so distressed at his potential departure that they became unable to function on a day-to-day basis. Representatives of six of Stoke's leading firms organised a protest meeting at the local King's Hall. 'Our slogan is "Matthews Must Not Go!"' said T. B. Roberts, concerned industrialist. 'We have been inundated with protests from workpeople. They are unable to do their work properly!' Over 3,000 locals attended. Brows were furrowed. Impassioned speeches were made. Something had to be done!

Two days later Stoke's directors announced they had refused to put Matthews on the transfer list. 'This is a body blow to me,' cried Matthews. 'Why should Stoke want to keep a player who is uncomfortable and not happy with the club? I expected them to let me go.' A deputation of increasingly frantic factory owners sprang into action as go-betweens. A prepared statement was rush-released: 'We have had a very long and frank discussion with the directors, the result of which we have informed Matthews we are satisfied that real and genuine efforts will be made to make him happy and comfortable in the future. Stanley Matthews has authorised us to say that he is extremely glad of this happy termination and wishes to assure everyone he will continue to do his best for Stoke!'

The truce lasted barely 12 hours. Up with the lark, Matthews informed the press of a change of heart. 'I agreed to the statement last night, but I do not like it today.' There was, however, very little he could do in practice, tied as he was to the club contractually. He was out on the pitch in a Stoke shirt later that same day, and his first game since his transfer request proved something of an emotional maelstrom. 'If he didn't get the ball for five minutes,' noted the *Daily Mirror*, 'other players were accused of deliberately starving him, though it wasn't noticed that the man on the other wing often went longer without a kick. Matthews was as good as any forward on the field, but how he played in such an atmosphere is a mystery.'

Preston made a firm bid for Matthews at the end of the season, as did Manchester United. Matthews, away with England in Paris, was contacted by the papers and informed of the interest from Old Trafford. 'I don't think it would be a bad move for a player in my position,' he replied. His desperation to leave at any cost couldn't have been more explicit: Stoke were a progressive top-half concern, while United had only just won promotion from the Second Division and were little more than a yo-yo club at the time. But his relationship with McGrory was untenable. He just wanted out. Anywhere would do.

Matthews did indeed find alternative employment a year later, albeit making shells for the war effort in a local foundry. With top-drawer football suspended, plans were made for a regional War League to keep spirits high. Stoke were given a place in the Western League, which they won in 1940, though celebrations were understandably muted given the circumstances. The contribution made by their star man was limited. Matthews worked Saturday mornings in the foundry, so could only turn out for Stoke in their home games, plus any away matches that happened to be close enough by. A delicate artist, he was also often out injured. McGrory would cynically name him in the team anyway to ensure punters streamed through the gates, before announcing a late line-up change once everyone had coughed up their admission. Matthews was also in demand for representative matches around the country: in order to maintain morale, the great entertainer was allowed to bust out of work for those.

Matthews was then posted to an RAF unit near Blackpool, the sea air clearing out his pipes and turning his head. He initially travelled back to play for Stoke, but soon concentrated on making guest appearances for Blackpool instead. He also guested for Rangers and Morton, and, having enjoyed his visits to Scotland, tried to force through a transfer to Airdrieonians. Between December 1940 and January 1944 he didn't play a single game for

Stoke. Upon being demobbed in 1945 he decided to stay in Blackpool, where he invested in a hotel. He ran it himself, guests flocking to stay in the home of the famous host. It's safe to assume McGrory, who considered the venture an unwelcome distraction bordering on deliberate personal affront, didn't make a booking.

The Football League didn't restart immediately in the autumn of 1945. It was decided to initially maintain the regional arrangements of wartime, to give everyone space to rediscover their peacetime groove. Early in the League North season, Stoke travelled to Newcastle United in the hope of going to the top of the division. They were battered 9–1. Albert Stubbins, scorer of 221 goals in six wartime seasons for the Toon, found the net five times. It would not be the last time he'd cause Stoke pain.

The FA Cup resumed, though. In the fourth round, Stoke welcomed in-form Sheffield United, destined to end 1945–46 as champions of the League North. Matthews was not long off his sickbed, his throat cut to ribbons by the flu. He was prescribed two suspicious looking pills by the club quack. Matthews inspired Stoke to a speedy 2–0 victory, then went home to clean and reorganise all of his kitchen cupboards, brush the carpets, rake the leaves from his garden, and scamper off on a lengthy midnight run. He finally got some shut-eye just after 3 a.m.

Stoke saw off Sheffield Wednesday in the following round, and were drawn with Bolton in the quarter-final. For one season only, each round of the FA Cup was a two-legged home-and-away affair, to help clubs generate a little extra money as they regrouped. Bolton won the first leg at Stoke 2–0. The second leg at Burnden Park attracted a crowd of 85,000 spectators, each and every one excited to rediscover the simple joys of top-class sport after six years of untold misery. The mere presence of a big-name attraction in Matthews added to the fervour. But those in charge failed to manage the crowds properly. A terrible crush developed, and 33 people had the life squeezed from them. The injured, dying and dead lay at the side of the pitch, bodies encroaching onto the field of play. A line of sawdust was thrown down, serving as a new touchline. Two confused and sickened teams played out a listless, irrelevant goalless draw. An enquiry was held. English football learned nothing from it.

Disaster wasn't enough to quell excitement over the return of the Football League in August 1946. After a seven-year hiatus, identifying a likely winner was quite the task, just as it had been in the wake of the First World War. Everton were the reigning champions, though a side which in 1939 had looked good enough to dominate for some time – Tommy Lawton up front, Joe Mercer in midfield, T. G. Jones at the back – was now robbed of momentum. War was the glaringly obvious stick in the spokes, though the club hadn't helped themselves much either. Before the restart, they inexplicably allowed Lawton to leave for Chelsea in a big-money move. Mercer meanwhile fell out with manager Theo Kelly over the seriousness of a cartilage injury, and in a fit of pique quit to become a grocer on the Wirral. It didn't take Arsenal too much time or effort to persuade him into a rethink. Mercer was allowed to stay in the north and run his shop, training at Anfield during the week and travelling south for matches at Highbury, his kitbag teeming with tasty under-the-counter treats, precious fare to share during rationing. A well-fed Arsenal would win the title with Mercer in 1947–48.

Jones was also alienated by the autocratic Kelly, resulting in similar self-defeat. A ball-playing defender ahead of his time, Jones was, like Mercer, accused of putting on the agony over injuries and dropped to the reserves by way of punishment.

Arsenal, Manchester United and Roma showed interest in resurrecting his career, but Everton flatly refused to sell to a domestic rival, while a glamour move to Italy was strangled by red tape. 'Their attitude was "nobody leaves Everton",' Jones recalled. He subsequently proved himself to be equally capable of spite, walking out in 1950 for non-league Pwllheli, a career choice that ensured Everton didn't benefit from a penny in transfer cash: 'It cost them a lot of money. I like to think it cost them a place in the First Division the next season!' Everton were relegated for only the second time in their history in 1950–51.

Wolverhampton Wanderers were most people's favourites going into 1946–47. Like Everton, they were in fine fettle just before the outbreak of war, and were left to wonder what might have been had sense prevailed. But the runners-up of 1937–38 and 1938–39 made it out the other side in better nick. Major Buckley was gone, despite his £1,500-per-year 'contract for life'. He had been enticed away in early 1944 by third-tier Notts County, who offered him a £4,000 salary, the biggest in football history. He made an 'earnest request' to be released by Wolves, and the club agreed, taking into account the £150,000 he had earned them in transfer fees during his 17-year stint. Buckley was soon at it again at his new club, too, signing the striker Jesse Pye from Sheffield United, then offloading him for £10,000 ahead of the big restart to (of course) Wolves.

The Major was replaced at Molineux by the rather less charismatic Ted Vizard, though Wolves still had plenty of star quality. Popular captain Stan Cullis was joined in defence by Billy Wright, future captain of England. Winger Johnny Hancocks, 'a pint-sized Matthews' according to the *Sunday Express*, was signed from Walsall. Pre-war scoring sensation Dennis Westcott was still in his prime at 29. And the new boy Pye was described by *The*

Times as 'an inside-forward of great possibilities'. This pack of Wolves looked highly dangerous.

Hope was also high at Derby County. The Rams had enjoyed several high-placed finishes during the thirties, but were never seriously involved in any title race. They finished second in 1935–36, albeit as a speck in Sunderland's rear mirror. They even topped the table for a couple of months during 1938–39, but fell away well before the business end. Close, but no cigar, despite fielding plenty of talent during that time: Jack Bowers scored pretty much a goal a game; Hughie Gallacher came in from Chelsea; prolific David McCulloch arrived from Brentford; Dai Astley was a goalscoring threat from the wing. But now their team contained two influential title-winners of the thirties: Raich Carter and Peter Doherty. And this time there was tangible success. Derby thrashed Charlton Athletic 4–1 in the 1946 FA Cup final, former Manchester City striker Doherty scoring the decisive goal. Carter, who had lifted the Cup for Sunderland in 1937, became the only man to win the famous trophy before and after the war.

Charlton themselves were expected to do something too, despite having come up short at Wembley. Manchester United, with a new manager, the former Manchester City and Liverpool captain Matt Busby, had gathered together a 'Famous Five' frontline: Jimmy Delaney, Charlie Mitten, Johnny Morris, Stan Pearson and Jack Rowley. Chelsea had spent big again: £29,000 on new players, including Lawton and West Ham inside-left Len Goulden. Sheffield United meanwhile had just won the League North, and were fancied to kick on, especially after agreeing a new contract with stubborn talisman Jimmy Hagan who, unsure about the sustainability of a sporting career in uncertain times, had landed a job as a trainee chartered surveyor.

And then there was Stoke, with the world's most famous player-cum-B&B-owner on their books. Opportunity beckoned for the Arsenal of the North.

The Arsenal of the south weren't in such good nick. The team of the thirties had seen out that decade with a 2–0 pre-war win over Brentford at Highbury. That match was caught on camera and used for the action sequences of *The Arsenal Stadium Mystery*, an oft-cited but rarely watched 1939 thriller in which a poisoned player drops dead during a match against George Allison's team. Outlandish enough, but nothing compared to Arsenal's return to League action on the opening day of 1946–47: a 6–1 humiliation at Wolves, Jesse Pye helping himself to a 20-minute second-half hat-trick. Their second away appointment, an evening fixture at Everton, proved similarly farcical. The train to Liverpool stopped at Chester due to a freight derailment, necessitating a dash to Goodison in a fleet of taxis. The team made kick-off just in time, whereupon they were given another fearful chasing by the hosts. A 3–2 defeat was flattering in the extreme. The once-mighty Arsenal propped up the entire First Division.

Their plight caused some of the nation's biggest soccer writers to totally lose the run of themselves. Frank Butler of the *Express* worried what might become of Arsenal if they fell into 'the red glow of the Second Division . . . it will be one of the great tragedies of modern football, because the Old Gunners are still the glamour boys of English football in the eyes of the wide, wide soccer world . . . the long, long trail back would be a life-and-death struggle'. Meanwhile a tear-stained John Thompson in the *Daily Mirror* insisted that 'Arsenal are still a magnet'. Totting up their average attendance of 44,685, he insisted that 'every First Division club would regret their downfall. No! The glamour hasn't faded!'

Meanwhile an increasingly frantic Allison was changing the team by the week. Perhaps the most notable name on a long roll call of players was striker Albert Gudmundsson, at the time an amateur but destined to become Iceland's first professional at Nancy and AC Milan. Gudmundsson was also later to embark on a career in politics, defeated in the 1980 Icelandic presidential election by Vigdís Finnbogadóttir, the first woman in the world to be democratically elected as a head of state.

Arsenal were still in the relegation places in early December, whereupon the enticing of Mercer from his grocery store on the Wirral was the catalyst for an upsurge in form. They were decent if not spectacular for the second half of the season, and ended up comfortable in 13th place. But the stress had proved enough for Allison, who stepped down in favour of right-hand man Tom Whittaker. 'I'm tired,' said the old boy, who had told reporters he was 'somewhere around 50' years of age, despite being in fact 63. 'I want to take this opportunity of getting away from the constant strain of big-time soccer, and get back to my less strenuous interests.' Those more relaxing pastimes? 'Films, radio and journalism', a portfolio which included working for *American Weekly*, a magazine with a reach of a mere nine million readers, and broadcasting to the overseas forces on all matters Arsenal. Naturally, his decision to quit was front-page news.

But so much for the much-vaunted trio of Derby, Charlton and Sheffield United. The Blades started slowly, a result of all the faffing over Jimmy Hagan's contract, and were always on the periphery. Derby meanwhile got rid of two of their Cup-final heroes in Peter Doherty and winger Dally Duncan. After shipping 13 goals in three matches during November against Manchester United, Liverpool and Bolton they found themselves just outside the relegation zone, one place above Arsenal, though six wins from their next seven saw them safe enough. Charlton also flirted with the drop, struggling for much of the season after losing eight out of nine matches between November and Christmas. But they squeaked clear too, and made it back to Wembley for another FA Cup final, this time emerging victorious over Burnley. (The day after the game, Jimmy Seed dropped the cup en route to a celebratory dinner, tasking a local mechanic to solder the lid back together. Charlton's boss had woken that morning to a crate of whisky sitting on his front doorstep, a thank-you from a gleeful fan. A cause–effect correlation was never established.)

Chelsea never got going either. They lost their second match 3–0 at home to Busby's all-new Manchester United, then went down 7–4 in a weird affair at Anfield. Liverpool went six goals up, before Chelsea pulled four back. Had stand-in Liverpool keeper Charlie Ashcroft not denied Alex Machin at full stretch with ten minutes to go the comeback to end all comebacks was on. But the save was made, and Willie Fagan settled nerves on the Kop with a seventh. Chelsea ended the campaign in 15th, as yet another season of high spending ended in anti-climax. Tommy Lawton kept finding the net, though his heart wasn't really in it.

Manchester United were the form horse in the early stages. They won their first five games, the highlight a 5–0 whacking of Liverpool at Maine Road. It was clear that United under Busby would be a very different proposition from the rabble of the thirties. Stan Pearson scored a hat-trick, combining effortlessly down the right with winger Jimmy Delaney, a former Scottish Cup winner with Celtic and Busby's only notable addition to the squad he found upon his arrival at the club earlier in the year.

Manchester United were exhilarating on their day, but proved a little too inconsistent to build on their early lead. Liverpool, meanwhile, responded to their humiliation by purchasing the hottest striker in the land. Albert Stubbins had scored 232 goals for Newcastle United during the war, a tally that included 18 hat-tricks, six four-goal hauls and five five-goal games. Stuck in the Second Division at 27, he put in a transfer request in the hope of tasting top-flight football. It looked like his destination would be either Everton or Wolves, but Liverpool chairman Bill McConnell heard the jungle drums and, in the immediate wake of his team's drubbing in Manchester, travelled straight to Newcastle to throw his hat in the ring.

Nine times out of ten Everton would have got to Stubbins first. When McConnell arrived at St James' Park he found Theo Kelly already sitting in the foyer. But he'd not managed to speak to the player, who was out enjoying a meal with his wife. That gave McConnell a chance to make his pitch. When Stubbins was finally contacted, he made his way to the ground where, legend has it, he tossed a coin to decide which club to join. Liverpool won, though the heads-or-tails story is almost certainly apocryphal. McConnell knew Stubbins had ambitions to move into journalism and promised to use his influence at the *Liverpool Echo* to get him a column. He also revealed Liverpool had plans for another tour of the USA at the end of the season, which appealed to the striker greatly, not least because he had lived there as a youngster.

Stubbins moved to Anfield in a bargain £12,500 transfer – the papers had convinced themselves a £15,000 deal would supersede Bryn Jones and Arsenal's eight-year record by a grand – and was an instant catalyst for an upsurge in form. Stubbins scored the winner on his debut against Bolton, and by the middle of November, 11 unbeaten games later, Liverpool were top of the table for the first time since 1923, the year of their last title win. (Newcastle used the money to buy Len Shackleton from Bradford Park Avenue. Shack scored six on his debut, a 13–0 rout of Newport County.)

Nobody had seriously discussed Liverpool as possible champions. But their pre-season preparation was beginning to look like a stroke of genius. Chairman McConnell, a caterer by trade, had picked up nutritional tips while on a government-funded fact-finding mission to the States. He subsequently sent his team across the Atlantic, ostensibly to play a few friendlies but mainly to gorge on steaks, vegetables, fruit, butter, syrup, ice cream and malted milks all summer. Quite literally beefed up, the players came home half a stone heavier, an energy store that would serve them well during a long season in ration-book Britain.

Striker Jack Balmer was certainly fuelled up. The pencil-moustached David Niven-lookalike wasn't hugely popular with the rugged Liverpool crowd on account of his suave, middle-class ways. That state of affairs didn't take long to change when he embarked on a berserk scoring spree: a hat-trick of hat-tricks in consecutive matches against Portsmouth, Derby and Arsenal. It was the first time the feat had been managed since Dixie Dean's rampage towards the end of his 60-goal season in 1927–28 and the beginning of the next one. Balmer followed it up with another five goals in four games. Manager George Kay was able to take some credit, having thrown an off-form Balmer the captain's armband to motivate him for the game against Portsmouth, though the player himself was quick to praise both his teammates and the benefits of good nutrition. 'Really the credit should go to the rest of the team for providing the chances. And some of it to my wife for her cooking. Her meals put power in my boots!'

It wasn't long, though, before second-placed Wolves came to Anfield and taught Liverpool a lesson. Dennis Westcott scored four in a 5–1 thrashing, gambolling in space created by the clever runs of Jesse Pye. Up the other end, Stan Cullis was the boss of Stubbins, not allowing the striker a single run on goal. Liverpool were outclassed in every department. 'They always went to meet the ball and we didn't,' sighed captain Balmer after the game. 'That was the trouble.' And so the pre-season favourites Wolves reached the top of the table. Balmer tried to look on the bright side. 'Remember, lads, the last time we had five goals scored against us, we went 12 unbeaten!' But between Christmas and the end of January, Liverpool lost five out of six, allowing Wolves to pull clear at the top. It looked a one-horse race.

Not quite. Stoke City were coming up on the rail, piecing together a title charge amid a febrile atmosphere at the Victoria Ground. Stoke had started the season awfully, with a draw and three defeats. But then they embarked on a six-game winning run which pulled them towards the top. Stanley Matthews had been struggling with two separate injuries so, ahead of a high-profile visit to Arsenal, Bob McGrory decided that the winger should get back to full fitness in the reserves.

Either through incompetence or sheer devilment, the manager informed the press of his decision before telling the player himself. So when Matthews had the news broken to him by a journalist after a round of golf near his B&B in Blackpool, steam began to parp liberally from his ears. He phoned McGrory to discuss the matter in depth. 'I got up from a sick bed to play against Sheffield United in a Cup tie last year,' an irate Matthews told the press, perhaps wisely omitting the bit about his subsequent speed bender. 'I got out of bed to play for their convenience! There was no question of the reserve team, then. I have played on other occasions when I have only been half fit.'

There were also rumours of a rift in the dressing room. Should Matthews be guaranteed a return to the team once fit, at the expense of in-form replacement George Mountford? 'It is not the fact that I have been left out of the first team that matters. But I was rather hurt when I heard that the other players had told the board they would complain if I went back in George's place. I cannot believe they want me out of the team. If it is true, it would change my whole outlook. At the moment, it is premature to talk of leaving Stoke.' At which point he jumped in his '10 h.p. car' and sped off for another round of golf. Blackpool were favourites for his signature, though Chelsea and Arsenal were also very interested.

Matthews was eventually restored to the XI. He posed for hilariously bogus 'happy family' photographs with McGrory and Stoke chairman Alderman H. Booth, and gained plaudits for his performance in early December at home to, of all teams, Blackpool. He set up three and scored the other in a 4–1 win. Stoke were in the title race all right, and, come Easter, they stepped on the gas again, winning seven matches in a row. But the sequence proved to be the endgame between Matthews and McGrory, as a decade-long antipathy came to a head.

The first of those wins was a 5–2 victory at Grimsby on Good Friday in which Matthews played no part. According to the player, he had asked to be left out to rest, with a busy Easter schedule and the England–Scotland international coming up. McGrory, however, insisted that Matthews had cited the 'business pressure' of running his hotel, and simply not turned up for work. Apoplectic with rage at his winger's priorities, and emboldened by the big win on Humberside, McGrory made a big show of not recalling Matthews to the team for the next match against Huddersfield. He told Matthews in private on the morning of the match that he'd be playing, only to hook him from the changing room minutes before the game, instead sending out the same XI who did for Grimsby. A 3–0 win vindicated McGrory's decision, if not necessarily the way he went about implementing it.

Matthews was left out again for another win over Grimsby, and missed a victory against Blackpool while playing for England. He returned for a 3–1 triumph over Brentford, though later discovered he had only been recalled because Bert Mitchell had picked up an injury. His nose put out of joint yet again, he demanded a transfer to Blackpool at the end of the season. Stoke and McGrory, tired of fighting, finally acquiesced. Matthews played in wins over Blackburn and Leeds, matches which should have been Stoke's last of the campaign. But a freezing winter had extended the season, and they still had three rescheduled fixtures to fulfil. Matthews would miss the first two of those anyway, away on a continental tour with an FA representative team, and seeing Blackpool had completed their season, McGrory decided to bundle Matthews out of the door early. On 9 May, an £11,000 deal was struck in a bedroom of a Glasgow hotel. Matthews received £300 accrued benefit plus £10 for signing on. Stoke were annoyed that Manchester City had been willing to pay £15,000, but Matthews did not countenance the move. Matthews would effectively only miss Stoke's final game at Sheffield United. What harm could his absence possibly do?

While Stoke were winning and winning, Wolves stuttered. Top and with games in hand at the end of April, a first English title was in their sights, just as it had been in 1938 and 1939. Once again, they started to feel the pressure. They drew at Portsmouth, then only picked up one point in two home games against Everton and Blackburn. Meantime Liverpool had regained their verve, closing the gap with an impressive late-season run that included victories against Manchester United, Charlton and Arsenal. And so the situation eventually boiled down to this. If Wolves beat Liverpool in their last game, they were champions. If Liverpool won, they'd leapfrog Wolves into first place themselves. But Stoke would still be able to leapfrog them in turn, with their better goal average, providing they won that last game at Sheffield United (a match scheduled *two weeks* after the Wolves–Liverpool showdown).

'Wolves should make sure today,' announced the *Sporting Chronicle* as Liverpool arrived at Molineux for what they assumed would be the big climax. The hosts were hot favourites, on account of the five-goal lesson they'd handed Liverpool earlier in the season. Yet uncertainty hung in the air. For a start, the man who had found the net four times at Anfield – Dennis Westcott, with 38 goals the division's leading scorer – was out injured. More surreally, the mood at a sun-baked stadium had been drastically altered when a dramatic PA announcement was made 60 minutes prior to kick-off: this would be Stan Cullis's last-ever match! He was hanging up his boots on medical advice, having taken one too many blows to the head during his long career. The tension was now beyond bearable. Wolves simply *had* to deliver a valedictory title for their beloved captain.

Wolves started the quicker, but couldn't turn possession and territorial advantage into any meaningful attack on goal. Jack Balmer made them pay by opening the scoring on 21 minutes against the run of play. Then on 38 minutes, Bob Priday launched one down the middle for Albert Stubbins to chase. Stubbins had been in Stan Cullis's pocket at Anfield, but now he outpaced both the Wolves captain and Billy Wright, toe-poking it past outrushing keeper Bert Williams and into the corner. 'I had no idea Stubbins was so near, and then I saw his red head flash past,' sighed Cullis. Wolves pulled one back in the second half, but Stubbins's personal revenge over Cullis proved the decisive moment.

The pair shook hands at the final whistle. Tears rolled down Cullis's cheek as the realisation sunk in that he would never win a medal. 'That was as big a blow as our defeat in the 1939 Cup final,' he observed. In later years he was asked why he never tugged Stubbins back as the striker raced past him. 'I suppose I could have done, but I didn't want to go down in history as the man who decided the destiny of a championship with a professional foul.' Shades of 'Peerless' Jesse Pennington in the 1912 Cup final. Karma would pay back the sporting Cullis, like it had the West Brom legend, given time. Meanwhile Liverpool – who had gone top in the absence of manager George Kay, improbably away scouting for players in Ireland – now faced a two-week wait to find out if the title would be theirs. Having done all they could do, they toasted their best efforts with glasses of lemonade.

Few thought a champagne moment was heading their way. 'Stoke should grab the League title today,' trumpeted the *Mirror* a fortnight later. But while Liverpool had played their final game of the season in balmy conditions, Stoke arrived at Sheffield United just as the heavens opened. United named 38-year-old Jack Pickering in their XI. It was his first appearance of the season; his first competitive outing in eight years. After two minutes and 25 seconds, he scored with a pea-roller that totally foxed Stoke keeper Dennis Herod and dribbled in off a post. Alec Ormston equalised for Stoke immediately, but Pickering would not be denied: just after the restart, he sent Walter Rickett through on goal for United's second. Stoke still had time, and desperately tried to get back into it. Frank Mountford had a shot fingertipped onto the crossbar, then got in the way of his own man Syd Peppitt during a penalty-box mêlée that nine times out of ten would have resulted in an equaliser. But their overall play lacked cohesion and confidence; they were desperately missing the departed Matthews. The final whistle sounded. Stoke hadn't even finished second;

Matt Busby's Manchester United, mathematically never in the hunt due to the way the final fixtures fell, claimed that spot.

Back across the Pennines, Liverpool were playing Everton in the final of the Liverpool Senior Cup. An invader made his way onto the pitch to inform the players of the good news. The match stopped. Everton, the reigning champions of England for the last eight years, warmly congratulated the successors to their crown.

Bob McGrory considered leaving Stoke for Portsmouth, where long-serving, FA Cup winning manager Jack Tinn had just stepped down. But he stayed put, Bob Jackson taking over on the south coast instead. Stoke went nowhere fast without Matthews. McGrory left in 1952, and the club were relegated a year later. Three days after Stoke slipped out of the First Division, their former star winger set up goals for his Blackpool teammates Stan Mortensen and Bill Perry in an FA Cup final that would come to define him. Matthews had a winner's medal at last. Stoke still haven't won the League or Cup.

10

Dennis slips on a pebble
(1947–48 to 1954–55)

Tommy Lawton – protégé of the famous Dixie Dean, teenage inspiration behind Everton's title win of 1939, and scorer of 20 goals in 19 games for England – was the most famous, and the best, striker in the country. His big-money move to Chelsea hadn't worked out, though. Not quite. On the one hand, his 26 goals in 1946–47 broke the club's scoring record – not bad going in a team that finished 15th. But he'd fallen out with manager Billy Birrell and wanted away. A hectic scramble for his services ensued. His next destination? Either six-time champions Sunderland, five-time League winners Arsenal – who tried to sign him when he left Burnley for Everton in 1937 – or 1946 FA Cup winners Derby County. Surely?

Instead he rocked up at Notts County, ambitious spendthrifts, albeit ones fourth from bottom of the Third Division (South). The transfer made the front pages, alongside the resignation of Chancellor of the Exchequer Hugh Dalton, paying the price for absent-mindedly leaking his upcoming budget to a political correspondent. In other financial news, Lawton's record £20,000 move ensured he'd earn enough money to become the first footballer to pay 'surtax', a super-tax on high earners. He had also been promised the pick of four-figure-salary jobs in Nottingham once his playing days were over, and handed the keys to a modern detached house on the city's outskirts.

'That Lawton has made a sound financial move is proved,' noted respected *Express* columnist Frank Butler, 'but whether he has made a sound professional move by transferring to the Third Division at 28 can only be answered in the next two or three seasons.' Lawton was following a path to Meadow Lane well trodden by some legendary names – his mentor Dixie, the famous Hughie Gallacher – but those lads had arrived at County in their dotage as mid-thirtysomethings, with careers in steep decline. Lawton was still at his peak.

After two minutes of his November debut at Northampton Town he turned on a thrupenny bit and nearly threaded home a shot from 25 yards. After four he flashed a header into the top corner. An instant return. Back at Stamford Bridge Chelsea decided to keep supporters abreast of how Lawton was doing at his new club. The home fans indulged in a little gallows humour at half-time as County's winning scoreline was posted on a pitchside board; their own team were losing against Stoke City and struggling badly. But Chelsea rallied in the second period, with 23-year-old Ken Armstrong – billed as Lawton's successor by the press – scoring a hat-trick in a 4–1 win. 'Don't congratulate me,' insisted Armstrong after the game. 'Team spirit did it. We've got quite a lot of it at Chelsea.'

Armstrong went on to establish himself at Chelsea, becoming a fixture in their team for the next decade, albeit on the wing rather than following Lawton up front. The old Lawton, meanwhile, eventually led Notts County to promotion to the Second Division in 1950, though for such a brilliant player this was taking faffing around at the margins to ludicrous extremes (and his England career had long gone south).

Arsenal didn't need Lawton anyway. While flailing around the bottom of the First in late 1946, they signed 35-year-old Fulham forward Ronnie Rooke as a temporary striker. Rooke helped Arsenal to a mid-table finish with 21 goals in 24 games, whereupon the old boy shifted up a gear. Rooke was a relentless presence as Arsenal got off to a flyer in 1947–48. A six-match winning start included two victories over FA Cup holders Charlton Athletic to the aggregate tune of 10–2. Sunderland, Sheffield United, Bolton Wanderers and the previous season's runners-up, Matt Busby's Manchester United, were also swatted aside.

Arsenal didn't taste defeat until the end of November, and maintained their momentum. A draw at Huddersfield with five matches to go sealed the title, though the team had to wash and dress so quickly to catch their train back south that they only found out they were champions when Denis Compton – the England Test batsman who also played on the left for the Gunners – sprinted to a newsstand at Doncaster station and grabbed a paper which confirmed defeats for distant challengers United, Burnley and Derby. Rooke ended the season as leading scorer with 33 goals, the last four coming in an 8–0 humiliation of relegated Grimsby Town.

As ever, though, Arsenal's success had been built, first and foremost, on solid foundations at the back. Joe Mercer marshalled a back line happy to sit deep and deny opponents space to break; they only conceded 32 times in 42 matches, 16 goals fewer than second-placed Manchester United, 79 fewer than the 111 poor Grimsby managed to ship. Critics and neutrals weren't particularly enamoured, though it was unlikely that new boss Tom Whittaker paid them much heed. Arsenal now matched Aston Villa's record total of six titles. Herbert Chapman, who loved a bit of rugged defending as much as the next purist, would have been proud.

Jack Tinn wore the same pair of lucky spats to every match of Portsmouth's 1939 FA Cup run. Before each round, the superstitious Pompey boss would get one of his players to tightly fasten the guards over his ankles, a ritual that paid handsome dividends as the team won the trophy at the expense of Wolverhampton Wanderers and their heartbroken captain Stan Cullis. When the war sirens sounded, Tinn folded his spats very carefully and placed them in a safe at Fratton Park, alongside the famous old can itself. He later smuggled the Cup home, storing it under his bed for even safer keeping during its enforced seven-year residency on the south coast.

The lucky spats meanwhile lost a little of their supreme potency. A couple of months after Portsmouth's Cup win, captain Jimmy Guthrie was seriously injured in a car crash on blackout manoeuvres as an Air Raid Precaution warden. Guthrie thankfully recovered but the combination of accident and war rudely truncated his playing career. Meanwhile another Cup legend, Tommy Rowe, became a bomber pilot and was shot down during a mission over Frankfurt; he spent two years in a prisoner of war camp before returning to Portsmouth as a very different sort of hero. When footballing hostilities replaced real-life ones, Pompey immediately lost their grip on their trophy in January 1946, defeated by Birmingham City over two legs, the decisive strike an own goal by Reg Flewin, nominative determinism in full effect. After flirting with relegation from the First Division in 1946–47, Tinn decided to take off his spatterdashes for good after 20 years in charge.

Portsmouth's good fortune hadn't totally run out. With huge numbers of servicemen stationed on the south coast during the war, Pompey were in perfect position to snaffle some of the best talent from the army and navy. The fact that Field Marshal

Montgomery had been elected as club president in 1944 wouldn't have harmed the recruitment drive. The balletic inside forward Len Phillips joined from the marines: 'He should receive a fee from the magic circle for making the football sit up and talk without the use of a wand,' opined the *Portsmouth Evening News*. Jack Froggatt, a powerful winger who could also dominate at centre back, was demobbed from the army. The rugged but clever right-half Jimmy Scoular waltzed down the gangplank of HMS *Dolphin*. Tinn was replaced by Bob Jackson, whose first act was to sign powerful striker Ike Clarke from West Bromwich Albion. Clarke would share the goalscoring load with Duggie Reid and right-winger Peter Harris. Dependable young midfielder Jimmy Dickinson completed his navy service and formed a solid central partnership with Scoular, and by the time of Portsmouth's golden jubilee season in 1948–49, the pieces were in place for a tilt at the title.

Nobody – absolutely nobody – factored them into the pre-season equation. But if Portsmouth thought they could surreptitiously climb the table to execute a silent smash and grab, they were sadly mistaken. Their cover was blown pretty much from the off. After an opening-day draw at Preston, they won their next six in a row. Two routs of giants Everton marked everyone's card: 4–0 at Fratton Park, 5–0 at Goodison, Froggatt running riot down the left, scoring two and setting up a couple more. Top at the start of September, they were soon locked into a three-way battle with Derby County and Newcastle United.

Newcastle in particular had wind in their sails. They were newly promoted, having slummed it in the Second since a team packed with internationals somehow managed to get themselves relegated back in 1934. (They nearly slipped into the Third Division (North) in 1937–38, but escaped what would have been, at the time, an unprecedented fall for a former champion club. It was the closest of shaves with ignominy: they lost the last three games of the season, the final fixture 4–1 at Luton Town, squeaking clear by one tenth of a goal.) But now, thanks to local striking sensation Jackie Milburn, they were back in the big time, resurgent. And by April, a three-way battle had become two: it was between Newcastle and Portsmouth for the title.

Pompey travelled to a St James' Park crackling with the anticipation of 62,000 Geordies. They plunged the place into complete silence, playing the game of their lives. Froggatt scored a hat-trick and Harris a couple more in a 5–0 rout. All of the goals were headers. Pompey were now almost certain of the title. (One of the victorious men in blue, Jimmy Scoular, later joined Newcastle and lifted the FA Cup as their captain in 1955.) They tied up their prize a couple of weeks later at Bolton, eventually finishing five points clear of Manchester United, who had enjoyed a late surge to claim their third second-place finish in a row.

Busby's United were one of a number of clubs who wondered how the hell they didn't win the following title. The 1949–50 championship was one of the tightest on record, though initially a couple of clubs threatened to run away with it. First up, Wolverhampton Wanderers, who had won the 1949 FA Cup under old captain and new manager Stan Cullis, and were rocking an effective no-nonsense long-ball system. They established an early lead after going unbeaten for their first dozen matches, before being overhauled by George Kay's Liverpool, who had rediscovered their title-winning moxie of 1946–47 after a couple of mediocre seasons.

Kay's side was pretty much the same as their championship team, with Billy Liddell and Albert Stubbins still the focus of their attack. (Stubbins had agitated to return to Newcastle a year earlier, before simmering down when the club refused to sanction the move. He was back on a rolling boil a couple of years later, threatening to go on strike over a minor contract dispute. Was this rock 'n' roll disdain for authority the reason the Beatles put him on the cover of *Sgt. Pepper's Lonely Hearts Club Band*? 'Long may you bob and weave,' wrote Paul McCartney, in a note accompanying a copy of the long-player he sent to Stubbins in 1967.)

Liverpool went 19 unbeaten from the start of the season to the middle of December. They were still top come Good Friday, by which point they had already reached the FA Cup final and were within touching distance of the Double. But on Easter Saturday they got spanked 5–1 at Newcastle, where Stubbins was withdrawn with concussion. They never recovered from the jolt, losing three of their last four, finishing a distant eighth, and went down meekly in the Cup final to Joe Mercer and Arsenal. They weren't the only team to capitulate on the run-in, either. Manchester United once again narrowly missed out, winning only one of their last ten matches, and that when it was too late to be useful. Sunderland meanwhile ultimately proved themselves as inconsistent as their maddeningly mercurial star Len Shackleton, losing three of the last five, one of those reverses a miserable home defeat to relegation-bound Manchester City.

Liverpool had finished five points off the pace; United three; Sunderland just the one. It wouldn't have taken much for any of them to have made up the difference. Wolves got even closer, winning seven and drawing two of their last ten games. But a miserable two-month winless run during the autumn was just too much to overcome. They lost out on the title by 0.4 of a goal to Portsmouth, who became the first club to win the championship on goal average since Huddersfield pipped Cardiff in 1923–24, and the first to retain the title since Arsenal in 1934–35.

Pompey prevailed despite a slow start of three defeats in their first six. Jackson's men gathered themselves to stay in contention, and were nothing short of superlative during the run-in. While almost everyone else was crumbling, Pompey demonstrated the grit of champions, winning seven of their last nine. A crucial victory came in the last five minutes at Manchester United, Duggie Reid and Jack Froggatt coming up with late goals. That was followed by a turnaround win at home over Liverpool, Reid and Froggatt again the heroes, cancelling out an opening goal by Stubbins. They also had to do without the influential Scoular for the last two matches of the season, the hair-trigger right-half suspended after being sent off for trading blows with Johnny Morris of Derby. Pompey thrashed Aston Villa 5–1 on the last day, Reid's hat-trick breaking Wolverhampton hearts like it was 1939 all over again.

Cullis telegrammed his opposite number Jackson offering 'heartiest congratulations'. The Pompey boss also received instant wire communication from two children in Canterbury, who remembered how Jackson had once gone out of his way to collect the entire squad's autographs for them. 'In the giant entertainment industry which soccer has become,' purred an op-ed piece in the *Mirror*, 'Portsmouth have kept the human touch. Their players have proved again that it is the size of a man's heart that counts in the end.'

Twenty miles along the coast, not long after football's post-war resumption, a grocer's assistant who had become a sergeant in the Duke of Cornwall's Light Infantry broke into the first team at Southampton. Word was that the young man never stopped talking tactics. 'You can't better this type of player!' cooed manager Bill Dodgin of his new right-back. 'The player who thinks football, talks football, and lives football is the man who makes good!'

Alf Ramsey would make good all right. But his stratospheric achievement of 1966 tends to obscure how influential he was as a player too. He moved from Saints to Tottenham Hotspur in the summer of 1949, becoming a crucial component in Arthur Rowe's fluid, exciting side. Spurs had been exiled from the top flight since 1935, but bust their way back into the First in stunning fashion. They won the 1949–50 Second Division by scoring 81 goals, letting in only 35, and racking up 61 points, nine more than second-placed Sheffield Wednesday. If they hadn't taken their foot off the gas upon wrapping up the title in early April – they only picked up one point from their last five matches – all manner of records would have been smashed. As if to further emphasise how they were far too good for the second tier, they battered Sunderland, who finished two places and one point behind League champions Portsmouth, 5–1 in an FA Cup tie.

Tottenham's methods were simple enough to modern eyes, but thoroughly groundbreaking in their day. Rowe preached the virtues of passes that were short, accurate and most importantly fast. He drummed several mantras into his players' heads. A rolling ball gathers no moss. Make it simple, make it quick. He who stops is lost. Time means space. The philosophy became known as push-and-run, though Rowe never cared for the monicker, preferring another of his slogans: give-it-and-go. Ramsey more often than not started each move, receiving a throw from keeper Ted Ditchburn – another eye-opening change from the norm – and playing out quickly from the back. Wingers Les Medley and Sonny Walters, and strikers Len Duquemin and Eddie Baily, were more than able to finish them off.

Spurs took a little while to warm up on their return to the First. An opening-day White Hart Lane crowd of 65,000 witnessed

Stanley Matthews toy with Rowe's newly promoted side. Matthews was mesmeric, Tottenham over-anxious, and Blackpool won 4–1. A small child ran onto the field to get the famous winger's autograph. A policeman, in hot pursuit, slipped and fell flat on his face in the silent-movie style – small scraps of comedic entertainment for a disappointed home support. A week later Spurs should have beaten Arsenal at Highbury, but Ramsey's defensive partner (and fellow managerial legend-in-waiting) Bill Nicholson hacked down Doug Lishman to concede the equalising penalty in a 2–2 draw. It later transpired Nicholson, who had been knocked unconscious during the early exchanges, spent most of the afternoon seeing double. Further defeats at Liverpool and Wolves soon followed.

But when the give-it-and-go game clicked, it really clicked. In late September, Spurs went to Aston Villa, fell behind twice, then saw midfielder and captain Ronnie Burgess reduced to a limping passenger on the wing. Burgess and Spurs nevertheless scrapped their way to a 3–2 victory. The result inspired a sequence of eight wins of exponential import: six goals past Stoke City, five against the champions Portsmouth, and seven against a Newcastle team good enough to lift the FA Cup the following April. Arsenal had been the early pacesetters, but lost five out of six in December. The sixth was a 4–4 home draw with Blackpool, Arsenal having been 3–1 up and coasting at the break, Matthews running them ragged in the second half. Spurs saw out the year at the top.

Middlesbrough, fuelled by the goals of Wilf Mannion, stayed on Tottenham's shoulder awhile, but Rowe's side won five in six around Easter to shake them off. Matt Busby's Manchester United also gave good chase, but finished second yet again, perennial bridesmaids it would seem. With two games to go Spurs were in a position to claim the title at home to Sheffield Wednesday. As if to illustrate just how far they'd come in a short time, Wednesday, promoted alongside them the previous season, were in desperate relegation bother. Len Duquemin's drive secured the win, and Tottenham's first League championship, though it had been close: with six minutes to go, Wednesday's Dennis Woodhead swivelled to send Harry Clarke the wrong way, shaped to shoot into an open goal, then stepped on a loose stone and slipped over. 'If I hadn't trodden on a pebble, I'm certain I would have scored,' he sighed.

A Wednesday equaliser would only have postponed Tottenham's title celebrations by a week; as things panned out, the new champions beat Liverpool 3–1 in their last match anyway. Spurs became only the third team, after Liverpool and Everton, to win back-to-back Second and First Division titles. But Woodhead's misfortune had massive repercussions for Wednesday, who were now perilously close to the drop. Had they drawn at Spurs their destiny would have been in their own hands. Now they needed to beat fellow strugglers Everton on the final day, and hope Chelsea – who had won their previous three in a late, desperate spurt – found themselves unable to beat Bolton at home. Wednesday dispatched sorry Everton 6–0, sending the Merseysiders down for only the second time in their history. But that wasn't enough to prevent Wednesday joining them in relegation, as Chelsea won 4–0, their fourth victory in a row, and pipped them to safety by 0.04 of a goal. Small pebble, big consequences.

All the sympathy was with Wednesday, none with the terrible Toffees. Donny Davies in the *Manchester Guardian* summed up the prevailing mood. 'To abuse Everton at this stage,' he quipped, 'would be too much like picking up a person badly mauled from a street accident and reading him a lecture on the folly of jay-walking.' It was the start of a miserable decade for Merseyside. Everton did make their way back to the First in 1954, at the very point Liverpool were heading the other way to begin an eight-year exile. Manchester, however, was a city on the rise.

Portsmouth spent the close season sunning themselves in Brazil, where they took on several of the leading clubs: Santos, América, São Paulo, Palmeiras. They didn't win a game on tour, and in a 2-1 defeat to Fluminense, Jimmy Scoular was once again caught throwing hands, this time in retaliation to some saucy South American shirt-tugging. He was sent from the field, then dispatched back home, alone in disgrace, by air from Rio. Still, if nothing else, it proved the outgoing champions still had plenty of fight left in them.

Bob Jackson's men made a good fist of trying to reclaim their title in 1951–52. Despite having to do without Scoular for the first couple of weeks of the season – he was suspended by the FA and fined £10 – Pompey won five of their first seven to grab a slice of the action alongside functional but effective Arsenal, and a Manchester United whose near misses were beginning to get old: they had finished second in four of the five seasons since the war, and a close fourth in the other.

Come April, all three clubs were neck-and-neck at the top. It was at this point the influential Scoular got himself suspended again, this time for 14 days after 'making an objectionable remark which was likely to bring the game into disrepute' to Peter Doherty, the erstwhile Manchester City title winner now at Doncaster Rovers, in the midst of a set-to during an FA Cup tie. It didn't immediately look as though Scoular's absence would be costly, as Pompey beat leaders United at Fratton Park. But the indiscretion eventually told, and they lost their last four games, Scoular only returning to the team when it was too late. Pompey finished fourth, the end of an era as Jackson upped sticks in the summer for an unsuccessful spell at Hull City.

United, by contrast, rallied brilliantly after the reverse at Portsmouth. A tactical lightbulb pinged above Matt Busby's head: he moved young left-back Roger Byrne up the wing and into the attack. Byrne scored United's goal in a draw at Burnley, then twice against Liverpool in a 4–0 rout, and another couple in a 6–1 thrashing of Burnley. With two games to go, United and Arsenal were level on points, and the pair would meet at Old Trafford in the final game of the season. But the Gunners, their squad stretched by injury as well as exhaustion to key players such as 38-year-old Joe Mercer, had been running on empty. Mercer was stood down for a trip to West Bromwich Albion, which was lost 3–1. Meanwhile at Old Trafford, United skipper Johnny Carey raked home a 30-yarder as Chelsea were seen off 3–0. It meant Arsenal had to beat United by seven clear goals when the teams met in Manchester on the final day. Busby's men were pictured after the Chelsea win celebrating in the bath, swigging ostentatiously from china cups filled with champagne.

Premature? No, just realistic. Seven goals were scored in the last match at Old Trafford all right, but six of them by United. Jack Rowley hit a hat-trick to bring his season's total to 30, though his most magical moment was a long dribble to the byline followed by a cutback to set up Byrne for a tap-in. Stan Pearson got the other two, ending the campaign with 22. John Downie, forgotten these days but in 1949 an £18,000 record signing from Bradford Park Avenue, was United's other main goalscoring source that season with 11. Arsenal, down to nine men after further injury setbacks, left the field bedraggled. The usually suave Mercer was caught effing and jeffing at the referee, his linesmen, and several United players, though he had the good grace to apologise almost immediately. 'Put it down to old age,' he laughed, before congratulating Busby's team. Arsenal lost the FA Cup final to Newcastle a week later.

United didn't put up much of a title defence the following season. In fact at one point they found themselves scrabbling around at the foot of the table. The avuncular Busby told a restless fanbase to cool their jets. 'There is no deep cause for worry although we have slumped for the moment,' he shushed, in the manner of a man who knew something everyone else didn't. 'We have £200,000 worth of skill in our youth and reserve sides.'

Sheffield Wednesday, unfortunately relegated by such a slender margin in 1951, bounced straight back in style. They rattled in 100 goals en route to the Second Division championship, having unearthed an uncompromising scoring sensation in Derek Dooley. Described by *The Times* as a 'long-striding, rough diamond of a centre-forward', the big number nine scored 46 goals in 30 games, at one point racking up 22 in a nine-game spell. Top-tier defences all around the country tooled up for battle.

Initially, it was Dooley who came off second best. First Division defenders opted to fight fire with fire, and the young striker struggled to stand up to the big boys. Dooley failed to find the net in his first four appearances of 1952–53 and was dropped, though manager Eric Taylor was at pains to stress that his player hadn't done much wrong. 'If we had kept Derek in the team it would have meant breaking his heart, or breaking his limbs. He is the record scorer, the big fellow, and therefore the marked man. And, believe me, after four matches, he is marked, literally. There is no law in football that allows the use of fists on a centre-forward, but that is just what Dooley has been getting. He has needed more attention from our trainer than any other player, yet the fouls are being given against him. This boy is being penalised because of his physical advantages, because people are apt to bounce off him. We are not worried because he hasn't scored. He would get goals if he were permitted to play.'

Dooley went away to lick his wounds. He scored twice for the reserves against Sheffield United, then notched a hat-trick against Liverpool's second XI. He had literally rediscovered his scoring boots, having started the season with brand new ones, only to return to his tatty but trusted old pair upon losing his first-team place. He won a recall, and was soon scoring freely again: he went on to hit 16 goals in 24 games. But he remained a controversial figure. The last of those 16 goals came in a loss at Tottenham, where he managed to ruffle some established feathers. Dooley's no-nonsense approach disrupted Tottenham's slow build from the back, and he was tripped and shoved from pillar to post for his trouble. Spurs captain Ron Burgess lost his rag after coming off second best in one challenge. Ted Ditchburn complained of some trash talking. A laconic Alf Ramsey, raising a post-match eyebrow, was uncharacteristically diplomatic: 'Let's say he's unusual and leave it at that.' Dooley required police protection from irate home fans as he left the pitch.

Three weeks later, Wednesday faced Preston at a frozen Deepdale. In the 14th minute of the second half, Albert Quixall slipped a ball through the North End defence for the speedy Dooley to chase. Preston keeper George Thompson raced from his area, and got his foot to the ball first, though Dooley deflected it back towards goal. The ball rolled inches wide while, in a totally innocent collision, Thompson clattered into Dooley, who broke both bones of his right shin. Dooley left for Preston Royal Infirmary in an ambulance as Tom Finney secured victory for the hosts against ten men. The striker was expected to be routinely discharged on Monday, but a nurse, signing his cast, noticed no reaction as she accidentally knocked Dooley's toes. A doctor was called. Gangrene had set in, the result of dirt getting into a small scratch on the back of his leg. Amputation was necessary to save Dooley's life. 'It was all right if it was the only way,' the stoic young man said later. 'I will soon be all right.'

Dooley was offered a job by the *Mirror* as a 'Sports Adviser', and his first assignment was the super-dramatic 1953 FA Cup final. Dooley's analysis pulled no punches. 'I was shocked at Wembley by the number of people who had no right to be there. They are the spectators who left the stadium with Bolton leading 3–2 and the match boiling up to its crisis. The four biggest policemen in London could not have dragged me away.' Despite the dreadful fate which had befallen him, his fighting spirit couldn't be quashed.

'The Matthews final' came 24 hours after an equally dramatic denouement to an otherwise tepid title race. Workmanlike Arsenal were in a chase with Preston, who were somewhat unkindly known to quipsters of the day as 'the plumber and his ten drips'. Tom Finney – tradesman and wing genius – was certainly the superstar of the piece, though they were far from a one-man outfit, also starring pacy goalscorer Charlie Wayman and combative Scottish international midfielder Tommy Docherty. Arsenal found themselves two points clear of Preston with two games to go, but Finney and Wayman did for them at Deepdale in the penultimate match of the season. That left both teams level on points, but Arsenal with a marginally better goal average. Down to the wire.

Preston played their final game two days before Arsenal. Finney's decisive penalty at Derby meant the Gunners had to beat Burnley, a side good enough to have been on the fringes of the title race, in their last match at Highbury. Roy Stephenson gave Burnley an early lead, but Arsenal responded with three goals in

15 minutes through Alex Forbes, Doug Lishman and Jimmy Logie. With 15 minutes to go Billy Elliott reduced the deficit, but Arsenal hung on, their famously cultured fans cheering every walloped clearance. Proud Preston, champions in 1888–89 and 1889–90, were beaten to a third title by 0.099 of a goal. Joe Mercer took to the steps of Highbury stadium and announced his retirement: 'This has been the most splendid day of my life!'

Truth be told, late mathematical drama apart, it had been a fairly mediocre season. So Arsenal staged a title defence to match. They lost six of their first eight games in 1953–54, bottoming out with a 7–1 humiliation at Sunderland. It proved to be the last time 38-year-old keeper George Swindin – who had just secured a third championship medal, having won his first in 1937–38 – played for Arsenal in the League. Some way to bow out. Tom Whittaker responded by finally signing Tommy Lawton! The pre-war golden boy was now 34 years old, but there would be no Ronnie Rooke-style Indian summer It took Lawton over six months to score his first League goal; Arsenal finished 12th. Having recently completed a run of seven titles in 16 seasons, they wouldn't be a serious contender for another 15 years.

West Bromwich Albion had romped to the championship in 1919–20 with one of the most free-flowing sides the League had ever seen. Four decades later, history looked ready to repeat itself. Manager Vic Buckingham had spent most of his playing days at Tottenham as a defensive midfielder. His career ended just as Arthur Rowe's reign began, so he missed the club's titles of the early fifties, moving into management instead, test-running his progressive ideas with combined Oxford and Cambridge university outfit Pegasus. But Rowe acted as his mentor, sending Buckingham one of his famous pithy slogans – 'Make it simple, make it quick!' – by telegram ahead of the 1951 FA Amateur Cup semi-final between Pegasus and Hendon. Pegasus won the game, then beat amateur giants Bishop Auckland in the final. In the wake of victory, Buckingham set out his personal philosophy of perpetual motion, one that could have come straight out of Rowe's playbook: 'Whether you are playing well or badly, all of you must want the ball and look for it.'

By 1953–54 Buckingham had arrived at West Brom, implementing a Tottenhamesque style which also gave a nod to the achingly modern Hungary team which, during the season, thrashed England 6–3 and 7–1. 'The basis of Albion's style – and for that matter of Hungary's – is simply the business of keeping possession of the ball,' noted the *Observer*. 'This demands accuracy in passing, and such accuracy demands in turn reasonably short passes that seldom rise much above the ground. Seldom does the man in possession hold the ball for long . . . his teammates are always moving into position for a pass.'

West Brom were irresistible. Ray Barlow bossed the midfield, linking up with lightning wingers Frank Griffin and George Lee, as well as roaming striker Ronnie Allen and poacher Johnny Nicholls. Come March they were top of the League, a couple of points clear of slightly more pragmatic Wolves. Allen and Nicholls had scored 55 goals between them. Five had been put past Chelsea and Liverpool, six past Cardiff City, seven past Newcastle.

But momentum was stalled in tragic circumstances, seven games from home. After 37 minutes of a match at Sunderland, with Allen and Nicholls both away on international duty and the team already a goal down, keeper Norman Heath came out to smother at the feet of Ted Purdon. Heath jarred his spine and was carted off to hospital. What at first appeared a garden-variety injury soon revealed itself as something much more serious.

Almost total paralysis set in. Heath's career was over, and though he would regain some use of his limbs, he used a wheelchair for the rest of his days.

Barlow took over in goal for the remainder of the match, and though ten-man West Brom forced an equaliser, the match concluded in inevitable fashion, with Purdon scoring the winner. Heath's tragic fate was a vicious blow to morale. The next fixture – impeccably poor timing, this – was the visit of Wolves. Allen and Nicholls were still missing, Wolves defender Bill Shorthouse put an early, effective reducer on Barlow that had the influential midfielder hobbling for 82 minutes, and striker Roy Swinbourne hooked a second-half shot past Albion's half-fit second-choice goalie Jim Sanders. To be fair to Wolves, they were missing key players as well: captain Billy Wright and Jimmy Mullen were with Allen and Nicholls on England duty, busy beating Scotland 4–2 at Hampden Park. The West Brom duo both scored in that game, a bittersweet success seeing their club had been knocked off the top.

Still reeling, a demoralised West Brom lost at Cardiff. The sequence of three straight defeats was costly. They went into the penultimate match at Aston Villa two points behind Wolves, with an inferior goal average. They needed a win, and for Wolves to stutter. Wolves lost at Huddersfield, but West Brom went two down in the first ten minutes against Villa, and were thrashed 6–1. It was effectively all over: Wolves would have to lose their last match at home to Spurs by four goals, while West Brom would require an 8–0 win at Portsmouth. As it was, Wolves won, West Brom lost, and the difference at the end was a rather flattering four points.

All the luck during the run-in had gone the way of the Wanderers, though in fairness they had shown impressive resolve in finally winning the title after coming so close so often down the years. Few could begrudge nearly man Stan Cullis some League success at last. And accusations of a one-dimensional, bludgeoning style could only fly so far, given their smash-and-grab forward line of Swinbourne, Dennis Wilshaw and Johnny Hancocks had whistled in 74 goals between them.

Three days later, Wolves boarded a plane at Birmingham airport that would take the new English champions on a celebratory tour of Denmark. As the team made their way up the gangway, a small chartered craft landed nearby. An ambulance drew up to the plane, doors were flung open, and a stretcher was lowered to the ground. On the stretcher: Norman Heath, being transferred from hospital in Sunderland to a ward nearer his home. The Wolves squad, to a man, made their way across the tarmac to wish the stricken keeper their best. 'Congratulations,' Heath smiled. 'You deserve to be champions.' Sportsmanship beyond the call. Four days later, on a television set by his bedside, Heath watched his teammates lift the 1954 FA Cup at Tom Finney's expense. Finney, one of the greatest players in English history, never won a medal of any sort. But as the misfortunes of Dooley and Heath illustrated, there are far worse fates.

Pipe-smoking Billy Birrell, 55, known as the 'silent man of soccer', took his leave of Chelsea in trademark style. He avoided relegation to the Second Division in 1950–51 by 0.04 of a goal, and having endured another battle to escape the drop the following year, decided it was time to quit. 'I am getting a bit too old for this sort of thing,' he admitted. As his players lunched ahead of their third-last game of the season against Charlton, he tapped on a glass, cleared his throat, and announced in his gentle Scots burr: 'Do your best in the last three games. I want to finish on a good note because I will not be with you next season.' He silently left the room.

Chelsea saw off their boss with a couple of nondescript draws plus a defeat, which was about right for a mediocre reign. But Birrell wasn't the only old soldier whose tenure at Chelsea came to an abrupt end in the summer of 1952. Ted Drake, 40, the pre-war Arsenal scoring sensation, succeeded Birrell by announcing: 'I know there's something wrong here, and I'm determined to find out what it is.' His first act was symbolic. Chelsea's nickname, 'the Pensioners', referenced the residents of nearby Royal Hospital Chelsea, a nursing home for veteran British army campaigners who spent their dotage sitting around in bright scarlet coats and ostentatious pointed hats. A line drawing of a Chelsea Pensioner adorned the cover of every matchday programme. Drake immediately got rid of it, replacing the Pensioner temporarily with the letters CFC entwined on a shield in the Rangers style, then commissioning a coat-of-arms featuring a rampant lion, the design that remains the basis of the club's badge today.

'No offence to the old timers, we all know what the country owes to them,' Drake said. 'But I'm sure the Pensioners tag can do us no good. We don't like its implications and we want to lose it. The old gag – Yes, and they play like Pensioners! – wears a bit thin. We aim to become modern, to move with the times.' Drake then turned his attention to the team, which he built around defenders Peter Sillett (brother of Coventry's 1987 FA Cup winning boss John) and future West Ham and England manager Ron Greenwood. Roy Bentley provided the threat up front; Ken Armstrong, who had replaced Tommy Lawton all those years ago, was still out on the wing. By the start of the 1954–55 season the *Mirror* gave them an outside chance for the title: 'Their high-spirited flamboyant style will make them the people's choice!' By the end of October Chelsea were in the bottom half after a four-match losing streak. A very young Manchester United came to

Stamford Bridge and won a wild game 6–5. Dennis Viollet (three), Tommy Taylor (two) and Jackie Blanchflower put the Busby Babes 6–3 up before Chelsea debutant Seamus O'Connell – who spent the majority of his career as an amateur, splitting his days between football and cattle farming – completed a hat-trick of his own. Another of Chelsea's goals that day was scored by a second debutant, Jim Lewis, also juggling football with a less glamorous day job, in his instance selling Thermos flasks.

The Babes went top that day, though were still too callow to mount a consistent title challenge. Reigning champs Wolves took over and looked odds on to retain their crown, but this time they faltered over the final furlongs, winning only four of their last 12. Chelsea by comparison lost only four times after their depressing October run. (One of those losses was a Christmas Day defeat at Arsenal. The scorer? Who else? Tommy Lawton.) They effectively wrapped up the title in early April with a hard-fought home win over Wolves, whose captain Billy Wright handled a goalbound O'Connell shot, Sillett slotting home the decisive penalty.

Chelsea still hadn't won the Cup, of course, so Norman Long's whimsical 1933 number still had currency. But, by landing their first League title, they'd finally won a major trophy, rendering the popular nicknames of the day – 'the Unpredictables', 'the Circus Side', the ever-so-slightly harsh 'Clowns of Sport', and of course 'the Pensioners' – old hat. Mind you, normal service was resumed soon enough. Chelsea finished 16th the following year, and after a series of mid-table finishes, followed by a sluggish start to 1961–62, Drake was sacked and replaced by Tommy Docherty. The Doc's first game was a 4–0 humiliation at Blackpool; Chelsea ended the season relegated. The Unpredictables were back!

11

Matt and Billy pick up the pieces (1955–56 to 1958–59)

The *Manchester Guardian* could not be accused of regional bias. In their preview of the 1955–56 season, they didn't name-check local concern United at all. Wolverhampton Wanderers were certain to challenge champions Chelsea, they said, while Portsmouth and West Bromwich Albion were expected to come good again. The general consensus was that United were still too young and inexperienced: only Roger Byrne and Johnny Berry, aged 26 and 29, remained from their 1951–52 championship team. In addition, they were surely far too inconsistent: they'd lost 15 matches the previous season, failing to take advantage of a decent start.

United's first match of the new campaign was at newly promoted Birmingham City. Matt Busby's side went ahead twice, conceded two equalisers, and were left hanging on by the end, all those pre-season predictions made flesh. United remained erratic for a couple of months, but then a statement victory in early October changed everything. Wolves had begun the season no less erratically, and were in mid-table, a few points off the early pace. Still, when they were on song, they hit the high notes, beating Huddersfield 4–0, Manchester City 7–2 and Cardiff 9–1. They went to Old Trafford, and were widely expected to get the favourable result that would give their campaign fresh momentum. They went 2–1 and 3–2 up, but United levelled twice – then, with two minutes to go, Johnny Berry's corner was powered home by Tommy Taylor to earn the home side a 4–3 win. The cavernous walls of Old Trafford crackled with noise, and an electric sense that something special was in the air.

Adulation was the top note in Manchester that weekend: across town, exactly 24 hours later, a hysterical crowd of teenagers, barely held in check by 20 constables, a sergeant and an inspector, swarmed the Midland Hotel as poor old Johnnie Ray tried to work out how to get from the back of his saloon car to the safety of his room. Busby's Babes would soon be afforded similar hero worship. By the end of the calendar year, United had thrashed champions Chelsea 3–0, put four past West Brom and five past Charlton, going top in the process. Taylor and Dennis Viollet were scoring regularly; Duncan Edwards made strutting between both boxes as though he owned the place appear laughably easy. They glided clear of the pack. Blackpool and Stanley Matthews tried to keep within touching distance, and just about managed to hold on by the fingernails. With three matches to go, the Seasiders visited Old Trafford knowing only a win would keep them in with a distant shout. United weren't in the best place mentally. Matt Busby and assistant Jimmy Murphy had been in a car crash four days earlier; Busby was also dealing with the death of his mother-in-law, and would be away for the funeral. For a while, their unease showed: David Durie headed home Jackie Mudie's early cross, a lead Blackpool maintained at half-time. But a giant crowd of 62,277 pushed the home side on. Johnny Berry levelled with a penalty, Taylor scored his 25th of the season, and United's fourth title was secured.

Job done, no fuss. Club secretary Walter Crickmer breezily informed the crowd that there would be 'no presentation today, chaps. So don't swarm across the pitch, if you please. Out in the normal way, through the exits, that's right, thank you very much. See you later!' It was left to the man from *The Times* to purr. 'There seems little reason why their authority should diminish, for there is still much wealth of young talent in the background. That is where their strength lies, and not in the power of the cheque book. The more clubs that learn that lesson, the better for English football.'

United retained their title in 1956–57, flying out of the blocks and leading from the front. They scored 103 goals and were champions by Easter, finishing well clear of an emerging Tottenham Hotspur side influenced by playmaker Danny Blanchflower. United would have won the first Double since Aston Villa in 1897, too, had Villa themselves not beaten them in a controversial FA Cup final effectively decided when Peter McParland ludicrously slammed into Ray Wood, fracturing the United keeper's cheekbone in a very dubious challenge. In fact they weren't far away from a Treble, having also reached the semi-finals of the glamorous new continental competition, the European Champion Clubs' Cup.

United set out again in August 1957 hoping to become the first team since Arsenal in the thirties to win the League three times in a row. They started slowly, held goalless at newly promoted Leicester City for the first 70 minutes of the opening game of the season. At which point Billy Whelan scored a hat-trick in 480 seconds.

They registered another 3–0 victory, against Everton at Old Trafford, before putting four past Manchester City. They should have won their fourth game of the campaign, too, but in the early-season return at Everton, shipped a two-goal half-time lead and were forced to settle for a disappointing 3–3 draw. No matter: Leeds United were then spanked 5–0, while Blackpool were hammered 4–1. Could they beat the long-standing League points tally of 66, set by Arsenal during their first-ever championship season in 1930–31? They'd registered 64 the year before, after all. And now they were a couple of points clear at the top already, having scored 22 goals at a rate of over three-and-a-half per match. Only six other sides in the division had managed to clock up double figures. The next best haul was 13, jointly achieved by sixth-placed Portsmouth and Wolverhampton Wanderers, languishing in ninth with only a couple of wins to show for their not-quite-so-free-scoring efforts.

A gulf in class? Perhaps. Yet things started to go awry for United, quickly and spectacularly. Burnden Park was a ground where United hadn't tasted victory since the forties, despite winning three titles in the interim. Busby's side were thrashed 4–0 by Bolton Wanderers. The *Manchester Guardian* witnessed 'talented players buffeted about like bathers in an angry sea . . . No sooner was the ball at their feet than some questing boot or thrusting limb would roll it away, and if the challenge were renewed into play could come a pair of magnificent shoulders'. It wouldn't be the last time Wanderers strong-armed United into submission that season.

Then Blackpool, in another of those old-school, early-season fixture-list quirks, paid United back for the spanking at Bloomfield Road with a 2–1 win at Old Trafford, despite being without Stanley Matthews, injured but still regarded a menace at 42. Jackie Mudie scored twice in the first half; Duncan Edwards scrambled a consolation with four minutes left. An unexpected defeat, and one very much worth highlighting, for it was a highly significant moment, if only in hindsight. On the same night, 18 September 1957, newly promoted Nottingham Forest spanked Burnley 7–0 and took over from United at the top of the table. The Busby Babes would never reach the pinnacle again.

Forest were not built to last, an autumnal flash in the pan. The real threat to United was stirring down the table a little. Wolves had certainly started erratically: a defeat at Everton was followed by a 6–1 thumping of Bolton and a 5–0 win over Sunderland. Then the pendulum swung back again: a 1–1 draw at Bolton, a 3–1 reverse at Luton Town. This was mid-table form. But Cullis's side strung together a six-game winning run which propelled them to the top. The sequence became more impressive by each step: home wins over Blackpool and Aston Villa; a pair of 3–2 triumphs at Leicester and Villa; the final result of the run, a comprehensive 4–0 victory over Tottenham. And just before that, the most crucial scalp of all, a 3–1 win over Manchester United at Molineux in which Norman Deeley, with two goals from the wing, was the hero. United had a ready-made excuse for their defeat: they were missing Roger Byrne, Eddie Colman, Billy Whelan and Dennis Viollet thanks to an influenza virus which the previous day had forced 530 Manchester bus drivers to call in sick, and 30,000 children in the city to miss school.

United continued to splutter as the previous season's ultimately futile attempt to land a treble finally took its toll. In the next couple of months, a tired side lost 3–0 at home to Portsmouth, 4–3 at West Brom (future England manager Bobby Robson scoring twice for the Baggies), 4–3 at home to Tottenham, and 1–0 at Old Trafford against Chelsea. By mid-December United were fourth, ten points adrift of Wolves, who were unbeaten since early September. Deeley, Jimmy Murray and Peter Broadbent – whose trademark body swerve influenced young Wolves fan George Best – were all in fine goalscoring fettle. The only thing troubling Wolves was their continued inability to garner praise as a result of their direct and domineering style. The *Manchester Guardian* referred to them as 'sloggers rather than artists' and berated tactics which 'ought to be preserved in a museum of Roman antiquities alongside the ballista'.

Chelsea's win at Old Trafford turned out to be another significant milestone in the history of the Babes: their last-ever defeat. Busby responded by breaking the British record for a goalkeeper, paying Doncaster Rovers £24,000 for Northern Ireland international Harry Gregg. Busby threw Gregg straight into the team at the expense of Ray Wood, while also dropping three forwards, Johnny Berry, Billy Whelan and David Pegg, in favour of Kenny Morgans, Albert Scanlon and Bobby Charlton. United beat Leicester City 4–0; they could easily have had ten. Gregg had nothing whatsoever to do.

Wolves stuttered a little in December and January, losing at Spurs and Blackpool, and being held by a staunch Luton at Molineux. Their only League victory in over a month came at Sunderland, who were en route to the first relegation in their long, storied history. Sunderland – the English champions of 1935–36 and FA Cup winners in 1937 – couldn't get going again after the war. They pushed hard, enticing a series of big-name, big-money signings such as Len Shackleton, Ivor Broadis and Trevor Ford to the club, but the investments paid no dividend. Non-league Yeovil Town dumped them out of the FA Cup in 1949. A sluggish end to the season in 1949–50 handed the title to Portsmouth. An FA Cup semi-final in 1955 was lost to Manchester City; adding insult to injury, north-east neighbours Newcastle triumphed in the final. Another Cup semi ended in failure in 1956 at the hands of Birmingham. And that was it.

Shackleton, it was rumoured, kept himself entertained by imparting industrial levels of spin on passes to Ford, just to make the striker look inept, and ensure his status as fans' favourite remained intact. In 1957 Sunderland were found guilty of making illegal payments to players above the maximum wage. They were fined, and manager Bill Murray resigned. Alan Brown took over at the start of the new season, shipping out the underperforming stars and sprinkling the team with youthful talent, following the trend set by Busby. But it wasn't quite as easy as the Babes made it look, and Sunderland went down, the first time they had slipped out of the First Division since joining it in 1890.

Wolves' slow start to the calendar year allowed United to close the gap to six points by the end of January. Busby's side had re-energised the title race, which had been in danger of turning into a procession. On the day Wolves lost at Blackpool, United thrashed Bolton 7–2 at Old Trafford. Despite the result, Bolton keeper Eddie Hopkinson played a blinder, and the three saves from Tommy Taylor he made that day proved the difference between mere humiliation and record-book-bothering shame. It was also the day Bobby Charlton scored a hat-trick, showcasing for the first time his trademark combination of shoulder-drop, body swerve and thunderous shot, a thoroughly modern manoeuvre which would reach its apotheosis in the semi-finals of the 1966 World Cup. He had, according to the *Manchester Guardian*'s Donny Davies, 'crossed the borderline between promise and fulfilment and became a serious contender for the rank of master footballer'.

Wolves responded magnificently in their next League game, on the first day of February, hammering Leicester City 5–1 at home. Just as well, because at the same time, down at Highbury, United were rattling in the goals once more, embroiled in an instant classic with Arsenal. Duncan Edwards opened the scoring on ten minutes with a low drive. On the half-hour Harry Gregg sent Albert Scanlon away down the left. The winger tore past

Derek Tapscott and, at the end of a 70-yard run, rolled the ball inside for Charlton. The in-form inside-forward – 'tubby', according to the man from the *Express* – bashed home. Tommy Taylor gave United a 3–0 lead at half-time. The reigning champions were on song against a bland mid-table troupe. Surely this match was over?

Not by a long chalk. After 60 minutes, the score remained the same. By the time the 62nd minute had been and gone, the teams were level. Arsenal captain Dave Bowen lobbed through for David Herd, who sidefooted past Gregg on the volley. Gordon Nutt's left-wing cross was headed down by Vic Groves, and Jimmy Bloomfield whistled a snap shot home. Then Nutt delivered again, low from the left, Bloomfield diving forward to skim the ball in with his eyebrows. But United seemed unfazed. Scanlon crossed from the left for Dennis Viollet, who flashed a header past Jack Kelsey to reclaim the lead. Taylor made it 5–3 from a ludicrously restrictive angle, and though Derek Tapscott scampered through the middle of United's defence to welt a low shot into the net, the visitors held on for the 5–4 win. Highbury was abuzz. Meanwhile the highest standards were demanded at Molineux, where the home fans greeted the final whistle of Wolverhampton's five-goal win over Leicester with groans, having spent the last portion of the match chanting, 'We want six.'

The title race was perfectly poised, the fixture list the dramatist's friend. Because scheduled for the following Saturday: Manchester United versus Wolverhampton Wanderers! A draw or a win for Cullis's men, and the League title would surely be heading to Molineux. A victory for Busby's team, though, and the gap would be down to four points, very manageable with 13 games still to play. It promised to be one of the great summit meetings in the history of the Football League. The anticipation was palpable. First, though, United had a commitment on the Continent.

Had Matt Busby been granted a wish at the start of the season – one trophy this season, but that's your lot – he'd almost certainly have plumped for a third League title in a row, his evangelism for the European Cup notwithstanding. Championship hat-tricks don't come along too often; European glory could always wait another year. But with the League not going exactly to plan, progress in the European Cup suddenly offered some welcome succour.

United had reached the quarter-finals, where they faced Red Star Belgrade. In the first leg, Eddie Colman secured a 2–1 win at a misty Old Trafford, the man from the *Express* squinting through the fog at players who 'looked like phantoms'. The return match in Yugoslavia was played without assistant Jimmy Murphy, who instead went to Cardiff to oversee the World Cup qualification of Wales at Israel's expense. That Wales were still in with a shout was an outlandish long shot: having initially failed to qualify from their group, they were drawn as a lucky loser to face the Israelis, who were having trouble finding countries prepared to face them in their Asia and Africa qualification section. A lucky lottery win, and one that may well have saved Murphy's life.

He missed a ferocious 3–3 draw in Belgrade, enough to see United through. Busby's team left the pitch to a shrill cacophony of disapproving whistles, pelted with hundreds of snowballs. The local press pack was barely more appreciative, questioning United's 'fair play'. The *Borba* newspaper claimed they 'felled opponents in an impermissible manner', while the man from *Politika* was even more strident: 'There was not a single professional trick they did not use to bring themselves out of difficult positions. It is amazing how many fouls there were. They stalled the play by throwing the ball. They obstructed their opponents in making a free-kick. They were often unscrupulous when they tackled someone and they pushed and tripped up.'

On the way home, United's BEA jet, the *Lord Burghley*, stopped over at Munich airport. When it attempted to take off again, it was unable to attain the necessary speed on a slush-drenched runway, and with no space or time to abort, crashed through a fence and into a nearby house. The disaster would claim 23 souls; 11 of the victims were players or staff of United. Also among the dead was the 1936–37 title winner Frank Swift, Manchester City's goalie turned *News of the World* reporter.

Confusion reigned in the wake of the tragedy. Red Star, Milan, Real Madrid and the West German and Yugoslavian federations supported a plan to anoint the Babes, posthumously, as honorary winners of the 1958 European Cup. There was also talk that Manchester City might take United's place in the competition should their stricken neighbours choose not to continue. Neither scheme came to fruition, as the world of football eventually decided to trudge along its predetermined path. It was an attitude shared by United. 'Even if it means being heavily defeated, we will carry on with the season's programme,' promised chairman Harold Hardman. 'We have a duty to the public and a duty to football to carry out.'

United's summit meeting with Wolves, the centrepiece of the fixture list for Saturday 8 February, was naturally postponed. The rest of the League programme went ahead. There were two-minute silences, flags flown at half mast, black armbands worn by every player. United eventually got back on the horse 13 days after the disaster, under floodlights against Sheffield Wednesday in the fifth round of the FA Cup. The football family rallied round: Blackpool, Liverpool and Nottingham Forest offered loan players, while Aston Villa manager Eric Houghton coaxed an initially unwilling Stan Crowther into an emergency transfer by driving him to Manchester under the pretence of watching the comeback Cup tie. 'I should help them out,' Crowther told Houghton en route, his conscience kicking in, 'but I haven't got my kit with me.' Houghton was one step ahead: 'Don't worry, I've got your boots in my bag.' Crowther signed an hour before kick-off, and turned out at a sepulchral Old Trafford. A comprehensive 3–0 win represented catharsis – as much as any football result could. Any relief was short lived: two days later Duncan Edwards succumbed to his crash injuries.

The rest of the season was all about United's emotionally charged – and scarcely believable – run in the Cup. Their makeshift team somehow made it all the way to Wembley. But their League campaign, by comparison, was a complete write-off. United's inexperienced and hastily assembled side won only one of their 14 remaining fixtures after the tragedy, and that against relegation-bound Sunderland. Back-to-back games against West Brom highlighted the difference between the seeming spiritual destiny of their Cup heroics and struggles with the weekly grind: United beat the Baggies 1–0 at Old Trafford in an FA Cup sixth-round replay, but at the same venue three days later in the League were trounced 4–0.

A week after that harsh lesson, United travelled to Burnley, where they were walloped 3–0 in an eye-watering encounter. It was a rugged affair from the get-go, and United's composure collapsed completely on the half-hour when 17-year-old inside-left Mark Pearson scythed Burnley striker Les Shannon to the ground and was sent off for his part in the wide-ranging exchange of views that followed. Harry Gregg lost control of the ball and took offence when Alan Shackleton challenged for it, adopting a boxer's stance and threatening to pepper his opponent around the ears accordingly. Shackleton fell backwards and Gregg pinned him down; the United keeper was very fortunate to escape with a lecture. Stan Crowther was also lucky to stay on the park, having hacked down Les Shannon while already on a booking.

The ill feeling was not confined within the white lines. Murphy, holding the fort for the still-hospitalised Busby, was lectured by the referee for refusing to return the ball from the dugout. After the game, Murphy barged into the Burnley changing room in high dudgeon to remonstrate with Shannon over a tackle on Bobby Charlton. Complementary post-match refreshments were also sent back from the United dressing room.

The trouble had been in the post. In the immediate wake of Munich, United enquired about the possible transfer of Burnley winger Brian Pilkington and striker Albert Cheesebrough. Clarets chairman Bob Lord, a bluff Lancastrian businessman, took disproportionate umbrage at the request. 'I am just sick and tired of the whole business,' blasted the wholesale butcher, a mere ten days after the disaster. 'If United want to pick up other clubs' best players so that they can with the League Cup, European Cup, Central League and Youth Cup, they had better think again. When clubs offered to help it was with players sufficient to keep United ticking over until they could rebuild, not to supply them with the cream of the country's footballers.' Lord warmed to his theme, going out of his way to appear unsympathetic. 'United may be in a jam, but if they think they are coming to Burnley to pick roses off the tree, they better have second thoughts! Football is a business, a competitive one, and while one can have sympathy with United, one cannot be guided by emotions. United went into this with their eyes open. I am very sorry for them. They have come unstuck. But they'll just have to fight their way out of it. They went into it of their own accord.'

Not totally surprising, then, that it all kicked off when the teams met. Lord ramped up the ill feeling even further after the battle, accusing United of 'running around like Teddy Boys. Let this lot run roughshod, and it could upset the whole of organised football. It looks as if they don't like losing. If Manchester United continue to play like this, they'll lose the sympathy the public have for them. They must remember there are other clubs in football.'

An incensed Murphy – 'Shocking! Disgraceful!' – pointed out that United were hardly in a position to get precious about defeat, as they'd been fully expecting to lose every match after the crash. 'All we wanted to do was to keep the flag flying until the end of the season, when we could start to reconstruct. So the question of losing does not enter into it.' Lord refused to apologise for his comments, blaming a passing journalist for scribbling down and publicising a private boardroom conversation. In any case, he claimed that '80 per cent of the letters' he had received were 'in complete agreement with my views'.

Shocking as it may appear in hindsight, this was not a totally outlandish and cold-hearted stance by the standards of the time. In the *Burnley Express and News*, the paper's football correspondent Sportsman suggested that United were 'destroying the feeling of warm-hearted sympathy so freely offered' and 'becoming very much like bewildered Babes who have realised suddenly that the world is not all sympathy and adulation but a place of grim struggle and stern justice.' If that could be written off as partisan, similar thoughts were publicly aired by *The Times* correspondent Geoffrey Green, a writer usually favourably disposed to United (and later the author of the club's official centenary history). 'Mr

Busby, their manager, once said "I aim to make footballers of my boys." They had better remember that and not grieve their leader, still lying in a Munich hospital, or tarnish a fine name. There is a limit to sympathy.'

Wolves meanwhile embarked on an astonishing run, scoring 31 goals and winning nine out of ten games between Munich and Easter. They clinched the title with three games to go, beating nearest challengers Preston North End 2–0 at Molineux, Peter Broadbent setting Norman Deeley free to score after a long dribble from deep inside his own half. Gordon Milne's own goal sealed Wolves' second championship in the most underwhelming of circumstances. In the wake of such an extreme tragedy, there was no other manner in which the title could be won.

Their first match as champions-elect saw them travel to Old Trafford for the fixture postponed in the immediate wake of Munich. The summit showdown, hotly anticipated back in February, was a sick joke now. United, long past caring, laboured in ninth place. Dennis Viollet made his first appearance since the accident. Wolves won 4–0, Ron Flowers, Eddie Clamp, Norman Deeley and Peter Broadbent the scorers. A win in the final game for Wolves, away at bottom club Sheffield Wednesday, would have equalled Arsenal's record points total of 66, the mark so eagerly eyed by Busby at the start of the season. Wolves, setting the seal on the mother of all anti-climaxes, lost 2-1.

The disaster at Munich has turned the 1957–58 championship into the biggest what-if story in the history of the Football League. Would Manchester United have won the title had the tragedy not occurred? Chances are, probably not. Even if the Babes had beaten Wolves on 8 February at Old Trafford, it would have been a big ask, given the late-season form of Cullis's side. United would have still required 12 wins from their final 13 league games, plus a draw, to pip Wolves at the top by a single point. With a European Cup semi-final looming against Milan such a run would surely have been beyond even the beatified Babes. The damage had been done earlier in the season, and their free-scoring opponents – who ended the campaign with 103 goals – were simply too strong. Too relentless. Too good. Wolves might have been denied due credit in extraordinary circumstances, but they were deserving champions, and in a style that belied their workaday, long-ball reputation.

The remainder of the season was understandably underwhelming for United. They lost an emotional FA Cup final to Bolton Wanderers, who had physically worked the Babes over at Burnden Park early in the season and did so again at Wembley, Nat Lofthouse bundling Harry Gregg into the net for the signature goal of an uninspired 2–0 win. It wasn't a popular result – perhaps United had retained the nation's sympathy, after all, proving Bob Lord's cynical prediction well wide of the mark. Finally, they were comprehensively beaten in the European Cup semi-final by Milan. The most harrowing campaign in English football history was over, and not a moment too soon. A final against Real Madrid would have been, almost certainly, too much of an emotional load to bear.

A neat narrative arc has been grafted onto the next phase of the Manchester United story, as the club go into a post-Munich decline before being hauled out of it in the mid-sixties by the famous triumvirate of Bobby Charlton, Denis Law and George Best. But it's not quite as neat and tidy as that. In fact, a new United team built around Charlton, Dennis Viollet, British record signing Albert Quixall and winger Albert Scanlon challenged strongly for the title in the immediate post-Munich season of 1958–59.

One day after the first anniversary of Munich, United won 3–1 at Tottenham Hotspur. 'Their eyes once more are on the European Cup,' reported *The Times*, who praised United's 'subtlety and fluid movement in attack . . . qualities of a higher intellect.' United admittedly missed 'the towering authority of an Edwards' and 'the neat linking of a Colman' but 'in the place of the majestic old order we now find a tremendous driving spirit'. A tough-tackling 22-year-old wing-half called Wilf McGuinness was singled out for special praise. Soon after, they saw off League leaders and reigning champions Wolves 2–1 at Old Trafford. By the end of March they went top with a 6–1 evisceration of Portsmouth, their 16th win in an 18-match sequence stretching back to November. The *Manchester Guardian* cooed over their 'inspired demonstrations of craft, skill and understanding'.

But yet again Cullis's side proved too strong over the long haul. 'The team have mastered the art of doing just enough to win without overtaxing their strength, stamina and skill,' wrote the *Mirror* after two Mickey Lill goals at Preston reclaimed the divisional lead, a mere 24 hours later. 'They set up an attacking plan which was the essence of direct, purposeful simplicity.' Wolves were on a fine run themselves: they lost only one of their last 17 games, ironically that match at Old Trafford, to end the season six comfortable points clear of Busby's speedily reconstructed side.

The run-in was tainted by more tragedy. On a Saturday in March Birmingham City and England right-back Jeff Hall played in a 1–1 draw at Portsmouth. On the Sunday he starred in a five-a-side spectacular staged at West Bromwich and transmitted live by ITV in the Midlands region. On the Monday, he was taken ill and diagnosed with polio. He died a fortnight later, the shocking sudden loss of a fit, famous professional athlete causing nationwide panic and a rush for vaccination. Hall had played 17 times for

England, partnering Roger Byrne at the back. The pair lost just one game together, enjoying victories over Brazil, Spain, West Germany and Yugoslavia. Byrne had perished at Munich; now they had both been spirited away.

So it was two titles on the bounce for Wolves, at the end of another goal-strewn campaign. They had racked up 110 this time, Murray, Broadbent and Deeley sharing 58 of them. Captain and defensive linchpin Billy Wright took the opportunity to retire at the very top. Outstripped by Liverpool's Albert Stubbins at the cost of the 1946–47 title, and part of the England team humiliated by the USA at the 1950 World Cup, he ended his club days as a back-to-back League champion, before signing off as an international with an 8–1 win over – who else could it be? – the United States of America. Despite all the hammer blows, football still retained its ability to conjure up the odd feel-good fairytale.

12

Yvonne stokes a militant mood (1959–60 to 1961–62)

The quiz show *Double Your Money* was a ratings smash during the early days of ITV. The genius of the format lay in its simplicity. Contestants answered questions on their chosen subject, doubling their cash prize up to a maximum of £32. If they got an answer wrong they lost everything. If they made it to £32 they could return over the following weeks to continue their quest on the 'Treasure Trail', which involved them being bundled into a glass isolation booth as they tried to multiply their way up to £1,000. The heat was deliberately turned up in the claustrophobic cupboard to make contestants appear even more flustered and uncomfortable than they already were. Standing outside, asking the questions, your elastic-faced host Hughie Green, hamming it up to ensure maximum tension! The daddy of *Who Wants to Be a Millionaire? Double Your Money* was magnificent television, to which millions tuned in.

In January 1959, four sports stars were invited onto a special edition of the hit programme. Olympic runner June Paul was quizzed on cookery; fellow sprinter Roy Sandstrom, assisted by his wife Susan, fielded questions about geography; Middlesex cricketer John Warr chose classical music as his specialist subject; and Bobby Charlton of Manchester United and England was tested on pop music. Charlton proved the best of the bunch, getting all of his questions correct, making it to the Treasure Trail. But as he edged closer to the jackpot, the more he fretted and sweated. 'This guy takes a bigger beating in the box than anyone else I have ever had on the programme!' quipped Green, ever the showman. 'He really gets me worried because he's so nervous in there!'

Upon reaching £512, Charlton flatly refused to go back into the booth for his final £1,000 question, instead demanding to be quizzed on the stage. 'I don't like being shut in there, not being able to see anyone. I start to shake as soon as I get inside the box.' A flustered Green closed that week's show in a gurning panic. 'I'll have to ask the management! Come back next week and we'll let you know the result!' The suits at Associated-Rediffusion compassionately relaxed the rules, making a link between Charlton's claustrophobia and his experience at Munich only 11 months earlier. He was allowed to think outside the box, scooped the big cash prize, and bought his dad a car with the winnings.

So one of the world's most talented footballers, playing for England's most famous club, felt the need to go on network television to dance for beans. That fact should have given the folk running the sport pause for thought. But it didn't. And so the authorities kept blithely on, unaware that a perfect storm was brewing. There was money in football, and irritated players wanted a fairer piece of the pie. A pincer movement over the maximum wage and retain-and-transfer systems would soon be launched. The whole brouhaha would result in higher wages and more freedom for the best players, though it would have the unfortunate knock-on effect of tilting the table in favour of the larger clubs from the big conurbations. Before the big bang, a couple of modestly sized provincial outfits had just enough time left to make a mark.

Bob Lord might have been an awful blowhard, but the man knew how to run a football club. After joining the Burnley board in 1950 he ploughed thousands of pounds into a successful youth scheme and state-of-the-art training facilities. He could also spot up-and-coming managerial talent when he saw it. And in 1958 he saw it in Harry Potts, the 35-year-old Shrewsbury Town manager who had played inside-left for Burnley in the 1947 FA Cup final, hitting the bar during their defeat to Jimmy Seed's Charlton. It didn't take long for things to come together under Potts. A forward thinker, having briefly coached under Stan Cullis at Wolves, he was one of the first managers to seriously dabble with the 4–4–2 formation. Potts inherited a fine squad – playmaker Jimmy McIlroy; captain and engine room Jimmy Adamson; winger John Connelly; young striking partnership Jimmy Robson and Ray Pointer; erstwhile Manchester United target Brian Pilkington out on the left – and he got them passing, ordering his players to 'get a smile in your boots'.

Wolves were favourites to retain their title in 1959–60 and match Huddersfield and Arsenal's feat of three championships in a row. Nobody cottoned on to Burnley, and even though they hovered on the fringes of the title race all season, all of the attention fell on the tussle between Wolves and Tottenham Hotspur, now managed by Bill Nicholson. After finishing a distant second to Wolves a couple of seasons previously, Spurs started the 1958–59 season badly and were in relegation bother when manager Jimmy Anderson was sacked. Nicholson took over and won his first game, at home against Everton, 10–4. 'It can only get worse,' deadpanned team heartbeat Danny Blanchflower, tinder-dry as he ambled off the pitch.

Spurs bodyswerved the drop, Nicholson signed wing-half Dave Mackay from Heart of Midlothian, and things could only get better. They started the new season fast, hammering five past Newcastle, Manchester United and Preston. The 12th game of an unbeaten run saw Wolves turn up at White Hart Lane for a first-versus-second summit meeting. In the press box, lending a little glamour to proceedings, was actress Jayne Mansfield and her husband Mickey Hargitay, the 1955 Mr Universe. Spurs did their best to turn a starstruck crowd's gaze back towards the pitch, thrashing the champions 5–1. Bobby Smith scored four, the pick of his goals an overhead kick guided into the bottom right from a cross by a rampant Mackay.

'A goal in a thousand,' admitted Wolves boss Stan Cullis, though he did harrumph a caveat. 'I don't like seeing goals scored with the bicycle kick. It can be dangerous!' Meanwhile the 'English starlet' Yvonne Buckingham, who had accompanied Mansfield to the match, stoked the militant mood brewing in dressing rooms across the country, observing of the afternoon's four-goal hero: 'They tell me Mr Smith earns only £20 a week. Why, I earned that in one day as a beginner in films!'

Alongside Mansfield, Buckingham and Mr Universe in the stands was Tottenham's latest big-money signing, John White from Falkirk. The gossamer genius was the last significant addition to Nicholson's midfield, and by late February he looked to have sent Spurs on their way to the title, setting up three goals from the right wing in a 4–1 win at Blackburn Rovers. But three days later they came unstuck at Burnley. White didn't make it to Turf Moor in time from his army station at Berwick-upon-Tweed – the young man was still seeing out his period of national service – and promptly did a U-turn back to barracks. His teammates missed him, and this time it was the opposition who won the game from the right flank: John Connelly set up the opener, then cut inside and scored, his trademark move. Burnley's 2–0 win kept them in the hunt, just behind Spurs and Wolves.

The rest of the season became a topsy-turvy, tortoise-and-hare tale. Spurs never truly regained their rhythm after the Burnley loss; three defeats in four games around Easter eventually did for their hopes. Wolves took over, and having lined up an FA Cup final appearance against mid-table Blackburn, thrashed Burnley 6–1 at the end of March. A Double looked on.

But Spurs still had a role to play. They demolished Wolves 3–1 at Molineux in the penultimate game of the season, White the inspiration. It was too late for them, but it left the door open for Burnley, who had regrouped after the Wolves rout and were still hovering. Wolves won their final fixture of the season, 5–1 at Chelsea, to top the table. But Burnley could leapfrog them if they won their game in hand on the Monday night at Manchester City.

A crowd just a few faces short of 66,000 gathered at a supremely tense Maine Road; the population of Burnley itself was only 87,000. After four minutes Brian Pilkington cut in from the left and reached the byline; he flashed a shot at Bert Trautmann from the tightest of angles, and it flew in, the ball pinballing off the flapping keeper and his post. Three minutes later the same player should have made it two, but alone, ten yards out, sent a shot wide.

The miss could have been costly. On 12 minutes City's Ken Barnes clipped a free-kick into the Burnley box from the left. Superstar striker Denis Law miskicked when it was easier to score; Joe Hayes prodded home anyway. But on the half-hour, Burnley took the lead again when reserve winger Trevor Meredith, five foot five and 20 years old, met a ball squirting from a penalty-box stramash and volleyed it sweetly past Trautmann.

It proved the decisive act. City were the dominant team in the second half, but failed to get on terms, Burnley keeper Adam Blacklaw making a series of fine saves, Law missing another kick from close range. In the dying seconds, City left-half Alan Oakes zipped clear but shot straight at Blacklaw, who held onto the ball for dear life before launching it upfield. The whistle blew on Burnley's 2–1 victory. For the very first time that season, they were top of the table. A run timed to perfection.

Bob Lord cracked open the champagne. 'I think we are very worthy champions and I am very happy about it indeed!' Bill Nicholson, reacting to the result from afar, agreed. 'Burnley fully deserved the championship, they are a good footballing side and did well in the last three games to win five out of six points.' Stan Cullis was rather more abrupt. 'I am disappointed and do not wish to make any comment.' Wolves did have the consolation of winning the FA Cup five days later, beating Blackburn in a spectacle so miserable that, as they took their victory lap, they were pelted with orange peel, apple cores and screwed-up pages from the match programme. Poor Wolves, never quite getting the credit they deserved.

The new League champions immediately departed on a VIP cruise liner for a pre-arranged trip to the USA. It's fair to say there was no outburst of Burnleymania. The Clarets had agreed to take part in a new venture called the International Soccer League, an invitational tournament devised to drum up interest in soccer Stateside. The trip was a public-relations disaster from the off. Burnley considered their Brooklyn hotel to be sub-standard, having disliked the meal of stewed chicken and mashed potatoes

Above: Aston Villa's early movers and shakers: William McGregor (standing, second left), George Ramsay (holding the ball) and Archie Hunter (seated, second right)

Right: Preston's Invincibles: Jimmy Ross, as goalscoring star, gets to leave his hat on

Below: Sheffield United keeper William 'Fatty' Foulke: portly but nimble

Left: Ned Doig of Sunderland sports his trademark cap. Baldy head not pictured

© POPPERFOTO/GETTY

© BOB THOMAS/POPPERFOTO/GETTY

Above: Tom Watson (the hat on the right) with his Liverpool title winners of 1905–06

Right: Peerless Jesse Pennington, captain of West Brom's 1919–20 championship side

© POPPERFOTO/GETTY

Above: Colin Veitch: scholar, playwright, impresario, composer, conductor, educationalist, politician, socialite and captain of Newcastle United

Above: Blackburn's Bob Crompton, left, a haughty presence before kick-off

Left: Newcastle defender Bill McCracken, whose sly genius would transform football in the 1920s

Charlie Roberts, erstwhile Manchester United
legend and nearly man with Oldham

Alex Jackson, a scoring sensation at
Huddersfield, and a tabloid sensation at Chelsea

George Camsell (59 goals in 1926–27) makes like Dixie Dean (60, a year later)
with a towering header

Left: Jimmy Seed, bottom right, catalyst of The Wednesday's golden era, earns an England cap for his trouble

Right: Wee jinking genius Hughie Gallacher walks one in for Chelsea at Liverpool

Shy, retiring Arsenal manager George Allison holds a team talk and photo session at the same time

Raich Carter, the brains behind Sunderland's final title

Manchester City star Peter Doherty: 30 goals for the champions, another 23 when relegated the following season

Arsenal striker Ted Drake, shortly after being hit upside the head at Brentford during the 1937–38 title run-in

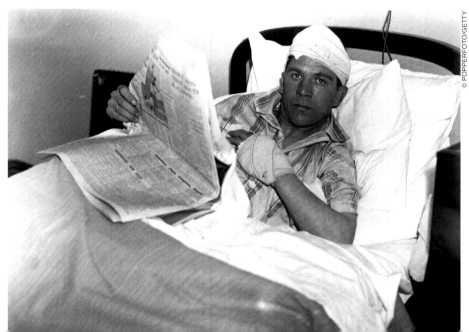

Major Frank Buckley and Jesse Pye together during their brief time at Notts County. Both men very nearly won the title with Wolves – Buckley as manager before the war, Pye as a striker after it

Bert Sproston, Leeds and England defender who had Hitler clocked as an 'evil little twat' from the get-go

Tea and telegrams of congratulation for new Liverpool signing (and future Sgt. Pepper's cover star) Albert Stubbins

Portsmouth's two-time title winners. Jimmy Scoular, back left, exudes an air of no-nonsense

Tottenham manager Arthur Rowe preaches progressive tactics to Vic Buckingham, the mastermind behind West Brom's near miss in 1953–54

Billy Wright, the epitome of golden glamour in the 1950s

Above: Roy Bentley leading
the line for Chelsea's 1954–55
title winners. The No.10,
Seamus O'Connell, was also
a cattle farmer

Right: Fulham chairman and
comic Tommy 'You Lucky
People' Trinder catches the
train with player Jimmy Hill.
Hill's work with the union
would end up costing Trinder
a pretty penny

Above: Duncan Edwards ushers the ball out of play at Arsenal, in the last League game the Busby Babes would ever play

Right: Burnley chairman Bob Lord: a gloriously entertaining blowhard

Below: Tottenham's 1960–61 Double winners sharpen their skills at White Hart Lane

Left: Ipswich Town's Ted Phillips, the man with the hardest shot in football, according to Matt Busby

Below: Denis Law catches some much-needed shut-eye after single-handedly winning the 1963 FA Cup for a not particularly vintage Manchester United (and celebrating accordingly)

Left: Johnny Carey, the genial boss of Everton, Orient and Nottingham Forest, sucks thoughtfully on his signature pipe

Above: Merseyside buddies Alex 'Golden Vision' Young of Everton, and Liverpool's Ian St John, enjoy a day out at the 1967 Open golf. (Roberto De Vicenzo beat Jack Nicklaus by two strokes, for the record.)

Below: Malcolm Allison and his mentor Joe Mercer, all pals as title winners with Manchester City. Not for long, mind...

Above: Don Revie outside Elland Road with a cigar on

Above: Dave Mackay of Derby and Manchester United's George Best fail to demonstrate their status as two of the greatest players ever to pull on boots

Right: Ray Kennedy, 19, is drenched in sticky beverage upon clinching the title for Arsenal in 1970–71. He'd go on to sweep up more championships with Liverpool

Above: Archie Gemmill of Nottingham Forest, gliding across the pitch, despite the state of it

Above: Kenny Dalglish, in his pre-Hitachi-era shirt, welcomes Graeme Souness to Anfield

Left: Cyrille Regis. What was more pleasing to the eye? This West Brom side's play or their iconic kit?

Above: A celebration of Midlands soccer: Brian Clough of Forest, Ron Saunders, Peter Withe and Gary Shaw of Villa, and ATV pundit Jimmy Greaves

Right: Gary Stevens, Trevor Steven and Kevin Sheedy celebrate with the ersatz-bordering-on-risible Canon League trophy

© BOB THOMAS/GETTY

© GETTY/STAFF

Above: Ossie Ardiles and Chris Waddle look on as Diego Maradona flashes some thigh at the League's centenary party

Left: Michael Thomas, fresh from scoring the most dramatic title winner of all, celebrates at Anfield by placing the lid of the Football League trophy on his head

Below: Leeds line up as champions in 1991–92, like Preston did 103 years earlier

© GETTY/STAFF

served up on their arrival. They walked out, forcing organisers to source rooms in Manhattan at short notice. Bob Lord then took umbrage at the behaviour of the mayor of New York City, Robert F. Wagner Jr, who posed for a brief photo with the visitors on the steps of City Hall as he was presented with some Wedgwood china, then disappeared back into the building. 'That was that!' seethed a paranoid Lord, convinced Wagner had orchestrated an anti-English snub.

England's finest were subsequently beaten by Kilmarnock in an ersatz Battle of Britain, during which Harry Potts subjected referee Dennis Howell – a Labour MP who would later serve as minister for sport under Harold Wilson and James Callaghan – to a rolling critique in the Anglo-Saxon style. Potts was carpeted and fined £10 by the FA. According to the *Daily Express*, Burnley were 'told in the blunt language of which they make frequent use that even if they are League champions for the next ten years, they will never again be invited.'

Their first foray onto the Continent, in the 1960–61 European Cup, proved equally farcical. Against two-time finalists Stade de Reims, whose number included 1958 World Cup scoring sensation Just Fontaine, Potts instigated a free-for-all at the Parc des Princes in Paris. Reims midfielder Lucien Muller stole a few yards at a free-kick, then watched in astonished irritation as Burnley's manager raced onto the pitch and moved the ball back to the spot of the original foul. Muller grappled with Potts, tried to push him over, and swung a fist. The pair suddenly found themselves in the middle of a mob of officials and the odd spectator; Potts had to be extricated from the pickle by an army of gendarmes. A hail of stones whistling past his ears, he was marched to the stand, where he spent the remainder of the match absent-mindedly kicking the Burnley club official sitting next to him as he nervously played along with every ball. Potts was fined the haughty sum of 100 guineas (£105) by the FA for that one.

Ahead of their quarter-final second-leg against Hamburg in March, Potts fielded ten reserves in a League fixture against relegation-haunted Chelsea. The other teams near the drop zone raised Cain, as Jimmy Greaves scored a late equaliser in an absurd 4–4 draw to secure a vital point. In the end Chelsea survived easily, but Burnley were fined a whopping £1,000 by the League, a sum large enough to make front-page news. It was all for naught, as Hamburg made it through. 'Who is to say, better than a club manager, which men shall constitute the first team on any occasion?' seethed Bob Lord. 'The League Management Committee? I don't think so.' Lord, for all his bluster, may have had a point. In addition to narrowly missing out on the European Cup semis, Burnley finished a distant fourth in the League, and lost semi-finals in both the FA Cup and the new League Cup. A strikingly similar fixture pile-up, and selection uproar, would infamously scupper Don Revie and Leeds just nine years later.

Bill Nicholson's Spurs, with their stellar midfield of Blanchflower, Mackay and White, and Bobby Smith up front relentlessly banging them in, took the League with a swagger, winning their first 11 games, a First Division record, and never looking back. The elusive twentieth-century Double was finally landed, too, albeit with a slightly anti-climactic FA Cup final victory over ten-man Leicester City. 'I didn't have much heart for running around the stadium,' admitted Footballer of the Year Blanchflower afterwards. 'I looked upon it as a duty rather than an enjoyment. There were too many people there who did not care about the result.'

Blanchflower, the perfectionist-aesthete, was no doubt pining for Tottenham's early season form. Never mind that record-breaking winning start: up until the turn of the calendar year, they won 22 of their first 25 games, dropping just four points and scoring 81 goals along the way. This was travel at an unprecedented rattle. That record would have been even better, too, but for a very strange match at White Hart Lane in early December against the champions Burnley.

Spurs stormed into a four-goal first-half lead, only for the Clarets, inspired by John Connelly, to peg them back level. Nicholson shook his head sadly at his team's largesse: 'We scored eight goals and still only drew!' It was pretty much the only disappointment in an otherwise near-perfect season for Spurs. Meanwhile a slightly manic Harry Potts celebrated the unlikely point. 'We did it because we are the proudest team in the game! We are the greatest champions for years!' Given how Spurs were halfway to redefining the century, he was just taking the opportunity to say it while he still could.

All-star Tottenham, champions-elect with showbiz sass, the glittering go-to team of Jayne Mansfield, would have been the perfect side to usher in the all-new televisual age. Unfortunately, however, they didn't see it that way. Britain's new second channel, Independent Television, had thrown money at the game ever since its launch in 1955. Within a few months of start-up, ITV had transmitted live coverage of floodlit friendlies between Hibernian and Manchester City and Wolves and Dinamo Moscow, plus a glamour FA Cup tie between Arsenal and Bedford Town of the Southern League.

But it was Manchester United's early adventures in the European Cup that really gave telly executives the taste. Granada, the local ITV franchise in Manchester, was, as the name suggests, run by hispanophiles, so United's 1957 semi-final against Real Madrid was an obvious attraction. Granada got huge figures for the game. Nobody much minded that the first four minutes were lost to an ad break. ITV were cut some slack as it wasn't organisational or technical ineptitude on their part; the referee simply started the game early as he couldn't be bothered to hang around in the nippy Manchester air.

The football industry was playing hard to get. Or perhaps it was completely indifferent. At the start of 1960–61, ITV paid the Football League £150,000 for the rights to show live matches on Saturday evenings. There had been compromise. The selected game wouldn't kick off until 6.50 p.m., and ITV would only join the match at 7.30 p.m. for the last knockings of the first half. This would allow match-going punters time to get back from the afternoon's 3 p.m. kick-offs, balance a fashionable tray of TV dinner on their knees, and groove their buttocks into the sofa. The second half in its entirety would then be shown live. 'It's viewing with a KICK!' hooted cigar-sucking ITV impresario Val Parnell, all jazz hands, as he whipped up anticipation ahead of *The Big Game*.

Parnell knew a thing or two about putting on a show. He had, after all, autographed his name all over the title card of the channel's variety spectacular *Val Parnell's Sunday Night at the London Palladium*. However, there was one major problem: the League had decided to keep all the cash themselves, without bothering to discuss it with the clubs. When some of them realised they were being forced to jig for free on national television, they refused to play ball. A fixture between free-scoring Spurs and Aston Villa had been lined up as one of the early shows, but Spurs told the League where to go. Arsenal, whose game with Newcastle had also been pencilled into the schedules, followed their north London rivals in refusing permission to transmit. It was also strongly rumoured that most of the era's other big draws – Manchester United, Wolves, Villa, West Bromwich Albion, Everton and Sheffield Wednesday – were distinctly unimpressed with the paltry cash on offer, too, not to mention the presumptive way the League had acted.

Much rested on *The Big Game*'s big unveil in early September. With so many clubs in open revolt, ITV were banking on their first pick, Blackpool versus Bolton, being such a smash that everyone would meekly fall into line. The fixture had been selected due to the likely presence of Stanley Matthews, now 45 but still fighting fit and one of the biggest draws in the land. But a leg injury kept the superstar winger out.

To compound matters, the ITV production team suffered a collective loss of noggin, opting to place the main camera behind one of the goals at Broomfield Road, rather than level with the centre circle, as dictated by precedent and logic. Viewers could just about work out that Bolton won by a single goal in a very drab fashion. It didn't help that the ITV commentator Peter Lloyd spent most of the match misidentifying players. Adding insult to injury the subsequent blacked-out Arsenal–Newcastle game ended 5–0, while Spurs–Villa finished 6–2. ITV's luck was out. The series was binned. Songs from hit musicals sung by Howard Keel filled the football-shaped hole in the schedule, and armchair fans would have to wait another 23 years for live First Division action.

In February 1961, a few months after *The Big Game* débâcle, Danny Blanchflower, captain of all-conquering Spurs, was invited by the BBC to one of their radio studios on the pretext of an interview. Upon his arrival he was ambushed by Eamonn Andrews, who waved his big red book in the player's unimpressed face and informed him that, 'This Is Your Life'. Blanchflower demurred, becoming the first celebrity from any walk of life to refuse to appear on the hit programme.

Blanchflower later explained that he 'did not want to expose myself to the public without the right to say yes or no. You get shanghaied into this situation where you are suddenly exposed to something.' His decision went down well across the country. In a letter to the *Mirror*, J. B. from Leeds exclaimed: 'Cheers for Danny! Perhaps now the BBC will end this sickly, sentimental drivel, in which every man appears a saint, and no one ever seems to have made a mistake or an enemy.' H. R. Ashtead from Surrey agreed: 'Now all it needs is for members of the public to refuse to take part in *What's My Line?* and I will be really happy.'

Contrary to his very bones, Blanchflower agreed to be interviewed a couple of weeks later by boozing and carousing intellectual Henry Fairlie on the ITV show *Compass*. Prior to transmission, journalists enquired whether Fairlie had asked why Blanchflower turned down *This Is Your Life*. 'No,' came the reply. 'The subject never came up.'

While Blanchflower and Spurs were gliding their way to glory, Newcastle United were in the process of getting themselves relegated yet again. Few neutrals had much sympathy. Before the start of the 1960–61 season, their 23-year-old inside-forward George Eastham publicly requested a transfer. He had fallen out with the board over the habitability of the club house he had been given, then over money, and finally over the refusal to give his father a complementary ticket for the stand; Newcastle would only front the cash for a spot on the terraces. It transpired this was the third time Eastham had asked to leave in two seasons. 'I'm fed up to the teeth,' he sighed. He simply wished to leave, and wasn't wholly fussy about the destination.

So Eastham refused to re-sign for the new campaign. But as Newcastle didn't want him to go, and would not agree to a move, they were able to keep his registration under the retain-and-transfer system. Eastham was within his rights to refuse another contract, but he'd get no wages and wouldn't be able to join any other club unless Newcastle backed down. It was an appalling state of affairs. Eastham called Newcastle's bluff. 'I want the right of every free man to work for who and where I please. I do intend to leave Newcastle. They won't stall me any longer, because this is not just an impulsive action.' Out of contract, he left the sport and took up a career selling cork in the Surrey town of Reigate.

Arsenal, Tottenham, Blackpool and Fulham all offered Newcastle big money to sign Eastham and bring an end to the ludicrous stand-off. But the Toon board flatly refused. 'All this talk about Eastham being granted a transfer providing the price is right is tripe,' groused Newcastle chairman Wally Hurford. 'He stays on our books.' It had become a battle of pride versus principle. One board member was reported as saying he'd 'rather see Eastham shovel coal' than ever play again. Eastham served Newcastle with a writ for 'unreasonable restraint of trade' but, before the High Court could hear it, the club relented and accepted a £47,500 bid from Arsenal. Eastham pulled his boots back on and headed for Highbury. But he carried on with his legal case anyway.

Newcastle were as shambolic on the field as they were in the boardroom, although they were nothing if not entertaining. An early-season 7–2 thrashing of Fulham was no omen. They drew 4–4 with Wolves and 5–5 with West Ham, results which strongly suggested that in-game management was a foreign concept. They shipped five goals in defeat to Arsenal, Everton, Burnley and Leicester, and six to West Brom and Chelsea. They ended the season bound for the Second Division, 21st out of 22, having scored 86 times but conceded a truly remarkable 109 goals.

Eastham could have been forgiven for thinking karmic justice had been served. Not least because he had been jeered to the rafters on his return with Arsenal in February, pelted with fruit and hit by a snowball. He responded by setting up two goals and scoring the equaliser in a 3–3 draw. Lord Westwood, new to the Newcastle board, offered an olive branch: 'I have been watching football here for 30 years and I've always thought there was not a better or friendlier crowd in the game. But the reception accorded Eastham was ghastly. I was disgusted with the way our fans acted.'

Eastham's struggle, and the whiff of television money, gave the Professional Footballers' Association the confidence to push for an end to the maximum weekly wage of £20. The clubs dug their heels in: Burnley's Bob Lord was the only high-profile owner to admit the players might have a point. J. P. W. Mallalieu, the Labour MP for Huddersfield East, encouraged the players to consider industrial action: 'This is the only treatment the players can dish out. They have been acting peaceably for 40 years and achieving nothing. The League and the FA are hopelessly out of date.' Jimmy McIlroy, captain of reigning champions Burnley, also sounded the call: 'It's now or never. If the PFA take this lying down, it's the finish of the Association. If they say strike, I'll strike tomorrow. The PFA must go flat out for the abolition of the maximum wage.'

The union, led by Fulham inside-forward Jimmy Hill, eventually called a strike for January. Hill cleverly curried favour with the public by suggesting it needn't stop them having their weekly flutter on the pools: the players would be willing to stage a shadow programme of identical fixtures on the day of action, thinly disguised teams such as 'Manchester United Rovers' and 'Manchester City Pirates' turning out at parks and recreation grounds around the country. The League meanwhile sent a telegram to all clubs in an attempt to bring forward that Saturday's fixtures to Friday evening, effectively forcing players to play by bodyswerving the agreed strike date.

However, in a climate in which even Harold Macmillan's Tory government were said to be sympathetic to the union's demands, a League climbdown was inevitable. Before the strike could take place, they agreed to the lifting of the minimum wage, as well as the abolition of the retain-and-transfer system. The League would brazenly attempt to backtrack on everything a couple of months down the line, and though the wages genie wouldn't go back into the bottle, the wrongs of retain-and-transfer would not be righted until the courts effectively settled the Eastham versus Newcastle case in the player's favour in 1963. Even then, the issue of freedom of movement was never definitively settled until the Bosman ruling of 1995.

But clubs were now free to pay top wages to the top stars. Not that they were totally happy about it. Fulham famously quintupled Johnny Haynes' money, making him the first £100-a-week player, but only because popular comedian and chairman Tommy Trinder had rashly promised to cough up the minute the legislation was changed. The club also released Hill. 'This has nothing whatever to do with his PFA activities,' a Fulham suit told the press, admirably keeping a straight face.

Before football got too slick and professional, there was still time for one last charming call-back to a quainter, more innocent age. While Bill Nicholson had built up Spurs, another alumnus of Arthur Rowe's push-and-run side was constructing something equally special, albeit in more modest surroundings. In 1954 Alf Ramsey, the heartbeat behind Tottenham's title-winners of 1950–51, retired and started out in management at Ipswich Town of the Third Division (South). He wasted little time in getting the unheralded Suffolk club into the Second. Then in 1960–61, another promotion took Ipswich into the top tier for the first time in their history.

Town went into 1961–62, their inaugural First Division campaign, with pretty much the same squad that had risen from the Third. It was no surprise when they were written off before the season as innocent hayseeds. It was no surprise either when they lost two of their first three games, conceding four goals against both Burnley and Manchester City. But it *was* a surprise when they met Burnley again in the fourth match of the season, and handed them a solid 6–2 spanking.

Spurs were the next high-profile victims, seen off 3–2 at Portman Road in early October. The reaction of the *Daily Express* was something to behold. Beside a match report peppered with references to 'city slickers' and 'rustic, pop-eyed yokels', a cartoon featuring a character with a stalk of straw sticking out of his mouth gave his own running commentary of what had gone down: 'They foine gents the Hotspurs come down from Lunnon to play that there football game. They got kickers what cost more pounds than oi seen cows, which is plenty. Mister Jones scores a goal for 'em and oi touches me forelock to him. Then our Master Phillips gets all disrespectful loike and near busts that there string stuff at back of their sticks. Mister Jones scores agin which is only roight and proper. Then that there Crawford of arn forgets his station and scores for us'n dang oi 'e do it agin an us wins!'

Master Phillips and that there Crawford – Ted and Ray respectively – were the spearhead of the side, and would score 61 goals between them during the campaign. Matt Busby, whose Manchester United were rolled over 4–1 at Portman Road, claimed Phillips had the hardest kick in soccer. News surfaced that he'd once fractured a keeper's wrist with a shot while playing in the Third, and that Newport goalie Len Weare had been knocked out while attempting to cushion a piledriver with his stomach.

But the real star of the side was Jimmy Leadbetter, a wily old playmaker who would regularly take up unorthodox positions, causing havoc for defences not anticipating any of his strange behaviour. He would drop unnaturally deep, confusing defenders who didn't know whether to follow their man or stay put. Or maybe he would come in off the wing, dragging the full-back with him and leaving acres for Phillips to gambol into. Leadbetter's passing from distance was superlative, and he regularly found Phillips and Crawford with laser-guided accuracy, causing all manner of problems. In the days before saturation television coverage, Ipswich were able to spring this surprise tactic all around the country, and stayed with the title pace.

Even so, for the majority of the season, it looked like Burnley were on course to repeat their 1959–60 triumph. They had responded to that early-season defeat at Ipswich by stringing together seven wins on the bounce, and spent most of the campaign handing out some fearful thrashings: they put five past Fulham, six past Leicester and Manchester City, and 13 goals past Birmingham in two games. They travelled to Manchester United and beat one of the pre-season favourites 4–1. And in early March they whipped West Ham United 6–0, bringing their seasonal goal tally to 90 in 29 matches. They were four points clear of second-placed Ipswich with a game in hand, and five clear of Spurs with two matches over the Londoners. 'The Lancastrians can start planning for the European Cup next season,' predicted Geoffrey Green in *The Times*. 'Barring some earthquake, the league title should be theirs for the second time in three years.'

The earth moved under their feet, and the sky came falling down. No particular catastrophe befell Harry Potts's side, which to all intents and purposes was the same one which had prevailed two years previously. They simply stopped winning matches. Of the 13 that remained, only two were turned into victories. There was no obvious reason why a settled, successful side suddenly lost its rhythm, other than a suspicion that the legs of 1960, two years further down the line, collectively went at the wrong time.

Ipswich took full advantage. They won ten of their last 16, losing only one, an incongruous 5–0 thumping at Manchester United which, according to the *Express*, 'could have been 24–0'. At least they were spared a condescending cartoon this time. The signature victory was a 3–1 success at outgoing champions Spurs, Crawford and Phillips – now known countrywide as 'The Twins' – again doing the damage.

Even though Burnley had capitulated abysmally, a League and FA Cup Double was still within their grasp going into the final week. A win against relegated Chelsea, then another at Sheffield Wednesday, would have them nick the title off Ipswich on goal average. But they could only manage a draw against the Londoners, allowing Ipswich to secure the title with two late Ray Crawford goals against Aston Villa at Portman Road. Burnley were thrashed in their remaining League match 4–0 at Hillsborough, then lost the FA Cup final 3–1 to Tottenham. It was one of the most miserable end-of-season collapses.

Ipswich, tipped for relegation, were the champions! They became only the second team to win the title at their first attempt, after Preston in the League's inaugural season. Chairman and owner John Cobbold, a jovial booze hound, got stuck into a crate of champagne. The self-effacing Alf Ramsey, lauded as a genius, merely allowed himself a small sip and a satisfied smile. 'Headline writers insist on loading me with the credit, but I do not seek personal publicity. This championship has been won by the players, not by Alf Ramsey. I have been lucky this season . . . lucky to have intelligent players who think football and talk football.' Genuinely modest shtick, which the entire country would lap up again, four years later.

At the start of the following season, Bill Nicholson devised a simple plan to counter Ipswich: mark Leadbetter. Spurs beat them 5–1 in the Charity Shield, everyone else took notes, and the champions ended a shocking title defence in 17th place. Ramsey left to take over England, for whom he would devise another successful tactical masterstroke soon enough. But the days of the small-town fairytale appeared numbered in the post-maximum-wage era. Ipswich were relegated in 1963–64. Burnley, within touching distance of the title in 1962, never got as close again; they went down in 1971, and by 1987 found themselves in the Fourth Division, the founder members one match away from dropping out of the League altogether.

13

Johnny takes a taxi to the Orient (1962–63)

Everton had been a thundering non-event since the war. A series of low finishes culminated in their chastening 1951 relegation; it took the grand old club three long, painful seasons to get back up; and the remainder of the fifties was spent floundering in the bottom half of the First Division. But after they were humiliated 10–4 by Tottenham in late 1958, Johnny Carey, the mild-mannered captain of Matt Busby's first great Manchester United side, took control. Suddenly there was big money to spend. Thanks to a new and extremely ambitious chairman in John Moores, founder of the Littlewoods Pools empire, the era of the Mersey Millionaires was upon us. Carey bought well, signing striker Roy Vernon, right-half Jimmy Gabriel and forward Alex Young, a player of such elegant inspiration that he earned himself the nickname 'The Golden Vision'. Everton improved quickly, hovering around the fringes of the 1960–61 Tottenham title procession. They finished fifth, their best showing since winning the title in 1938–39.

Onwards and upwards, though not on a trajectory which satisfied Moores, who wanted a quick return on his investment. So with three games of that 1960–61 season to go, a few days after a 4–0 romp at Newcastle, Moores accompanied Carey to a

Football League meeting in London. Carey, a vocal supporter of the agreement to abolish the maximum wage, watched in horror as Moores and Everton voted against its implementation. On the way home, Moores sacked his manager in the back of a black cab. (Taxi for Carey!) He phoned home to break the news to his wife Margaret. 'I must be the most successful failure in the business,' Carey told her. Margaret told the press that 'it wasn't exactly a shock. There had been hints recently. He didn't sound very upset. The team are fifth in the League, what more do they want? They have obviously made up their mind that they want a new manager, and that's it.'

Moores had been goaded into action by the recent resignation of Sheffield Wednesday boss Harry Catterick, whose side had nudged regal Spurs even closer than Everton, eventually finishing second in 1960–61, albeit as a distant runner-up. Catterick maintained the purchase of a reliable striker would have made the difference, but the Wednesday board refused to meet the asking price for Hibernian sensation Joe Baker. So he quit in a huff, a lofty reputation suddenly on the market. Moores decided the disciplinarian Catterick would be a better fit for his ambitious project than the gentle, easy-going Carey. Catterick had also played up front for Everton just after the war, wanted to manage the club above all others, and was a personal friend of Moores. Carey was never going to win. Catterick took up the reins at Goodison with a couple of games of the 1960–61 season left to tidy up. Thanks to a quirk of the fixture list, his debut match was at Wednesday; Everton won it 2–1. Carey washed up at Leyton Orient in the close season. Tasked with keeping a struggling club in the 1961–62 Second Division, the *Express* immediately identified him as 'a man with a problem'.

Problem? What problem? The level-headed Carey quickly realised that 'Orient, though poor, were a club with tremendous heart and feeling. It is such a happy club that one cannot be part of it without feeling that happiness. People here are so good, so nice and seem to expect so little that you feel that if you don't do a good job, you are letting these people down.' He took a puff of his pipe and calmly organised his team: Malcolm Lucas, Sid Bishop and Cyril Lea provided a solid base at the back, while Dave Dunmore offered life up front. Dunmore scored 22 goals in Carey's first season. Incredibly, with a game to go, Orient just needed to better Sunderland's final result to grab the second promotion slot behind Liverpool (who under Bill Shankly were finally wriggling out of the Second after eight years).

The Mackems could only draw at Swansea, but Orient beat Bury 2–0, Malcolm Graham scoring twice in a state of high emotion. 'I couldn't stop the tears coming into my eyes,' he sobbed after the game. 'I'll never forget that moment.' Club director Leslie Grade, theatre impresario and brother of ITV mogul Lew, asked Orient's hero to name his reward. Graham, wrapped up in the excitement and giddy on bubbles, asked for nothing more than a refill. Years later, he recalled the exchange with a bittersweet smile. 'If I would have said, "Mr Grade, you can pay off my house bond," he would have joyfully done it.'

Manchester United had slipped back into the pack after finishing runners-up to Wolves in 1958–59. Two seventh-place finishes were followed by 15th spot in 1961–62. Something had to change. Matt Busby identified former Manchester City striker Denis Law, miserable in exile at Torino, as the catalyst. After a summer spent chasing elusive Torino president Angelo Filippone around Europe – a saga that included flights to Amsterdam, Lausanne and Geneva, plus a madcap car journey over the Alps to a meeting in Turin which the deliberately awkward Filippone didn't attend – Busby eventually got his man in a pricy £115,000 deal.

Law provided him with an instant return, scoring with a glancing header after just seven minutes of the new season. The goal put United 2–0 up against West Bromwich Albion, David Herd having opened the scoring after 90 seconds. The 51,685 inside Old Trafford bounced around noisily. But Albion scored twice in the last 15 minutes to force a draw. The mood of the 51,685 turned sour. 'One cannot recall having heard the slow handclap at Old Trafford so early in the season,' reported the *Guardian*. 'Is this a record?!'

So much for United's fast start. They went on to lose nine of their next 13 games, a run that culminated in a 6–2 humbling at Tottenham which sent them plummeting to the bottom of the table. It was promising to be a long season in Manchester, for City had started the season by going down 8–1 at Wolverhampton Wanderers. A 6–1 home defeat by West Ham United in early October meant City had shipped 27 goals in their first seven games. West Ham's fifth goal was hotly disputed by City keeper Bert Trautmann, who kicked the ball at the referee, successfully clocking the official upside the head. He then tore off his shirt, threw it to the ground, and stormed off the pitch without waiting for the inevitable sending off. Some of the crowd wondered whether Trautmann had simply thrown in the towel, given the referee had failed to make the internationally recognised signal for dismissal. 'I was sent off all right,' insisted the raging keeper. 'The referee just said: "That is you for the dressing room." Did I kick the ball at him? Well, I can't honestly say that I didn't.' It was Trautmann's first premature bath of a long and famous career.

One of United's early-season defeats had been to Johnny Carey's Orient. The minnows, tipped to go straight back down, started briskly enough: in a spectacular September, they beat United, West Ham, Fulham and, most impressively of all, the '£130-a-week Merseyside maestros' of Everton. Carey, sacked so ignominiously by the Toffees 17 months earlier, allowed himself a long, contemplative suck on his pipe after the satisfying shock of a 3–0 thrashing. Given that Everton had won six of their first seven games, pressmen wondered whether Orient were equipped to repeat Ipswich's tricks. Nope! The wheels came off. Orient didn't win another game until April, by which time they were miles adrift at the bottom of the division. The board offered to spend money on new players in February, but Carey, knowing full well the likely outcome, responded in selfless fashion: 'Gentlemen, don't waste your money.' Having taken the club as far as it seemed possible to go, he left for Nottingham Forest in the summer.

Wolves also dealt in early-season illusion. The most successful club of the fifties had flirted with relegation in 1961–62, finishing 18th, their lowest position since 1933. So Stan Cullis gave his squad a good shoogle. His new, youthful side – their Wolf Cubs nickname was cute but didn't stick – flew out of the blocks. The 22-year-old striker Ted Farmer scored four in that 8–1 rout of Manchester City. Spurs, once again the choice of the *cognoscenti*, were beaten 2–1 at White Hart Lane, 23-year-old forward Chris Crowe and 20-year-old winger Terry Wharton doing the damage. The defence was built around the 18-year-old David Woodfield. The Wolf Cubs sat top after their first 11 matches, unbeaten, having won eight.

Captain Ron Flowers, the three-time title-winning veteran (at 28) of the wild fifties scene, was bullish. After the poor showing of the previous season, most observers had concluded the Cullis long-ball style was outmoded. Flowers was having none of it: 'Many people claimed we were finished. I'm confident we have demonstrated that the Wolves style is still the best and most successful.' But Farmer was dogged by injury, while in 1962 the maxim that you win nothing with kids had yet to be disproved. A 2–0 home reverse to Everton set Wolves off on a miserable run: in their next 13 games, they'd only win twice.

Cullis's team still finished a creditable fifth, having scored 93 goals, but this was the Indian summer of a playing and managerial giant. Another average season followed. Then a poor start to the 1964–65 campaign did for Cullis, who had driven himself ill with stress. After taking a two-week break to recuperate, he was sent packing. Several loyal shareholders mobilised to demand the club legend's reinstatement, but new pipe-sucking chairman John Ireland, in the job a full seven weeks and the self-styled 'Iron Man of Molineux', refused to budge. Cullis was on his way after 30 years' service. Ireland replaced him with former Huddersfield and Scotland manager Andy Beattie, who had a reputation as a troubleshooter. One year and three days later, Wolves were languishing in the Second Division, and on the wrong end of a 9–3 walloping at Southampton. Beattie was on his way too, the all-gold golden era well and truly over, never to return.

Everton's two-goal victory at Wolves in October had been a classy one. Their slight but smooth captain Roy Vernon was, according to the *Guardian*, 'beyond reproach in all things' and 'had no equal. He arranged the variations of pace at which the game was contested and decided whether the long or short pass was suitable for each set of circumstances. Under this astute and experienced general, Everton scarcely could help but thrive.' Billy Bingham and the Golden Vision got the goals; Catterick's side went top. It looked like they were destined for a simple *mano-a-mano* title battle with Tottenham, who on the same day drew 4–4 with Arsenal but otherwise were in the middle of a six-game winning streak which featured a 4–0 win over Leicester, a 5–1 victory at Leyton Orient, a 6–2 demolition of Manchester United and a 9–2 felling of Nottingham Forest in which Jimmy Greaves scored four.

But the climate closed in, throwing an icicle in the works. Three days before Christmas, a freezing fog descended on Britain. Eighteen games were postponed, while eight more were abandoned midway through. By Boxing Day, the country was blanketed tip to toe by snow. Only three top-flight matches survived, Spurs beating champions Ipswich 5–0 on an afternoon when ordering bare-legged players to slide around in the ice and snow amounted to a brazen violation of human-rights legislation. (Greaves got a hat-trick nonetheless.) A mere ten matches took place countrywide on the following Saturday; the entire card was decimated on New Year's Day.

Somehow, the weather got even more extreme: 'the Big Shiver' would morph into 'the White Nightmare' and eventually 'the Big Freeze'. There were -20°C temperatures, 15-foot snowdrifts, and at one point along the Kent coast the sea stopped rolling altogether, turning into a mile-long ice rink of the deepest blue. The British winter hadn't been this harsh since 1739. Clubs staged matches when they could, but that was not always that often. There were only four First Division games played in the whole of January.

The Big Thaw wouldn't set in until early March, and the Big Hiatus caused a fixture pile-up which served as a metaphorical reminder of all those snowdrifts. Some clubs got off more lightly than others. Everton only got to pull on their boots twice in the League during the Big Freeze; Spurs managed four games. But

Leicester City played six. Their groundsman had recently re-laid the Filbert Street pitch using a blend of fertiliser and weedkiller that generated enough chemical heat to deal with the worst of the frost. The snow was cleared by the shovel-load, fans having answered a rallying cry in the local paper. The grass was then covered with straw, while the brave groundsman sat up every night to make sure braziers strategically positioned across the pitch were full of coke and kicking out enough warmth to stop the playing surface from turning to sheet ice.

A little luck and a lot of effort, but it was worth it. Matt Gilles had built a progressive 'switch and whirl' side around the playmaking of Davie Gibson, the flexibility and hard running of midfielder Frank McLintock, the wing-play of Mike Stringfellow and the goals of Ken Keyworth. But Gilles was clever enough for them to switch to a more basic, long-ball style on pitches battered by the harsh winter. Either way, they gained momentum while the other teams were kicking their heels.

Like Spurs, Leicester played on Boxing Day too, and came out 5–1 winners over Orient. It was the first of seven straight wins in the League, a run that included victories over Everton, Arsenal, Liverpool and Ipswich. It took them from fourth to joint top with Tottenham, and earned them the sobriquet of the 'Ice Kings'. The run ended with a controversial 2–2 draw with Spurs at Filbert Street, during which a Jimmy Greaves shot, mid-air and bound for the roof of the net, couldn't reach the goal before the referee blew his half-time whistle. Adding insult to injury most observers thought the official had mistakenly blown up on 44 minutes anyway. Leicester, having ridden their luck outrageously, kept their unbeaten run going for another four games before going down at West Ham. They regrouped, forcing a 2–2 draw with Manchester United at Old Trafford, then beating the same opposition 24 hours later, 4–3 on their own patch, Keyworth and Denis Law both scoring hat-tricks. The win took them top. Leicester's Ice Kings were five games away from wearing the crown.

The fixture chaos caused by the Big Freeze played havoc with the football pools. With so few matches played, the Pools Promoters' Association had to do something if they wanted to keep the wheels of the gambling industry turning smoothly. Four blank weeks had lost the betting companies a combined £12 million in revenue. This wouldn't stop John Moores of Littlewoods Pools bankrolling two huge deals for Everton during the cold snap: he landed Sheffield Wednesday wing-half Tony Kay for £55,000, and beat Spurs to Rangers winger Alex Scott with a £40,000 bid. The transfers brought the overall cost of Everton's team to a reported £296,120; this was spending on an unprecedented scale.

But something had to be done to keep the big money rolling in. So, midway through January, the pools moguls came up with a plan for a 'dream-up' scheme, which involved assembling a panel of experts who would kick into action whenever 31 or more matches were postponed, forecasting the results so the pools could always go ahead. It wasn't a popular idea. 'What a cheek!' spluttered one off-the-record First Division manager. 'Who has the right to say my team lost or drew?' A board member at Bolton suggested the idea reduced football to 'the level of ludo'.

The dice were rolled anyway. The first pools panel was held on 26 January, and consisted of six men: three erstwhile England stars in Tommy Lawton, Tom Finney and Ted Drake, the one-time Scotland full-back George Young, the 1950, 1954 and 1958 World Cup referee Arthur Ellis, and John Theodore Cuthbert Moore-Brabazon, 1st Baron Brabazon of Tara. This upstanding chappie was a former Tory MP and proud owner of the first pilot's licence ever issued in the UK. He had been a pioneer of aviation, strapping a wastepaper basket to the wing of a plane back in 1909, placing a small piglet in it, and taking the craft up for a spin, thus proving conclusively that pigs could fly. While the only amateur on the panel, Brabazon clearly knew his onions, having only a couple of years earlier claimed £1,500 on an eight-from-eleven perm, winnings he spent on repairs to one of his sailing boats. He had also gathered in 'oh, over £100' earlier in the season. 'That was a very complicated perm,' he yawned. 'I didn't think it was going to come in as much as it did.'

The 'findings' of the first pools panel were announced live on both BBC and ITV. Sure enough, not everyone was in agreement with the 'results'. Eyebrows shot up at the suggestion Leeds would beat Stoke, and that Peterborough could win at Derby. As the weeks passed, the public became more incredulous at what appeared to be increasingly whimsical conclusions. A panel chaired by another legend of aviation, the double-amputee wartime fighter pilot Sir Douglas Bader, insisted struggling Manchester United could eke out a draw at high-flying Burnley. Morecambe and Wise suggested that they could preside over the next one.

'This pools panel lark is a scream!' began Eric and Ernie. 'Let's face it, some of the results are so funny they couldn't have been bettered by a panel of comedians. So why not have one?' TV's top comic duo suggested an all-star line up of *Goons* star Harry Secombe, tickling-stick-wielding one-line merchant Ken Dodd, themselves, and music-hall legends Tommy Trinder and Bud Flanagan (chair). Secombe was up for it. 'A great idea!' he said. 'I won a first dividend three years ago. Now maybe I can fix my coupon again!' Meanwhile a demand for legal action against the actual panel was made by hot-faced Brigadier Terence Clarke, the

Conservative MP for Portsmouth West, who argued that the pools companies were effectively running an illegal and loaded lottery. The Attorney General wasn't interested. Morecambe and Wise had no luck either: their meta showbiz scheme fell by the wayside soon after, when spring finally decided to bring everyone some sunshine.

Leicester's advantage at the top of the table disappeared, both figuratively and literally, with the snow, and the return of regular football. Tottenham and Everton had games in hand, and both made up the ground. Spurs would end the season having scored 111 goals, an astonishing total in an age when teams were, slowly but surely, beginning to develop their defensive smarts. Two games against Liverpool over Easter showed how Bill Nicholson's swashbucklers really should have won the League, but also why they didn't. Jimmy Greaves helped himself to another four-goal haul at White Hart Lane in a 7–2 victory, yet found the critics cooing over the calm midfield prompting of Dave Mackay. Three days earlier, Spurs had travelled to Anfield, where they hadn't won since the RMS *Titanic* had sunk. Terry Dyson scored with a shot struck so ferociously that, upon hitting a stanchion at the back of the goal, the ball rebounded back to the halfway line. Spurs went two up, but five unanswered second-half goals condemned them to a big defeat. The Kop, feeling ever so pleased with itself, chimed up a version of 'London Bridge is Falling Down'. Spurs finished second.

Leicester slipped all the way to fourth, having used up too much fuel in a hard-fought FA Cup semi-final victory over Liverpool. Bill Shankly's emerging side had more than 30 shots on target, but all were turned away by an inspired Gordon Banks. Up the other end, Mike Stringfellow scored on the break to secure a win Frank McLintock admitted in later years was 'the biggest travesty of justice I witnessed during 21 years as a professional'. Leicester's form then went south. Injuries to Banks and the influential Davie Gibson didn't help matters but, after hitting the top following the Manchester United victory, they only picked up a single point from their last five games.

Everton by contrast turned on the hot jets at exactly the right time. At the start of April they embarked on a 12-game unbeaten run, winning eight. Kay and Scott gave good bang for Everton's buck during the run-in. The Toffees won their final fixture of the season 4–1 at home against Fulham, captain and leading scorer Roy Vernon netting a hat-trick. Meantime, Spurs lamely lost 1–0 at relegation-haunted Manchester City, while Leicester went down 2–0 at Bolton. Everton were the 'chequebook champions' of England, the first time they had won the prize in nearly a quarter of a century. As the crowd at Goodison lost itself in frenzied reverie, the chequebook's owner was relieved of his hat. 'It went after the second goal, I think,' laughed John Moores. 'I've been yelling my head off.'

Spurs eased the pain of missing out on the title by blitzing Atlético Madrid 5–1 the following Wednesday in the final of the Cup Winners' Cup, becoming England's first continental champions. Leicester also had a chance to rescue something from the season. They were hot favourites going into the FA Cup final against Manchester United, who had escaped relegation by the skin of their teeth, snaffling priceless late-season points in a draw at Manchester City gifted by a late and completely unnecessary Dave Wagstaffe backpass, and a 3–1 win over already relegated Leyton Orient. (City, it almost certainly goes without saying, went down with the Orient instead. They had conceded a reckless 102 goals.)

But Leicester failed to turn up for the final, in which Denis Law was imperious. Law had top-scored for United with 29 goals in League and Cup, though his first season back hadn't been totally plain sailing. In a 3–0 defeat at West Brom just before the Big Freeze, he missed a couple of relatively easy chances. After one particularly egregious scuff, match referee Gilbert Pullin let slip a loud guffaw and offered a capsule review of the £115,000 striker's abilities. 'What a waste of money!' he parped, before continuing his trenchant critique: 'You're a clever bastard. You can't play.' Law, momentarily shocked into silence, eventually gathered himself and replied in the Aberdonian vernacular, before adding: 'I have seen better referees in junior football.' Pullin considered sending Law off, but satisfied himself with another *bon mot*: 'And I have seen better players in junior football. Now stop acting like a big baby and let's get on with the game.'

United reported Pullin to the FA. At the subsequent hearing, Pullin claimed his patter had been of a more jovial variety, insisting he had merely quipped: 'Even the good players miss 'em!' He was carpeted anyway, so turned in his whistle, notebook and pencil in anger. The freshly retired official refused to shake the conciliatory hand offered by Law in front of newspaper cameramen, and his valedictory salvo wasn't without some merit: 'There seems little future for a referee if the only weapon he has against a player who uses a naughty word or passes an unkind comment is a sending off, while a forthright comment, designed to restore a player's sense of proportion, is to be rejected as a crime.' But it was a sad way for Pullin to complete his dealings with United, for he'd had the bittersweet historical honour, four years previously, of refereeing their rollercoaster 5–4 win at Arsenal in February 1958, the last match played by the Busby Babes in England.

A bronze penny for Pullin's thoughts, then, his feet up in front of the television set on FA Cup final day, as Law bossed the Wembley showpiece, scoring the opening goal, hitting the post and cavorting around with United's first piece of silverware since Munich. 'That was my greatest game,' Law claimed as he fell out of a London drinker 24 hours later, a few richly deserved celebratory refreshments to the good. 'I was great! Just great!' United had been reborn. Matt Busby's mad pre-season dash around Europe was utterly vindicated. A clever bastard? Damn straight.

14

Jimmy reverses into a canal (1963–64 to 1964–65)

Thanks to his daily regime of a mug of breakfast tea, 90 minutes jogging along the beach, a light salad and piece of fruit for lunch, and another brew in the afternoon, Stanley Matthews was still going strong as a professional footballer. In October 1961, aged 46, he'd been dropped by Blackpool for the first time in 14 years, so decided it was time to pack up and go home. He rejoined Stoke City, the club he first played for as a 17-year-old in 1932 but left acrimoniously during the last knockings of the 1946–47 title race. Stoke were now in the Second Division, short of cash, with low gates and even lower expectations. 'If we do not double our average attendance of 10,000 I shall be surprised,' announced Stoke chairman Albert Henshall, fingernails bitten to the quick. Henshall's father Ernest had been on the board when Stan departed in 1947 and hadn't wanted him to leave. 'But we have not signed him for his crowd-pulling alone. He will be a tremendous boost for the team.'

Any doubts that the old boy could still have a positive effect were dispelled quickly enough. Stoke's crowds had in fact plummeted to an average of 8,000 – the chairman had been desperately talking it up – but for Stan's comeback against Huddersfield Town, 35,974 clicked through the turnstiles. The old magic was still there. Matthews's dribbles were beguiling enough to send the left-back he faced, future England World Cup winner Ray Wilson, sliding around haplessly on his backside. Matthews had a hand in all the goals of a 3–0 win.

Matthews and Stoke eased away from relegation trouble, then went for promotion the following season. Their star-studded 1962–63 team also featured recent title-winner Jimmy McIlroy, sensationally jettisoned by Burnley after falling out with Bob Lord, Munich survivor Dennis Viollet, and Jackie Mudie, who had been Matthews's teammate in the FA Cup final ten years earlier. Stoke visited fellow promotion chasers Chelsea during the run-in. Tommy Docherty's young side were too wound up for the big occasion, and Matthews – now 48 – was twice dumped over the hoardings and into the stands. The needlessly robust challenges had the strange effect of turning a 66,000 crowd against their own team, in support of a legendary figure being roughed-up in his dotage. Different times. 'It was hard but I enjoyed it,' smiled Matthews as he dusted himself down. Stoke prevailed by a single goal and secured the Second Division title with a 2–0 win over Luton Town. Matthews scored one of the goals, and was offered a glass of champagne as the celebrations got under way. He turned it down. Instead, at the moment of his last great achievement, he took time to guide a blind fan around the changing room, introducing him to all the players. Luton manager Bill Harvey, whose team had just left the division in the other direction, couldn't help but smile anyway. 'Look at Stan. He deserves everything he gets. He's so human!'

Matthews's unexpected return to the First Division wasn't the perfect fairytale. Nonetheless, as a final page of the story, it satisfied enough. Injuries and age combined to severely limit his appearances as Stoke consolidated in 1963–64, but he was knighted in the

1965 New Year's honours list, and, during the midst of a February injury crisis, he was called up five days after his 50th birthday to play against Fulham. In what proved to be his final match, Sir Stan slipped an exquisite ball through the middle of the Fulham defence to set up John Ritchie for the decisive goal of a 3–1 win. A couple of months later, as the whistle blew on his Victoria Ground testimonial – guest-stars included László Kubala, Josef Masopust, Alfredo Di Stéfano, Jim Baxter and Jimmy Greaves – Matthews was chaired off by Ferenc Puskás and Lev Yashin. The least he deserved at the end of a 33-year shift.

As one legend embarked on his valedictory lap, a new talent arrived to fill some big boots. George Best was handed his debut for Manchester United against West Bromwich Albion in September 1963, though not everyone agreed with Matt Busby's decision to throw the 17-year-old winger into First Division action. Best's fellow youth teamer Eamon Dunphy thought it might be a little bit too soon. Dunphy blamed Best for United getting knocked out of the previous season's FA Youth Cup – 'He fucked around on the left wing all night!' – and hadn't witnessed much development in his game since.

To be fair, Dunphy wasn't far off in his analysis. Best prepared for his debut in typically laid-back fashion, sitting in the dressing room idly flicking through the *United Review*, popping out for a cup of tea with his pals, and only returning ten minutes or so before kick-off. He was then given a thorough going over by no-messing Baggies right-back Graham Williams, who meted out treatment rough enough to send Best scampering off to the other flank for refuge. Best did have a minor role in the only goal of the game, scored by David Sadler, but otherwise he was, as Dunphy noted, 'a schoolboy against men. And he played like a schoolboy as well.' Busby sent Best back to the reserves. Three months later, refreshed, slightly older and infinitely wiser, a more experienced Georgie Boy got his second chance against Burnley. He scored in a 5–1 win, then got his second League goal three weeks later at the home of his virgin tormentors West Brom.

United weren't quite the finished article as a collective either. They topped the early 1963–64 table after a couple of attention-grabbing wins over the previous two champions, 5–1 against Everton at Old Trafford, 7–2 at Ipswich Town. Denis Law was beginning to rattle them in at a prodigious rate: as well as the couple he grabbed against both Everton and Ipswich, he scored a hat-trick in a 4–1 win over Tottenham Hotspur and claimed four in a 5–2 stuffing of Stoke City.

But the team was gloriously inconsistent, and not a little hot-tempered. They went two goals down at Aston Villa in double-quick time, whereupon Law, frustrated by a couple of meaty challenges, kicked out at Villa defender Alan Deakin. He was sent packing, the fourth United player to be dismissed that season, and it wasn't even the middle of November. Law, whose righteous hair-trigger constitution brought legendary compatriot Hughie Gallacher to mind, was eventually banned for 28 days. His United teammates had a whip-round to cover the £500 Law lost in wages and bonuses.

Ten-man United eventually lost 4–0 at Villa. Everton wreaked revenge at Goodison by the same scoreline; the champions had also humiliated United 4–0 in the season-opening Charity Shield. United were also thrashed 6–1 at Burnley on Boxing Day. Despite it all, they remained good enough to end the campaign in second spot, though they were never seriously in with a shout during the title run-in. The end of their first European campaign since Munich told the story of their up-and-down season in microcosm:

a 4–1 home win over Sporting Club of Lisbon in the semi-final of the Cup Winners' Cup was followed up by a dismal 5–0 second-leg capitulation in Portugal.

United weren't the only team struggling to maintain their rhythm during a campaign where consistency came at a premium. For the third time in four seasons Tottenham ended up as top scorers of the division, with 97 goals. They started like a train as usual, winning eight of their first ten, though an alarm bell sounded in the distance when that run was punctuated by a heavy 7–2 loss at Blackburn Rovers. Age was catching up with Danny Blanchflower and dependable defender Maurice Norman. Dave Mackay then broke his leg during a Cup Winners' Cup defeat at Manchester United. Their new frailty was further emphasised on Boxing Day, when they blew a two-goal lead to draw 4–4 at West Bromwich Albion, contributing to a very famous classified check:

Blackpool 1–5 Chelsea
Burnley 6–1 Manchester United
Fulham 10–1 Ipswich Town
Leicester City 2–0 Everton
Liverpool 6–1 Stoke City
Nottingham Forest 3–3 Sheffield United
Sheffield Wednesday 3–0 Bolton Wanderers
West Bromwich Albion 4–4 Tottenham Hotspur
West Ham United 2–8 Blackburn Rovers
Wolverhampton Wanderers 3–3 Aston Villa

This 63-goal glut remains perhaps the most famous batch of results in Football League history, a legend cemented by some supernatural turnarounds in the return fixtures a couple of days later. Ipswich repaid Fulham 4–2; West Ham won 3–1 at Blackburn; Manchester United beat Burnley 5–1.

Tottenham's reunion with West Brom ended in a 2–0 home defeat. The result didn't augur well for Spurs' title aspirations, for the Baggies were otherwise in utter disarray. A couple of weeks before the festive double-headers, ten of their first-teamers demanded to be placed on the transfer list, citing autocratic boss Jimmy Hagan's 'old-fashioned training methods and unnecessary discipline . . . we are fed up with being treated like schoolboys instead of intelligent individuals. After all, we are grown men. We are being forced to work the old way, lapping and the same routine day after day. Training has become a bore.' Hagan's response was to simply sniff: 'Oh well. You have your opinion, and I have mine.' The matter escalated just before Christmas when 19 players walked out, Hagan having refused to let them wear tracksuit bottoms for training during temperatures of minus five centigrade. The brouhaha was infused with a delicious irony: the Baggies nickname had been coined when the club were the last in the country to swap their long Victorian breeches for shorts. But it was also beyond absurd. Not least because the players, having staged their walkout, brazenly returned to collect their Christmas gift from the club, a four-guinea shopping voucher handed to each of them in seething silence by a thin-lipped Hagan.

Farce nearly turned to tragedy in late January when Hagan made to leave West Brom's Smethwick training facility in his Vauxhall Cresta. Reversing near the entrance, his tyres skidded on some loose earth and the saloon car somersaulted backwards down an unfenced embankment, plunging towards a canal. Four of the players who had lodged a transfer request – Terry Simpson, Ronnie Fenton, Stan Jones and George Best's harasser Graham Williams – raced to save Hagan, only to find their hardy manager clambering out of the mangled wreck through the smashed windscreen. Before being taken to hospital with head and neck injuries, Hagan bollocked his rescuers for being out of breath. He eventually recovered, leading West Brom to the 1966 League Cup. The rebellious Williams scored in the final.

Spurs meanwhile bounced back with five wins in early 1964 which moved them top by the end of February. But the glory days suddenly started fading fast. March was super-costly. They lost to Everton, then Manchester United, then twice to Liverpool. The penultimate match of the season saw them belted 7–2 in the historic county of Lancashire once again, this time by Burnley. Spurs trailed in fourth, six points off the pace. They could very easily have won every single title between 1959–60 and 1963–64; as it stood, one of the greatest sides in history had managed to land just the one. Then, in a July storm, their midfield genius John White took refuge under a tree at Crews Hill Golf Club, and was cut down in his prime by a bolt of lightning. Tottenham's glory, glory days died with him.

The reigning champions Everton took over from Spurs at the top, but the Mersey Millionaires were quickly hoist by their own petard. Harry Catterick coughed a club-record £85,000 on Blackburn striker Fred Pickering, who replaced Alex Young's Golden Vision and scored a hat-trick on debut in a 6–1 rout of Nottingham Forest. But the introduction of Pickering upset the delicate Everton ecosystem. Three defeats and a draw in their last five matches put paid to any hopes of retaining the title.

The only team to hold it together when it mattered most was Liverpool. In 1962, Bill Shankly had extricated the five-time champions from an eight-year Second Division tangle, building a high-energy side around goalscorers Ian St John and Roger Hunt and defensive behemoth Ron Yeats. One season of consolidation back in the First was all that was required, and now a seven-game winning run during March and April sealed the club's sixth title with three games to spare. As well as beating Spurs home and away, they swatted aside their last realistic challengers Manchester United 3–0 at home, then climaxed by battering Arsenal 5–0 in front of a BBC documentary crew primarily there to capture anthropological footage of the Anfield crowd for their *Panorama* magazine show.

The Kop obliged by swaying with feeling, belting out a selection of Beatles and Cilla Black numbers. 'The gay and inventive ferocity they show is quite stunning,' cooed journalist John Morgan in his film, *The Other Mersey Sound*, transmitted the following Monday on the first night of BBC1, along with a report concerning the independence question in Southern Rhodesia. 'Throughout the match they invent new words, usually within the framework of old songs, to express adulatory, cruel or bawdy comments about the players or the police.'

Club captain Ron Yeats embarked on a lap of honour, hoisting a papier-mâché model of the League trophy above his head. Everton had refused to hand over the real thing ahead of Liverpool's big day, insisting on doing things 'by the book' and sending it back to the Football League's headquarters in Lytham St Annes, forcing it to be re-circulated far too slowly through official channels. Beyond petty, but only a churl would fail to acknowledge the humour.

The feelgood factor at Goodison was quickly evaporating. As Everton's campaign to defend the title sputtered out, and their championship trophy departed along its circuitous coastal route to Anfield, the *Sunday People* accused big-money wing-half Tony Kay of fixing a match during his time at Sheffield Wednesday.

Along with two of his teammates, Peter Swan and David 'Bronco' Layne, Kay had bet on his own side to lose against Ipswich Town in December 1962. Wednesday went down 2–0. Kay was immediately suspended. He was later found guilty of bribery and served 11 weeks of a four-month jail sentence before being banned from football *sine die* by the FA. Kay, like the big central defender Swan, had been tipped to play an integral role in England's bid to win the 1966 World Cup. As he left the FA tribunal, his dreams up in smoke, Kay momentarily dabbled in a little gallows humour, twirling a cigar around in the style of Groucho Marx for the benefit of the gathered press. But his heart wasn't really in it. And as the enormity of the situation hit home, his feelings quickly betrayed him. 'I feel sick, utterly sick. Football has always been my life. This is like someone cutting my legs off.'

Kay's fall was an indirect blow to Everton's grand old reputation, which had already taken a couple of direct hits earlier in the season when some of the new-fangled hooliganism broke out at Goodison Park. Spurs goalkeeper Bill Brown claimed to be the victim of an unpleasant bombardment one October afternoon: stones, marbles, 'rice blown from peashooters' and a dart rained down upon his cloth-capped noggin. 'When the dart came it was the last straw,' he fumed. 'Luckily I was wearing my cap at the time, and facing the pitch. If I had turned my head a few seconds earlier, it might have hit me in the eye. This is going too far!'

Brown's version of events was hotly disputed by an Everton fan who penned an open letter to the press, claiming the dart had been thrown into an unpopulated area during the half-time interval: 'While I do not condone the action of the idiot who threw the missile, you were nowhere near the goal when the dart was thrown. A few thousand people behind the Gwladys Street goal know it was there when you came to resume the second half.' Brown stood his ground, but as a result of this conflicting evidence, an FA committee found it impossible to censure Everton over the affair.

Still, a trend was set in motion, and a fortnight later a blue plastic arrow sailed through the east London sky at Leyton Orient, landing with a sickening cholt between the shoulder blades of Northampton Town inside-left Frank Large. On the same day, back at Goodison, bread, paper and spit cascaded down from the stands when pariah-in-waiting Kay was sent off for throwing a right hander during a 4–2 defeat by Blackburn Rovers. 'We want the referee!' chanted an irate mob of Evertonians, gathered outside the changing rooms after the final whistle. The official in question, Ken Stokes, tried to play the incident down: 'When I came out of the dressing room the street was practically deserted. Apart from catcalls from a few youngsters, there was no trouble. I even signed a couple of autographs.' Everton were fined £100 for that sorry scene. Kay was suspended for 21 days.

'When you get a crowd of 50,000 you are bound to get a little conduct that is not quite parliamentary,' shrugged one Everton director, miffed that his club was taking all the heat for a problem sweeping the nation. 'It doesn't only happen at Everton, of course. At a London match I've seen them throwing toilet rolls!' A special investigative report by the *Daily Mirror* noted, in the interests of balance, that over at Anfield, Leicester goalkeeper Gordon Banks had recently been served 'apple cores, orange peel and a chewed pork chop', a tasty barrage that covered most of the food groups but contravened FA policy. The Kop was clearly on far better behaviour the day *Panorama* came to town.

Early in the 1964–65 season, Goodison erupted again. Don Revie's Leeds United had been promoted as Second Division champions, and by the end of October were the surprise element in a title race featuring Manchester United, who with George Best now fully integrated were on the cusp of another golden age, and Tommy Docherty's peppy Chelsea side. The reigning champions Liverpool were never in it, their one notable contribution a 3–2 opening-day win over Arsenal that was featured on the BBC's groundbreaking new highlights programme *Match of the Day*. Leeds had shown early promise by thrashing Shankly's side 4–2, and against Chelsea served notice of their complete unwillingness to kowtow to any supposed betters at this new level.

'Not for a long, long time have I seen such a distasteful display from two teams at the head of the highest division in the land,' thundered Albert Barham in the *Guardian* after Leeds visited Stamford Bridge to give it a square go. Bobby Collins, in the grand tradition of the diminutive Scottish hard man, concluded a prolonged struggle with fellow toughie Ron 'Chopper' Harris by high-kicking the Chelsea player, the ball having long departed for the other side of the pitch. Eddie McCreadie responded with a challenge that saw Johnny Giles carted away on a stretcher. Chelsea ran out 2–0 winners of a game the *Observer* classed as a 'primitive contest'. Leeds, who had been fingered as the most ill-disciplined club in the country before the season began, thanks to a table published by the *FA News*, appeared to be living down to their reputation.

The stage was set for the mother of all donnybrooks at Goodison Park, the one place in the land where a hot welcome was guaranteed. The game sparked into life immediately. After four minutes Johnny Giles launched himself into Sandy Brown, scraping several six-inch grooves into the Everton left-back's chest with his studs. Brown threw a punch back, and was sent packing by Ken Stokes, the referee who had been so lovingly serenaded by a select Goodison choir the previous season. As retributive tackles flew in, all manner of debris sailed down from the stands. Leeds keeper Gary Sprake was showered by coins, the full Bill Brown treatment.

After 39 minutes, Willie Bell of Leeds and Everton's Derek Temple collided accidentally, knocking each other out. Temple was stretchered off, while a dazed Bell was chaired to the dugout by his teammates. With the crowd now in overdrive, referee Stokes took the players off the field for five minutes, giving 43,605 tempers in the stands, and the 20 remaining on the pitch, time to cool their boots.

It was the first time in the history of the League that play had been suspended, and players hooked, for the purposes of lowering the temperature. The match eventually resumed at a mere rolling boil, Norman Hunter and Roy Vernon putting in questionable tackles that nearly set the whole thing off again. Hunter was booked; Vernon, Collins and Billy Bremner all received long lectures from an increasingly jaded referee. Leeds won 1–0, Bell heading home a Collins free-kick from the right, but that was almost an afterthought. 'Something must be done!' cried League president Joe Richards. Don Revie immediately went into damage-limitation mode, launching a pre-emptive strike in defence of his team, noting that the infamous *FA News* statistics which had condemned his side were premature and misleading and effectively to blame for incidents like this. 'I am disgusted by attacks on Leeds for being a dirty side,' he blasted. 'They didn't point out that juniors and reserve players were included in that record, and they didn't point out that we had no players sent off. They just left Leeds high and dry, and we are now feeling the backlash. A lot of managers and players in the First Division have never seen us play, but they have read about Leeds being a hard, dirty side and [so] come out to play hard and tough against us.'

It was difficult to get a dispassionate take on events. Leeds defender Jack Charlton suggested that the referee 'deserved a medal . . . the way Everton played shook us. It was murder!' Sandy Brown pulled up his shirt to show his bruised and lacerated chest, claiming he had 'never been provoked like this before, I've never known anything like it'. Only Ken Stokes remained calm: 'I was the least worried man on the field. I had everything under control.' It was somehow possible to sympathise with everyone and no one. There were calls for points to be docked, though it would be another 26 years before the League pressed that particular nuclear button. Instead, Brown was suspended for 14 days for his dismissal, while Everton were fined £250 for the actions of their fans.

A week later Denis Law was sent off yet again, for sending a volley of abuse towards the ref in a match against Blackpool. Meanwhile in the FA Cup, several board members of amateur Athenian League outfit Hayes were involved in an unsightly slanging match at Third Division Exeter City over some half-time refreshments. 'We were literally pushed about!' spluttered Hayes president Maurice McNally, upon being bundled away with feeling from the entrance to the boardroom. Exeter chairman Reg Rose responded with a shrug: 'A man at the door asked for their tea tickets, which they could not produce.' Board members of the Athenian League; you can't take them anywhere. The fabric of modern society was indeed unravelling.

Chelsea led the 1964–65 table with six games to go. They collapsed in spectacular, typically glamorous, style. A run of three points from four matches cost them pole position, though with away games at Burnley and Blackpool remaining, they still had a mathematical chance. They set up a special training camp in a hotel on Blackpool promenade, but the sea air wafting across the Lancashire Riviera proved too heady. Three days before the must-win Burnley match, eight members of the first-team squad, including captain Terry Venables, George Graham, John Hollins, Eddie McCreadie and Barry Bridges, ignored manager Tommy Docherty's 11 p.m. curfew and stayed out for four additional hours of beer-fuelled ten-pin bowling. According to the night porter, the players finally came back to the hotel 'in high spirits' with a couple of 'pretty, good-looking girls' in tow. Docherty was waiting in the lounge to turn the women away and issue his players with train tickets back to London. One hotel resident heard an almighty rumpus as the title hopefuls debated the matter in parliamentary fashion. 'I thought we were being invaded,' spluttered a Mr Ken Midwood, Room 142. 'Doors started banging, people shouted along the corridor, and the noise was terrible. I felt like dotting someone on the nose.'

The players insisted they'd done little to deserve such a draconian punishment. 'People must be thinking there was a right orgy, but there was nothing,' an unnamed source said. 'No booze. No birds. Just a couple of drinks. This is awful!' Docherty sent out a second string at Burnley; a predictable 6–2 defeat put paid to any lingering title hopes. Docherty forgave the Chelsea Eight, welcoming them back into the fold for the final match at Blackpool; they went down 3–2. 'If I had known what the effect of my decision would have been,' admitted the Doc afterwards, 'I would rather have cut off my right hand.'

Chelsea weren't the only ones to throw it away. Leeds took over at the top, and were three points clear of Manchester United with five to play. But they failed to put up much of a fight when United came to Elland Road and made off with the points thanks to a John Connelly goal. Leeds then capitulated 3–0 at Sheffield

Wednesday. Instructively, an injured Billy Bremner had been missing from both matches. His absence proved costly, as Manchester United were in the midst of a decisive seven-game winning streak. A 3–1 victory over Arsenal in their penultimate fixture forced Leeds to match that achievement to keep the title race alive. Against an already-relegated Birmingham City side reduced to ten men for 82 minutes, Leeds froze, going three down before salvaging a farcical 3–3 draw.

It still wasn't technically over. The teams were level on points, but Manchester United had one game left, and if they lost it 19–0, Leeds would be gifted the title on goal average. If that wasn't unlikely enough, United were playing Aston Villa, a team they'd hammered 7–0 earlier in the season. Villa did in fact win the game, 2–1, and United's title-winning campaign ended in slightly anti-climactic fashion. But most of the celebrating had been done after the Arsenal match. And the nation's attention was elsewhere anyway, it being the night Puskás and Yashin ceremoniously chaired Matthews into retirement.

15

Malcolm speaks way too soon (1965–66 to 1970–71)

In 1965 the football club bearing the city of Liverpool's name finally won the FA Cup after 73 years of trying. It was 59 years since Everton had first managed it. Local wags suggested Bella and Bertie, the 18-foot stone birds perched atop the grand Royal Liver Building on the waterfront, might fly off to sea as a result of such an epochal shock, and the entire city would fall. To collective sighs of relief up and down the banks of the Mersey, the mythical pair stayed put. To this day Bella and Bertie remain *in situ*, spiritually and literally unmoved, happily chomping away on their sprigs of seaweed.

The club's League championship success of the following season was not infused with quite so much symbolism. Bill Shankly's tight-knit side went top in mid-November and stayed there, never seriously troubled. Their 1965–66 triumph was a tale better told in numbers: they finished on 61 points, six clear of Leeds United; they only conceded 34 times in 42 matches; World Cup hopeful Roger Hunt top-scored with 30 of his team's 79 goals; and the title was won using only 13 players. One of those 13, the injury-hit striker Alf Arrowsmith, only featured in five games; a 14th man, Bobby Graham, got his solitary run-out in the final match with the League already in the bag. Oh, and it was

Liverpool's seventh title, a figure which brought them level with Arsenal at the top of the all-time roll of honour.

Liverpool required a little good fortune to be able to operate with such a slim squad. Very few injuries meant a settled team. It also meant they didn't need to send on many of the new-fangled substitutes; they made only three such swaps during the entire campaign. This was the first season the Football League allowed managers to make substitutions, though initially they were only permitted to do so for genuinely injured players. 'We are going to investigate every single case of substitution and will deal firmly with any attempted abuse of the new regulation,' finger-wagged League secretary-despot Alan Hardaker. 'I will not accept that teams will be able to cheat and get away with it.'

Hardaker and his medical goons were quickly forced into action. On the opening day, 14 substitutions were made. The first was in the Second Division, where Charlton goalkeeper Mike Rose took an awful whack across his kneecap; defender John Hewie pulled on the gloves, while 20-year-old midfielder Keith Peacock came on to make history. In the top tier, the honour of being first second-choice went to Keith Bebbington of Stoke, who replaced Dennis Viollet after 78 minutes at Arsenal. Bebbington's every touch was booed by the Highbury crowd, which suggested Hardaker's hard line was more in tune with the mood of the day than one might now assume. Stoke boss Tony Waddington was forced to explain himself: 'Viollet was playing too well for this to be anything but an honest change!' It would be another two seasons before the rule was relaxed to allow tactical switches.

Those desperate for First Division thrills and spills had to look towards the bottom of the table. In the summer of 1964, popular comedian and Fulham director Tommy Trinder had got himself into a bit of bother by incorporating his club's struggles into his stage and radio act. Trinder's shtick was very much of its time, and would be unlikely to pass muster today. He would solemnly ask theatregoers to stand for two minutes' silence; once it had been gravely observed, an announcement came that it had been for Fulham Football Club. Trinder invented two Chinese players for the Fulham team: 'We Won Once and How Long Since.' He suggested that £100-a-week Johnny Haynes had a say in the club's transfer policy, adding with obvious sarcasm: 'We have bought some *stunners*.'

Haynes and his teammates became increasingly agitated at being the butt of the joke, and eventually threatened to strike if an apology was not forthcoming. 'We don't want to be associated with the music hall,' sniffed one unnamed player. Trinder was initially unrepentant. 'I'm not taking this seriously. I mean, look at Chelsea! Everyone tells jokes about *them*.' But, for the sake of peace and harmony, the comic eventually relented, meeting his irate squad and apologising unreservedly.

A year on, however, and it began to look as though Trinder might have had a point. Fulham, more or less perennial strugglers since their promotion in 1959, started the 1965–66 season by winning just one of their first ten games while losing six. An even more damaging run of 11 defeats in 14 games between November and February had them bolted to the bottom of the table, five points from safety. At which point runaway leaders and champions-elect Liverpool came to Craven Cottage. Fulham won 2–0, winger Steve Earle scoring twice, and though Earle admitted to using the devil's right hand in the build-up to his second, the Cottagers were good value for their win. Ian St John, a study in frustration, was sent off with a couple of minutes remaining for dusting Mark Pearson about the jowls. 'It was a beautiful punch,' admitted Pearson afterwards. 'I have no grumbles.' St John was not so generous in his analysis: 'I was savagely attacked! He grabbed me by the head and pulled my hair!'

Earle scored another brace in a 5–2 defeat of Aston Villa a week later, and a great escape was suddenly on. Johnny Haynes was back to something approaching his playmaking best, and attributed his form to young coach Dave Sexton, who had come in to work alongside manager Vic Buckingham, now a dozen years down the line from his near miss with West Bromwich Albion. 'Our improvement stems from the introduction of The System,' explained Haynes enigmatically. 'Things have been clicking since we started playing 4–3–3, with three strikers up front looking for goals.' Good old-fashioned New-York-or-bust, in other words. And it worked. The Liverpool game was the start of a run that saw Fulham win nine of their last 13; by way of comparison, Shankly's title-winning side only won five of their last 11.

The crucial victory came four games from home. Despite their improved performances Fulham were still in the relegation zone, two points behind Northampton Town, who had been in the Fourth Division as recently as 1961 and were battling for survival in their first-ever season at the top. Northampton had already beaten Fulham earlier in the campaign, 4–1 at Craven Cottage, in a match that saw enigmatic dribbler Rodney Marsh end up in goal. It looked like more of the same this time round: in front of nearly 25,000 at the County Ground, Town were 2–1 up when their striker George Hudson fizzed a shot goalwards. Fulham keeper Jack McClelland fumbled, and the ball rolled gently over the line.

In desperation, McClelland scooped it back out. 'It was just over,' Hudson insisted. But the nearest linesman had fallen face down in the mud, and referee Jack Taylor – who would later take charge of the 1974 World Cup final – didn't feel able to award the goal with any certainty. Fulham took advantage of their lucky break: two minutes later, instead of trailing 3–1, they were level at 2–2 thanks to the in-form Earle, who then added two more late goals to complete his hat-trick and a 4–2 win over demoralised opponents. 'We think we will stay up now,' trilled Fulham captain and England international right-back George Cohen, bang slap in the summer of his years. Cohen was right. Fulham leapfrogged Northampton and completed their escape from relegation bother. Those two points were the difference; the linesman's slip at the County Ground effectively the decisive moment in the battle to avoid the drop. Town went down instead; they were back in the Fourth by 1969. Tommy Trinder's famous cheeky-chappie catchphrase: 'You lucky people!'

'We won it!' And to commemorate England's big victory in the summer of 1966, the Piccadilly Jewellers of Piccadilly Circus and the International Jewellers of Oxford Street joined forces to offer the public 'the official FIFA-approved souvenir World Cup, 1¼in. high, for charm bracelets or key rings. Nine carat gold £7.0.0, sterling silver £1.5.0. Money returned if not satisfied after nine days.' But the feelgood factor wasn't all-pervasive. There were a few concerns that English football might struggle to live up to its new best-in-class status; that the refereeing in the League didn't pass muster; that the grumbling trouble on the terraces might get worse and worse; and that the all best players in the country would, in this modern, post-maximum-wage world, gravitate to the biggest clubs, leaving everyone else to fight for scraps.

World Cup winner Alan Ball's close-season move from Blackpool to FA Cup holders Everton was a case in point. The champions Liverpool, Manchester United and Leeds United all looked strong again; Tottenham Hotspur had just spent over a quarter of a million pounds on Chelsea midfielder Terry Venables and in-demand Blackburn defender Mike England; while West Ham United, argued Clive Toye in the *Express*, were just 'eight players short of the greatest team in the world', an arch nod to the summer contributions of Bobby Moore, Martin Peters and Geoff Hurst. Little attention was paid to Nottingham Forest, and that was fair enough: under Johnny Carey, they'd finished 18th the previous season. And they lost their first two games of 1966–67, too.

But Forest were about to emerge from a transitional chrysalis. The former England striker Joe Baker joined from Arsenal, while a young Ian Storey-Moore was in the process of establishing himself on the left wing. Terry Hennessey arrived from Birmingham City to firm up the back line, while link-up expert Frank Wignall bounced back from a broken leg. At the start of October high-flying Manchester United visited the City Ground. Baker gave world champion Nobby Stiles a comprehensive runaround, repeatedly streaming down the right, cutting inside, and playing a part in all of Forest's goals in a 4–1 win. Soon afterwards, a 14-game unbeaten spell fired Forest into a three-way title race with United and Liverpool.

Shankly's defending champions were top at the start of March, but a little weariness seeped into ageing legs; they only won two of their last 11 matches and trailed home fifth. Forest's unbeaten run meanwhile came to an end in a summit meeting at United in February, when keeper Peter Grummitt made an exceptional point-blank save to deny Denis Law with three minutes to go, only for Law to convert the only goal of the game from the resulting Bobby Charlton corner. United's win proved the season's decisive act. Forest did not crumble afterwards: they won eight of their last 11, despite Joe Baker suffering injury in a tumultuous FA Cup quarter-final win over Everton. But United were steadier throughout, unbeaten after Boxing Day. They eventually bettered Forest by four points; the game at Old Trafford had made all the difference. United put the lid on their seventh title with a 6–1 mastery of West Ham at Upton Park, Law, Best and Charlton all on the scoresheet. The Hammers, who lost seven of their final eight games, were eight players short of being the greatest team in the world all right.

Forest failed to build on their unexpected second-place finish, and slipped back into mid-table in 1967–68. Then five matches into the season after that, disaster struck. Forest were drawing 1–1 with Leeds United when the main stand at the City Ground, built just four years earlier at the cost of £120,000, caught fire. One policeman's quick reactions averted tragedy. Chief Superintendent Joe Smalley, sitting in the directors' box, spotted smoke belching from under the seats, the conflagration having broken out in the dressing rooms below. He marched to the front of the stand and ordered supporters out onto the pitch just before the fire took hold. His calm direction ensured there was no panic, and no casualties in a crowd of 31,126.

Players from both teams took the opportunity to file elaborate insurance claims for items lost in the blaze. 'I never knew footballers owned so many Rolexes,' quipped big defender Bob McKinlay, eyebrow still arched years later. But humour was otherwise in short supply. Forest were forced to play their next six home fixtures north of the River Trent at Notts County's Meadow Lane, where their form went south. Ian Storey-Moore scored 13 times in the next 13 games, but found himself on the winning side just the once. Then a visit to Queens Park Rangers, playing in the First Division for the first time in their history and nailed-on for relegation, ended in a 2–1 defeat, former Fulham star Rodney

Marsh teasing an increasingly frustrated Forest with his showboating skills during the final exchanges. John Winfield put an abrupt halt to Marsh's carry-on in the old-fashioned way, at the cost of a booking. 'I was merely being professional,' shrugged the cheeky victim. 'This is a highly professional game.'

The normally genial, pipe-sucking Carey kept his players in the dressing room after that 'rock-bottom performance' to administer a 75-minute bollocking. That it had come to this for a man everyone said was the loveliest around. Forest returned to a half-derelict City Ground in late November, and promptly went down 1–0 to Liverpool. Carey, famously offed in the back of a cab by Everton, was sacked again, albeit this time in a more dignified manner. 'Personally I don't think there is a nicer fellow in football,' sighed chairman Tony Wood. 'He is one of nature's gentlemen. In my book he is one of the greatest administrators in the game. But we think the time has come for a change.' Gentleman Johnny eventually resurfaced at Blackburn, where his managerial career had begun in the fifties. In 1971 he took them down to the Third for the first time in the grand old club's history. A sorrowful end to a managerial career of close brushes with success. A pipe, but no cigar.

Manchester United, however, did build on their magnificent 1966–67 performance. 'We would obviously like to win the championship again,' said Matt Busby between sips of celebratory champagne, 'but we all feel that we must have a real go at the European Cup.' As things panned out, they should really have won both prizes in 1967–68. They were top of the League with three games to go, a point ahead of Leeds and two clear of Manchester City. Busby, however, had attributed the previous year's success to being unexpectedly knocked out of the FA Cup by second-tier Norwich City in February. 'The Cup defeat, although a bitter disappointment at the time, proved to be a good thing. With only the League to worry about, we have been better equipped both physically and mentally.'

And so United set about proving that going for two major prizes at once is easier said than done. After beating six-time European champions Real Madrid at home in the first leg of the European Cup semi-final, they were humiliated 6–3 at West Bromwich Albion, Jeff Astle helping himself to a hat-trick. To further illustrate their up-and-down form, five days later they beat Newcastle 6–0 at Old Trafford, George Best claiming the first hat-trick of his career.

Leeds were incapable of taking advantage, finishing with four straight losses. Instead, it was Manchester City who grasped their chance. At the start of February they had been six points off the pace. But they won ten of their next 14. Jovial Joe Mercer and his brash sidekick Malcolm Allison had rescued City from a mid-sixties low of 11th in the Second Division, building an expressive team around the midfield triumvirate of Franny Lee, Colin Bell and Mike Summerbee. Unlike their neighbours, they could concentrate solely on the League. When United slipped at West Brom, City took their place at the top on goal average.

In the final games of the season, United hosted Sunderland while City travelled to Newcastle. 'The title is ours for the taking,' said Mercer, 'but if we fail, then I can think of nobody better I would like to see the championship go to than my old friend down the road, Matt Busby.' United had the easier task on paper, but went two down in little over half an hour. They could only pull one of the goals back. City meanwhile were in hot form at Newcastle. Summerbee, Neil Young and Lee scored, while Lee and Young had another couple disallowed. With five minutes to go, they were 4–2 up and on their way to the title. Whereupon Pop Robson pulled one back for Newcastle. At 4–3 a few City nerves began to jangle. But the club was long overdue a positive result in a crucial end-of-season fixture, and this time they held on for the win. A deserved second League title was theirs.

When the result was relayed over the PA at Old Trafford the United crowd reciprocated Mercer's pre-game sportsmanship with some good manners of their own, applauding long and loud in tribute to their neighbours. A couple of weeks later the European Cup was finally theirs. Allison, the super-confident new champion coach of England, predicted his team would match this glorious achievement: 'I think a lot of these foreign people are cowards. They play with a fear of defeat. I promise you that next season City will attack these people as they haven't been attacked since the old Real Madrid.' Sure enough, they were knocked out in the first round by Fenerbahçe.

On the opening day of the 1965–66 season Arsenal manager Billy Wright sent his team out in a new set of shirts. The distinctive white sleeves introduced by Herbert Chapman back in 1933 had gone; now their tops were just plain old red. Wright's team played as unimaginatively as they dressed, and finished 14th after a mediocre campaign. Banners calling for the manager's head appeared in the stands. Crowds dwindled to the point where only 4,554 paying punters turned up at Highbury for a match against Leeds. One of them unsheathed a bugle and gave a crisp, clear rendition of 'The Last Post'.

The former Wolves and England captain was asked by chairman Denis Hill-Wood to fall on his sword. Wright, ever the gentleman, obliged. 'I am very fond of Billy Wright and he is a good friend,' said Hill-Wood as he left for his stately pile near Basingstoke, where he was hosting a dinner party to celebrate the start of Royal Ascot week. Wright, who was not invited, remained magnanimous: 'I don't blame him. He was embarrassed. I felt sorry for him.'

Wright's celebrity wife wasn't having a bar of it. Joy Beverley, a member of the post-war, pre-rock, close-harmony singing sensations The Beverley Sisters, was in no mood to mince words: 'Billy is a wonderful man, a good man and a trier. He just isn't the resigning type. I know they told him to go and I don't see the point in being hypocritical about it. I don't see why he should cover up for the people who pushed him out. He came home this afternoon, put his arms round me, and suggested we should have a night out together. I knew immediately something was wrong. I burst into tears, and then he cried too. We both just sat there weeping. It's the most heartbreaking thing that ever happened to us.' Later that afternoon, Wright sauntered out into his garden, where he ostentatiously stopped to smell the roses, a coded stiff two-fingers to the world.

Within a week Wright took up a £5,000-a-year position at ATV as a major mover and shaker in its sports department: 'This is a tremendous opportunity, I'm turning my back on football management.' As England's record cap-holder took his leave of professional football at the age of 40 he made one last pointed defence of his regime: 'My youngsters had just won the FA Youth Cup. I am convinced I was on the verge of a breakthrough.' But it was his successor Bertie Mee who reaped that particular harvest. Mee was a surprise choice as Wright's successor, given he was the club physiotherapist and trainer, though he had played for Derby as a winger just before the war, only for his career to be cut short because of injury. Mee flanked himself with respected coaches Dave Sexton and Don Howe, and set about gently reshaping the team.

By the summer of 1968, Arsenal were ready to take their first serious pop at the title for 15 years. They flew in under the radar, pre-season odds of 25-1 looking extremely generous after they won seven of their first nine games. They went top after putting four goals past the champions Manchester City at Highbury, 21-year-old

John Radford scoring one and having a hand in two more. But the team weren't quite ready to end a trophy drought that stretched back to 1953. Having lost the 1968 League Cup to Leeds, they reached the final again in 1969 only to be swept aside in extra-time by Swindon Town of the Third Division. Swindon's shock 3–1 victory was a proper men-versus-boys rout, Don Rogers too powerful for a supposedly parsimonious Arsenal defence, though in fairness eight members of the Gunners team had been laid low the previous week by a virus. Either way, the result drained Arsenal of confidence, and they fell off the 1968–69 title pace set by Leeds and Liverpool.

Leeds turned up at Highbury in April and delivered a knockout punch. Arsenal striker Bobby Gould went up with Leeds keeper Gary Sprake for a high ball. In the *Observer* Hugh McIlvanney suggested he had done so 'with all the grace of a runaway thresh-ing machine'. Gould was rewarded for his agricultural methods with a ferocious haymaker to the chops. Sprake escaped a sending off, to the astonishment of everyone in the ground, including the keeper himself. 'It was a stupid thing to do, and I regretted it immediately,' he later admitted. A calamitous backpass by Arsenal defender Ian Ure gifted Johnny Giles an easy tap-in, and gave 11-man Leeds a 2–1 win. Liverpool were also unable to keep up with Leeds, Bill Shankly's increasingly superannuated sixties selec-tion once again running out of steam over the closing stretch. Leeds secured the title after a goalless draw at Anfield, whereupon the Kop sportingly serenaded the new champions.

Leeds had finally won the big one. In the final analysis they managed it with ease. They lost only twice, a League record for a full-sized First Division. They made it to 67 points, beating by one the previous best set by Arsenal in 1930–31. All of those points were parlayed from just 66 goals, a whacking 61 fewer than

Herbert Chapman's side scored all those years ago. In fact, it was the lowest championship-winning scoring tally since Huddersfield Town landed the 1923–24 title with 60 goals, a state of affairs so grim it had caused the offside law to be rewritten. Leeds were therefore saddled with a reputation of joyless efficiency, though as usual the truth is slightly harder to pin down.

In January the glamorous reigning European champions Manchester United had travelled to Elland Road. They were undone when Peter Lorimer floated a diagonal chip wide left to Mike O'Grady, who cushioned a header back down the channel towards Johnny Giles. The ball was instantly wedged back to O'Grady, whereupon the striker unleashed a curling half-volley into the bottom right. It was a team goal of intricate, instinctive, incisive brilliance. Leeds might have been catching hell for their grinding style, a reputation they'd never quite shake off, but Revie's lads could certainly play.

Leeds had won their title by going unbeaten for the last 28 matches of the season, then started the 1969–70 campaign by adding another six to that running total. The 34-match sequence surpassed the record of 30 games without defeat set by Burnley in 1920–21, and was ended by a harbinger. Early leaders Everton beat them 3–2 in late August, left-winger Johnny Morrissey the man of the match. Morrissey was one of only three survivors, alongside goalkeeper Gordon West and defender Brian Labone, from Everton's title-winners of 1962–63. Unlike Bill Shankly across the city, Harry Catterick had not shied away from breaking up his first great team.

The Golden Vision had long gone – Alex Young was sold to Glentoran in Northern Ireland a year before – so in lieu of melodramatic religious imagery, Alan Ball was joined in midfield by Colin Harvey and Howard Kendall to make up the Holy Trinity. The Dixie Dean of the day was 20-year-old Joe Royle, an alumnus of Quarry Bank school, the alma mater of John Lennon. The new working-class hero scored at a more sedate, modern pace than Dean – 23 goals this season – but Royle's efforts were enough to help Everton to their seventh title. They romped it by nine points from Leeds.

Chances are the race would have been closer had Leeds not been flailing around on all fronts, trying to land a Treble of League, FA Cup and European Cup. While still on their famous unbeaten run, the *Observer* had opined that Leeds 'gave the impression that they could climb Everest without oxygen'. But the air eventually got too thin. At the end of February they had reached the summit and were still in control of their own destiny. But six fateful games in ten days as March turned into April proved their undoing. This was an old-fashioned fixture pile-up, with shades of Burnley in 1961, caused by the FA's determination to finish the season early ahead of the upcoming World Cup in Mexico. Two days after beating Manchester United in a second FA Cup semi-final replay, Leeds hosted Southampton in the League. They were without six of their internationals, and went down to their first home defeat in 39 matches. Revie responded by naming a side of reserves for a match against Derby – a mere two days later – effectively giving up the defence of their title to Everton. Leeds would concentrate on the Cups instead.

The gambit backfired horrifically. Celtic won the first leg of the European Cup semi at Elland Road. On the same evening, Everton officially took over as League champions by easing past West Brom at Goodison. A mere 24 hours after that Leeds travelled to a League fixture at West Ham. En route Revie visited the Football League offices, where he was fined for fielding the under-strength side against Derby. Revie, echoing Bob Lord nine years earlier, was vehement in defence of his actions: 'What is the point of employing the services of a fully qualified medical officer if you don't take his advice? Our doctor declared that the players concerned were thoroughly tired, mentally and physically, and that, if they carried on, there was no knowing what damage might be caused. So we had no alternative but to take the steps we did. I could have wept for them.' To placate the suits, Revie named right-back Paul Reaney in his team at Upton Park that night. Reaney – who had been looking forward to the FA Cup final and the World Cup with England – broke his leg.

Finally, another 48 hours later, came the sixth game in the ten-day sequence, the visit of Burnley. Exasperated and incandescent, Revie named eight second-teamers. After ten minutes Eddie Gray floated a precision chip over Peter Mellor from 40 yards. Then in the second half, he picked the ball up on the left-hand edge of the Burnley area and embarked on a rococo dribble which consisted of two pullbacks, a couple of feints, a pair of jinks and one no-backlift snapshot to score a genuine wonder goal. Gray had only beaten four men in this sequence – Arthur Bellamy, John Angus, Eric Probert and Mike Docherty – though he embarrassed three of them twice. Poor Angus was sent skittering hysterically across the turf on his impotent cheeks on both occasions. 'The goal was one of the best I've seen since Eddie scored in an international youth tournament in 1966,' said Revie. 'He beat eight men then.' A tough man to please.

The 2–1 win embellished by Gray's genius was Leeds' only victory between their FA Cup semi-final win over Manchester United and the end of the season. Celtic knocked them out of Europe, while Chelsea finally put Norman 'A song, a smile, a piano!' Long in his box by winning the FA Cup final after a replay. Leeds had nothing whatsoever to show for their Homeric journey, the wheels clattering off in a style which owed a great debt to Ben Hur. And yet Gray had produced two works of art for the ages, two goals which occupy a more prominent place in the culture than anything Everton, Chelsea, Celtic or eventual European champions Feyenoord submitted that season. See, medals and trophies aren't *everything*.

Catterick's championship side of 1970 disintegrated with indecent haste. They lost a European Cup quarter-final to Panathinaikos the following season, and finished 14th in the League, a miserable defence of their title. Just before Christmas 1971 Alan Ball was shocked when surprisingly packed off to Arsenal, still at the peak of his powers. By 1973 Catterick himself was gone, dogged by heart problems.

Leeds kept on keeping on, though. 'It's better than not being involved at all,' shrugged Don Revie, sucking philosophically on a Slim Panatella in the wake of their multiple near misses of 1969–70. They characteristically decided to tackle abject misery head on, going balls out to reclaim their crown. And with four games to go of the 1970–71 season redemption was on! They were two points clear of Mee and Howe's Arsenal, who had two games in hand but were still required to visit Elland Road. At which point it all went belly up for Leeds at home to West Bromwich Albion.

After 20 minutes Jack Charlton miscued a simple pass straight to West Brom striker Jeff Astle. The ball was transferred to Colin Suggett, who shuttled it on to Tony Brown to score. Another Leeds defensive howler arrived on 70 minutes, as Norman Hunter romped up the left wing, hit Bobby Hope on the arse with an errant ball forward, then upon being gifted the rebound, shanked a second ball infield and into the path of Brown, who suddenly had a clear run on goal from the halfway line. Problem was, Suggett was standing miles offside at the time, albeit not interfering with play. The linesman put his flag up. Everyone, including Brown, stopped. And then Brown started running again as he realised referee Ray Tinkler, a farm manager by day, was ignoring the flag and waving play on. Brown romped down the right, then slipped the ball inside for Astle, who sidefooted home from the penalty spot with goalkeeper Gary Sprake and the desperately backtracking Paul Reaney helpless. Cue a pitch invasion led by several aged supporters who really should have known better, plus Don Revie, whose irate menace was negated by the tartan travelling rug tucked under his arm.

'Leeds will go mad and they have every right to go mad!' hollered BBC commentator Barry Davies, a soundbite that would become extremely famous indeed. That Davies appended the quote with a rather large caveat is now all but forgotten. 'Though one must add that they played to the linesman, and not the whistle.' The other linesman, who had played no part in the controversy, was felled by a tin can. Allan Clarke pulled a goal back, and had a late backwards header marvellously clawed out by Baggies keeper Jim Cumbes. But it wasn't enough. Leeds had lost 2–1. Arsenal meanwhile were grinding out a one-goal victory at home against Newcastle.

Don Revie admitted that he had 'never been so sick at heart. The ref's decision wrecked nine months' hard work. I regret the crowd scenes like anybody else, but I can understand why they cut loose.' Tinkler, who reviewed the incident on that night's *Match of the Day*, stood his ground. 'I saw nothing which caused me to change my mind. You will have noticed that Mr Revie did not say anything about Jack Charlton giving away the first goal. You can hardly blame me for *that*.' He went on to accuse an unnamed Leeds player of complaining, mid-rumpus, that the decision had 'cost us a lot of money. Not, notice, the match or even the championship. I found that a disappointing attitude.'

Revie and Leeds vowed to 'keep fighting to the last gasp'. Who would have expected anything less? They won their last three matches, including the home game against Arsenal, Jack Charlton breaching a packed defence for the only goal with two minutes to go. But even that dramatic intervention wasn't enough. Leeds, their work done, led the division by a point, but Arsenal still had their game in hand. Mee and Howe's team had ended Arsenal's long wait for a trophy 12 months earlier, winning the 1970 Fairs Cup, and now possessed the mental fortitude to get the job done.

To emphasise their new-found street smarts, they'd recently got themselves involved in a brawl with Lazio at an after-match Fairs Cup banquet. Having been given leather pouches as gifts, the not-yet-metrosexual Brits responded by prancing around in an exaggerated effeminate style for cheap laughs. The Italians, understandably irate, decided that if Arsenal wanted macho, they'd get macho. The meal spilled out onto the street, fists, boots and European carry-alls flying everywhere. This new robust Arsenal had won ten of their previous 12 games during the run-in, so a goalless draw at, of all places, Tottenham would have been enough to secure the title by 0.013 of a goal. But the 19-year-old striker Ray Kennedy flashed a header home with two minutes to play, and they won by a point instead.

Leeds were the first club to amass 64 points and fail to win the title. Adding insult to injury was one other mathematical fact: had Tinkler not waved play on that day, but everything else in the season remained constant, Leeds would have ended up with the same points as Arsenal but with a goal average superior by 0.034. But this is the way it was. Arsenal went on to secure the second Double of the twentieth century by beating Liverpool in the FA Cup final. With their eighth championship they once again became the most successful club in Football League history.

16

Brian takes off for Tresco (1971–72 to 1973–74)

The Watney Cup was a tournament way ahead of its time, a jamboree of nonsense designed to maximise revenue streams during the otherwise barren pre-season. It was Britain's first-ever sponsored soccer competition – four-bottle packs of Watney Mann Brown and Pale Ale cost 24p at the Co-op – and it proved very much not to Manchester United's taste.

Conditions of entry were strict and based on Byzantine logic: eight teams, the two highest-scoring sides from each of the four English divisions who had won neither promotion nor entry to Europe, contested a straight knock-out competition. The first edition, held in August 1970, was epochal in its own way. In the opening match Denis Law defied blisters to mastermind Manchester United's 3–2 win over third-tier Reading. Then in the semi-final against second-tier Hull City Law scored a late equaliser to set up the first-ever penalty shoot-out in competitive football.

Shoot-outs were a brand new method of deciding drawn matches in Cup competitions, considerably fairer than the old coin toss. The idea – described variously as a 'penalty system' or 'penalty series' – had been ratified a month earlier by the International Football Association Board during a convivial meeting in Inverness, and was now getting an early test run. Cue a series of firsts: Law, his feet still killing him, was the first player to miss; Ian McKechnie, who stopped Law's spot-kick, was the first keeper to make a save; McKechnie then became the first keeper to take a penalty himself; and having shaved the bar and sent the ball sailing over, McKechnie became the first player to miss a deciding kick.

United faced Derby County in the final. Derby had won promotion under fresh-faced manager Brian Clough in 1968–69, then finished a very impressive fourth the following year. That should have earned a place in the Fairs Cup, but Derby were banned from European participation for a season as a result of minor financial chicanery. So instead they contested the Watney Cup. Clough's side boasted notable young talent in defender Roy McFarland and right-winger John McGovern, but 35-year-old captain Dave Mackay, enjoying a late-career renaissance as a playmaking centre-back, was their inspiration.

The former Spurs man explained how Clough – whose direct mannerisms were the polar opposite of taciturn theorist Bill Nicholson – had introduced him to 'a world of four-letter insults and an underlying hint of physical violence'. Clough, in turn, spoke of Mackay bringing a 'swagger to the team and whole club' that made Derby feel 'unbeatable'. They certainly felt it against United, thrashing them 4–1, Mackay setting up the opener and scoring the fourth. Before the match, United's fans had serenaded Mackay with beneficial careers advice: 'Hang up your boots!' After it Mackay raised the 1970 Watney Cup along with an eyebrow. 'Aye, well, over the last few years an awful lot of people have been saying that. It was sort of funny, really. I didn't do too badly in the end, did I?'

After one more top-flight season, in which he was ever-present for the first time in his long career, Mackay took his leave of the big time and became player-manager of Swindon Town in the summer of 1971. Clough and Derby prepared to build further upwards. Manchester United meanwhile entered the Watney Cup again; a team starring Law, Best and Charlton were promptly sent packing 2–1 by Halifax Town from the Third Division. It was an inauspicious start for new manager Frank O'Farrell, who had replaced Wilf McGuinness, who in turn had replaced Matt Busby when the old boy called it quits in 1969. Going into the 1971–72 season, the 1968 champions of Europe didn't appear to be in very good shape at all.

George Best certainly didn't go into the new season in the most positive frame of mind. A week after the Halifax débâcle, he spent the majority of a not-so-cordial friendly at Fulham either deliberately teasing opponents with his skill or being lifted off the ground by the throat by way of retribution. A week into the season he was sent off at Chelsea, weeping, after swearing at the referee, though he escaped further FA censure by telling the disciplinary panel he'd been cursing at teammate Willie Morgan. The FA bought that explanation; Best admitted years later to lying through his teeth.

United effectively faced six away fixtures in a row at the start of the campaign. There had been a 'knife-throwing incident' at Old Trafford in February against Newcastle, and United had been ordered to play the first two home games of the new season at least 12 miles outside of Manchester. The club opted to play one of those matches at Stoke's Victoria Ground; the other, in a decision certain to widen modern eyes, was held at Anfield.

Against all odds United started the season in sparkling fashion. They quickly went two goals up on the opening day at Derby, Denis Law and Alan Gowling converting a couple of

Bobby Charlton corners. They were eventually pegged back to a 2–2 draw – a crucial point for Clough's side, as it would transpire – but the fast start gave United confidence nonetheless. Best's dismissal at Chelsea mattered not one jot: the ten men turned round a one-goal half-time deficit for a 3–2 win. Then in the 'home' game at Liverpool against Arsenal, Bobby Charlton curled a sumptuous free-kick into the top left at the Anfield Road End, while Best was named man of the match as he orchestrated a 3–1 victory. For once, the Kop went home happy after a United win.

United won ten of their first 14. By early December they had torn five points clear of Manchester City, Derby and Leeds, with Liverpool a further two behind. Southampton striker Terry Paine, who had witnessed United whistling five goals into his team's net at the Dell, admitted it was 'a privilege being out on the same pitch with them. They are a marvellous side.' Best, his early season troubles seemingly miles behind him, scored his second hat-trick of the season.

Soon after, the bandwagon derailed. United beat Forest at home, but drew their next three, then lost the following seven straight. Having slipped back into the pack, they travelled to title-chasing Leeds in late February. It was goalless at half-time; by the 74th minute it was 5–1 to Leeds, Mick Jones having helped himself to a hat-trick in a quarter of an hour. Revie's side then got bored, stroking the ball around in contemptuous fashion. At one point they held onto possession for one minute and 20 seconds, a sequence of 22 passes, cheers of 'easy' and 'ole' drifting down from the stands. 'The spectacle was almost that of the matador toying with a weary bull,' observed Brian Glanville in the *Sunday Times*. In their very next League match, Leeds would reprise this cape-swishing routine in a famous 7–0 win over Southampton, showcasing an even more elaborate series of feints, backheels and dribbles. That performance that would be repackaged by the BBC as one of their 100 Great Sporting Moments and wheeled out whenever there was a five-minute gap in the schedules during the 1980s.

O'Farrell's side picked themselves up and won five of their remaining 13 matches, but any idea that they had bottomed out at Elland Road proved well wide of the mark. United limped home in eighth spot, and instead of reporting for Northern Ireland's Home International match with Scotland, Best jetted off on holiday to a five-star hotel in Marbella. Sitting by the swimming pool, sipping on an iced beer, he announced his retirement at the age of 26. 'My mind is made up about football. I'm sorry, but it's over. I won't change my mind.'

Leeds took over from United at the top, though they quickly handed the leadership to Manchester City. Back in October City coach Malcolm Allison had taken advantage of some boardroom machinations to ease Joe Mercer to one side. Mercer, who had won the title, the FA Cup, the League Cup and the Cup Winners' Cup while in charge, was given the meaningless and patronising title of 'general manager', while Allison was granted sole control of the team. City, still boasting their famous trio of Lee, Bell and Summerbee, looked in fine fettle for a second championship in four seasons at the start of March: they were four points clear at the top. Then, hours before the transfer deadline, Allison made his first big decision while flying solo. He paid Queens Park Rangers £200,000 for Rodney Marsh, the prototype Seventies Maverick.

Marsh made an immediate impact, adding 10,000 on the Maine Road gate. A 53,000-plus crowd turned up to witness an instructive debut against Chelsea. His first touch of the ball came after five minutes, and it was, according to the *Guardian*, 'spectacular . . . a gliding effortless dribble which took him with ease past three Chelsea players'. Marsh then went close with two headers. But it was all downhill from there. He missed an open goal in the second half, then fell victim to cramp. City won 1–0; Marsh went back to London on the Chelsea bus. His contribution the following week, during a dismal goalless draw at Newcastle, was nondescript. City then lost back-to-back games against struggling Stoke and Southampton sides. Marsh's baroque doodlings on the wing were accused of playing havoc with City's speedy counterattacking style.

City did indeed lose their thread after the signing of Marsh. He had arrived with nine matches to go: beforehand, they'd won four out of five; afterwards, they lost three and drew a couple more. Given they were destined to finish a tight title race one point off the top, in fourth spot, this was a costly and disastrous loss of form. Years later Marsh was big enough to admit to throwing a spanner in a 'well-oiled machine . . . I provided star quality, but it was to the detriment of team play. They started to play around me and we lost the focus of what we were trying to do. I hold my hand up to say I was responsible for City losing the championship in 1972.'

Yet perhaps Marsh is more of a team player than he's usually given credit for. Because here's the question: is he retrospectively taking a hit for his teammates by giving in to received wisdom? Cause and effect is rarely binary, and Marsh wasn't the complete comic hindrance he's painted as nowadays. For a start, the City cogs weren't *that* well-oiled: in the month before Marsh arrived, they shipped a two-goal lead at Sheffield United in a 3–3 draw, and were comprehensively spanked 3–0 at Liverpool. Marsh's actual contributions after his arrival are also due a reappraisal. He scored twice in a 3–1 win over West Ham; came off the bench in the Manchester derby at Old Trafford to draw the free-kick that led to the winning goal, then found the net himself; and scored again in City's final match, an energetic solo effort from the right wing in a comprehensive 2–0 victory over title-chasing Derby. 'He stood revealed as a master craftsman,' reported Eric Todd of the *Guardian* after that game, putting down Marsh's early struggles at his new club to being 'neither sharp nor fit'.

Either way, City had blown it. The win over Derby was too little, too late. It put them top by a point, their season's work complete, but Derby, Liverpool and Leeds all had games in hand and a superior goal average. With Derby and Liverpool still to play each other, someone was guaranteed to overtake Allison's side. Mercer, having presided over a golden age, left in the summer for Coventry, hurt and humiliated. 'Malcolm and I never ever had a row, and he has done a great deal for Manchester City. He has just refused to co-operate or consult me since he was made team manager in October. We just didn't talk. And I don't think that was my fault, because I never stop talking.'

Liverpool made a late charge. Bill Shankly had been too loyal for too long to his beloved mid-sixties troopers, allowing the team to drift. A sentimental man at heart, he finally summoned enough bravery to get shot of Roger Hunt and Ian St John, albeit rather cack-handedly, unable to break the news himself or look them in the eye. Now the sap was rising again in a younger team: Steve Heighway on the wing, John Toshack a lightning rod up front, Kevin Keegan relentlessly buzzing, the Luis Suárez of his day. From a mid-table position in January, Liverpool suddenly clicked, winning 13 of their next 14 games and drawing the other. The sequence included a 3–0 win at Manchester United, a 4–0 derby victory over Everton, and a 5–0 thrashing of Newcastle. But having hauled themselves into contention, their unbeaten run came to a juddering halt in the penultimate game of the season, against fellow title-hopefuls Derby. Toshack battered the ball into Heighway's face; the winger eventually had to be hauled off with double vision. Liverpool's attack was severely blunted, with Colin Todd dealing imperiously with Keegan. The busy Archie Gemmill set up John McGovern for the only goal of the game. Derby went top, a point clear of Manchester City and Leeds. Like City, they'd completed their fixture list.

But Liverpool, two points behind, and Leeds still had a game in hand. A draw for Don Revie's side at Wolverhampton Wanderers, or a win for Bill Shankly's team at Arsenal, would be enough to snatch the title on goal difference. Clough, utterly impotent, left for a well-deserved break on the garden island of Tresco in the Scilly Isles. His players left to sun themselves in Majorca. 'If Derby can't win this title I hope it will be Liverpool who get it, because of that fabulous man Bill Shankly,' said Clough. 'He is just about the most honest man in football and I think it is only right that those people who try to play to the rules and have avoided conning people should be properly rewarded.' This was less a ringing endorsement of Shankly, more an unsubtle dig at Revie, whose pragmatism rankled Clough to high heaven, and who the Derby boss had long suspected of financial chicanery.

The reckoning came on a Monday night in early May, two days after Leeds had finally won the FA Cup by seeing off Arsenal at Wembley. Liverpool came awfully close to beating the losing finalists at Highbury, Emlyn Hughes hitting the underside of the bar with a 25-yard screamer, John Toshack turning Kevin Keegan's mishit shot into the net with two minutes to go. But Toshack's effort was ruled offside. A goalless draw was not enough. 'The referee deprived us of the title,' fumed Shankly. 'It is heartbreaking for my young players after their magnificent challenge.' But the general consensus was that the decision was correct.

That wasn't the case at Wolves, where Leeds had two very strong penalty appeals turned down, home defender Bernard Shaw at one point using both hands to stop an Allan Clarke shot. Wolves went two up before Billy Bremner pulled one back. In the closing minutes Peter Lorimer headed onto the crossbar. Leeds couldn't have come any closer to the draw they required. But for the second season in a row, an unjust non-intervention by a referee had cost them the title. 'It is just too much,' wailed Revie. 'When you get decisions like that, what can you do? But I'm even prouder of my lads than I was on Saturday. I heartily congratulate Derby on winning the title.' Clough was rather less magnanimous. 'I don't feel sorry for Don Revie,' he flatly admitted, before ordering champagne all round in the bar of his Tresco hotel.

Title races can't be nip and tuck every year, and the couple that followed were processional affairs. Both were staunch responses to failure. First up, Liverpool, who had been the form horse over the final furlongs of 1972–73. Kevin Keegan, in just his second top-flight season since joining the club from Scunthorpe, showed signs of impatience from the get-go. 'This is my real test,' he announced on the eve of the big kick-off. 'Make or break is a phrase you've often heard. In my case it's the phrase that fits best. At Liverpool we are aiming for four things: the League Championship, the FA Cup, the Uefa Cup and the League Cup. I know I am going to win something big with Liverpool!'

Two out of four ain't bad. Liverpool started with a 2–0 win over Manchester City, despite the dismissal of Larry Lloyd, sent off for being headbutted by Wyn Davies. They beat an increasingly dismal Manchester United by the same scoreline three days later.

A five-goal evisceration of Sheffield United in mid-September put them top, and they were never really troubled afterwards. Keegan ended the season as top marksman on 22 goals, netting the crucial late winner against Leeds in April that effectively put the title beyond distant challengers Arsenal. Bill Shankly celebrated by daintily draining some tea from a tiny china cup. Keegan then scored twice in the Uefa Cup final as Liverpool won their first European trophy at the expense of Borussia Mönchengladbach. After the big pre-season talk, the superstar-in-making had the decency to walk the walk.

Leeds meanwhile lost the FA Cup final to an inspired Sunderland, then suffered more outrageous ill fortune in the final of the Cup Winners' Cup. In what was fast becoming an annual folk tradition, they had three legitimate penalty shouts ignored in a big match, going down to Milan. Had Revie taken Leeds as far as he could? The rumour mill whirled wildly with suggestions that he was headed for Everton to replace the ailing Harry Catterick in a £250,000-per-year deal. It wasn't the first time a carrot had been dangled to tempt him away from Leeds – Manchester City and Torino had given it a go – but this time the gossip seemed to be backed up by fact: he was spotted one day wheeling around Merseyside, lost, looking for the home of Everton owner Sir John Moores. But talks floundered, Revie decided to stay put, and behind the scenes he threw down a gauntlet to his players ahead of what proved to be a valedictory fling. Could they go through an entire season unbeaten, like Preston North End in 1888–89, only with 20 more matches to play?

Rolling out a properly expansive and attacking style, Leeds made it as far as 29 games. The sequence smashed the previous unbeaten League run from the start of the season in a full-sized First Division, the 19 set by Liverpool in 1949–50. But having built a large lead at the top, nerves suddenly began to jangle after a shock home FA Cup defeat to Second Division strugglers Bristol City. Leeds lost their first League game of the season immediately afterwards, 3–2 at Stoke, which meant Burnley's single-season undefeated record of 30 in 1920–21 still stood. Soon after, a narrow defeat at Liverpool was followed by a 4–1 home capitulation against Burnley and another loss at West Ham. What had long looked a shoo-in was suddenly back in the balance.

Bill Shankly's reigning champions kept on winning, and got to a point where, if they won the three games they held in hand, they'd usurp Leeds at the top. But they took a couple of games to get past Leicester in the FA Cup semis, after which their focus slipped. Liverpool won only two of their last nine, saving their energies for an upcoming cakewalk against Newcastle United in the FA Cup final. All of which rather let Leeds off the hook; Revie's side, the pressure easing, won four of their last six and eased to their second title, a comfortable five points ahead of Liverpool, and 14 clear of Derby in third place.

The real drama had been unfolding at the other end of the table. Manchester United's downward spiral had continued apace. At the start of 1972–73 Frank O'Farrell's team lost their first three matches, didn't win for nine, and by mid-December had degenerated into a total shambles. One calendar year after topping the table, they were two points from the bottom. They went to Crystal Palace, the side propping up the entire division, and lost 5–0, two-goal Don Rogers bossing the show. United were in such a sorry state that they elicited tearful sympathy from the Palace president Arthur Waite: 'This is tragic! I find it hard to bear!' All O'Farrell could say was: 'Oh God.' Real Madrid, Derby and Chelsea prepared bids for George Best, who had returned to football in body if not in soul, as did Third Division AFC

Bournemouth. 'I do not want people to regard this as a gimmick, we are genuinely interested,' insisted their ambitious manager John Bond.

O'Farrell was sacked and replaced by Tommy Docherty, who just about kept United up. But the Doc was merely staving off the inevitable. Bobby Charlton retired, the last remaining link to Munich waved away with a pat on the back and the presentation of a shiny silver cigarette case. Denis Law found out he was being given a free transfer while watching television in an Aberdeen pub, and rejoined Manchester City. Then, on New Year's Day 1974, the George Best saga finally petered out as he played his last game for United, overweight and disinterested, at Queens Park Rangers. United's form, amid the maelstrom, continued to plumb the depths.

Ralph Coates gave Tottenham victory at Old Trafford in March, nailing this shadow of the famous Manchester United to the bottom of the division. They were three points behind Norwich City, five adrift of Birmingham City, and seven behind West Ham United, who were safe in 19th spot. The *Observer* washed their hands of Docherty's side. 'United must prepare for life in the Second Division,' the paper wrote, adding that 'a number of clubs at the top of the Third' were not as 'monotonously drab' as the relatively recent champions of Europe. It was at this point that United remembered who they were, scrambling a draw against the Burnley side who had thrashed champions-elect Leeds 4–1. Then they beat Norwich, Newcastle and Everton, scoring 12 goals in the process, and suddenly survival was a real possibility.

But a couple of games later, Everton gained revenge over United at Goodison Park, Mick Lyons scoring the only goal. That win was coupled with Birmingham's 4–0 rout of QPR. United were suddenly close to the brink, and on an afternoon of dangerously heightened emotion at Old Trafford, Denis Law of Manchester City backheeled an 82nd-minute goal to consign his old club to the Second Division. It was only a symbolic blow: Birmingham, who had played like men possessed ever since midfielder Howard Kendall joined in March, beat Norwich that day to rubber-stamp the paperwork and render whatever United did totally irrelevant.

Law, however, knew full well what his goal represented, the very moment the ball crossed the line. As Kendall frolicked in celebration of survival at St Andrew's, his first lap of honour since winning the title with Everton in 1970, the crowds rushed the field at Old Trafford. The Manchester derby was abandoned eight minutes early, but the result stood. Law walked straight off the pitch, the blood drained from his face. It wasn't his last kick in club football: he played a couple of Texaco Cup matches for City during the following pre-season, before deciding to hang up his boots. But this is the point when the credits roll.

17

Archie enjoys a kickabout in the street (1974–75 to 1979–80)

The summer of 1974 was a period of glorious flux, the grand old order in tumult. A tired Bill Shankly stepped down at Liverpool, who were addled enough by shock to briefly consider offering the job to Middlesbrough's long-ball merchant Jack Charlton. Bill Nicholson, disheartened by money-obsessed modern culture and increasing bother on the terraces, quit Tottenham Hotspur. Harry Catterick had already left Everton a sick man, while Bertie Mee was slowly winding down at Arsenal; neither club had built on their early seventies success. Manchester United were in the Second Division, for goodness sake.

And Don Revie finally said goodbye to Leeds, accepting the England job vacated by Sir Alf Ramsey. He was replaced, surreally and senselessly, by Brian Clough, who had spent the previous five years loudly accusing Revie and his players of cynicism and moral turpitude. Clough lasted 44 farcical days at Elland Road, unwanted, unforgiven and unloved, before being bundled down the M1 to become a man of leisure back home in Derby. Jimmy Adamson stepped in, and guided a famous collective to one last hurrah, a European Cup final against Bayern Munich in which – needless to say – Leeds had their hopes scuppered by some questionable refereeing decisions. That, at least, was a beacon of dependability in a fast-changing world.

Clough had not joined Leeds straight from Derby. He'd walked away from the Rams in October 1973 after falling out with chairman Sam Longson over his increasingly strident TV appearances. At one point the row got so petty that Longson changed the lock on the drinks cabinet in Clough's office. Clough's loyal squad staged a sit-in at the Baseball Ground, publicly demanding their manager's reinstatement and threatening to strike. But Clough's successor was not to be messed about. Dave Mackay, erstwhile club captain, publically shamed the players as 'a schoolboy eleven' and added, 'I am a man and I like dealing with men, not misguided children. I will fight them to the death!' The squad took one look into his fiercely blazing eyes and meekly backed down. They gave Mackay their unconditional support, and finished third in 1973–74. Clough resurfaced, incongruously, at third-tier Brighton and Hove Albion, where he lost 4–0 in the FA Cup to non-league Walton & Hersham and 8–2 at home to Bristol Rovers. No wonder he eventually accepted the call from Leeds.

Derby went two places better in 1974–75. Mackay's title-winning team is these days often assumed to be a continuum of Clough's 1971–72 championship side, but there were significant differences. Francis Lee joined from Manchester City, while Bruce Rioch arrived from Aston Villa – the pair contributing 27 goals between them. The most famous of those 27 proved to be this Derby side's signature moment. Against his old club, Lee turned on the left-hand corner of the box and, in front of none-more-seventies hoardings – WINFIELD ONLY AT WOOLWORTH, RADIO RENTALS COLOUR – unleashed an unstoppable riser into the top right. The screamer was soundtracked to perfection by BBC commentator Barry Davies, whose voice cracked with childlike glee and some career-defining creative energy of his own: 'Interesting! *Very* interesting! Look at his face! Just *look* at his face!!!'

Kevin Hector and Roger Davies added another 25, with Derby now committed to all-out attack. Mackay also had to do without the injured Roy McFarland, a mainstay of the Clough defence; his understudy, the perennial squad member Peter Daniel, stepped up to the plate and contributed the form of his life, earning himself the club's player of the season award. Derby were eighth at the start of March, but won eight of their last 12 games to breeze through a congested pack. They were deserved winners, ahead of a Liverpool side finding its feet under new pass-and-move disciple Bob Paisley – was Big Jack Charlton ever seriously a goer?! – though Billy Bingham's Everton, who finished just three points off the pace in fourth spot, would always rue two inexplicable and ultimately costly defeats to Carlisle United.

The Cumbrian minnows were enjoying their single season in the sun, having been the first beneficiaries of the League's new three-up, three-down promotion and relegation policy. (It had been a less fluid two-up, two-down affair ever since the Test Matches had been abolished in 1898.) They won their first two top-flight matches, at Chelsea and Middlesbrough, then beat Spurs 1–0 at Brunton Park, a penalty from Chris Balderstone – who also played first-class cricket for Leicestershire – sending them top. 'We've given our supporters the day of glory they wanted,' smiled manager Alan Ashman. It couldn't last, and Carlisle ended the season at the bottom, but they had left their mark, not least on Everton. Ashman, who won the 1968 FA Cup for West Brom, always rated this achievement as his greatest.

Meanwhile in Nottingham, after a few months spent licking his wounds, Brian Clough re-emerged at Forest in January 1975. As his old club Derby celebrated their second First Division title, the one he'd just taken over narrowly escaped relegation to the Third.

Manchester United were back for the 1975–76 campaign, along with similarly rejuvenated giants Aston Villa, the latter having bottomed out in the *Third* Division at the start of the 1970s. But neither of these behemoths – 13 championships between them – were seriously expected to take a tilt at the title. In the wake of Derby's successes, more modestly sized clubs were in vogue. This isn't to say the new-found dominance of the mega-clubs was being rolled back in any meaningful sense: the trend-busting seventies triumphs of Derby, and later Nottingham Forest, were set in motion by Clough, a singular genius raging against the dying of the provincial light. Rule-defining exceptions. However, the power men were yet to seriously apply boot pressure to the neck of the body politic – that would come during the eighties with the hogging rather than sharing of home gate receipts, stock flotations, advances in marketing know-how, TV money and the ongoing threat of some sort of fancy super league – so for now there was still a chink of daylight, and the smaller clubs felt it worthwhile to have a square go. Ipswich Town, Stoke City, Sheffield United and Middlesbrough – all coming off the back of high finishes – were, along with Derby, expected to push hard again.

It didn't quite pan out like that. Ipswich, under Bobby Robson, were still a couple of years away from entering their second trophy-winning phase, and finished well off the title pace. Big Jack's Middlesbrough ended the season in mid-table. So did Stoke, the wind taken out of manager Tony Waddington's sails when a gale whipped the roof off a stand at the Victoria Ground, eventually forcing the club to cash in on playmaker Alan Hudson and striker Jimmy Greenhoff. And Sheffield United were relegated despite the presence of Tony Currie, another of those celebrated seventies mavericks. It was up to another unsung club to take the good fight to the bigger boys.

Dave Sexton's Queens Park Rangers were 50-1 shots at the start of 1975–76. In their first match of the season they scored with a glorious pitch-long sweeping move, playmaker Don Masson stroking a pass forward for yet another maverick, Stan Bowles, who flicked sideways to Gerry Francis. The rangy striker exchanged a one-two with Don Givens and, at full stride, fizzed a shot into the bottom corner. The victims were Liverpool, priced as 11-2 second favourites. A week later QPR travelled to Derby (odds 4-1 f.); Bowles claimed a hat-trick in a 5–1 win. Dave Mackay brazenly insisted the result was 'cock-eyed' and argued that 'Rangers were rarely dangerous', but his captain and centre-back Roy McFarland was more willing to hold his hands up. 'I'm in a daze,' he admitted. 'Rangers blitzed us.' In pre-season friendlies QPR had scored four goals against both Borussia Mönchengladbach and Benfica; now, having thrashed the champions of Germany and Portugal, they'd put five past the champions of England too.

Manchester United (33-1) also started quickly, as if to make up for lost time. Having got used to regularly winning again during their sabbatical in the Second, Tommy Docherty's side clamed 11 of their first 12 points before losing to rampant QPR. Liverpool by contrast were a tad more sluggish out of the traps. After their defeat against Rangers they required a late John Toshack goal to salvage a draw against West Ham at Anfield, then soon after were beaten 2–0 at Ipswich, a result which caused the normally sanguine Bob Paisley to do his nut. 'It was the worst display I can ever remember from a Liverpool team,' said Paisley, who had worked at the club in one capacity or another since 1939. 'We had far too many big heads out there, men who think wearing the Liverpool shirt makes them stars. These people need cutting down to size. I'll cut them down, don't worry about that!'

In the wake of Paisley's righteous blast Liverpool lost just one of their following 23 matches. The run included a 3–1 home win over Manchester United in early November which knocked Docherty's team off the top spot, all the way down to fifth. One point separated United from the new leaders, the FA Cup holders West Ham; reigning champs Derby, QPR and Liverpool were sandwiched in between. Docherty went out and bought winger Gordon Hill from Millwall, a purchase which, the *Guardian* noted, enabled him to 'realise a long-standing ambition to play four front men with the ability to score goals'. This was old-school buckle-and-swash. The subsequent livewire antics of Hill, Steve Coppell, Stuart Pearson and Lou Macari encouraged the *Express* to claim that United boasted 'the most exciting team in England since the Spurs of 1960–1962 and the Busby Babes of 1956–1958'.

It was shaping up to be a tight, dramatic race, though West Ham fell out of it in preposterous fashion, winning just one of their 21 games after Christmas and finishing two places above the relegation zone. Manchester United had the title in their own hands going into April, with six games remaining, though a 4–3 win at Newcastle in late March, in which they were forced to make three scrambled clearances off the line, suggested they might not be fully equipped to see the job through. Sure enough, after beating Derby in the FA Cup semi and booking a date with Southampton of the Second Division at Wembley, a distracted and exhausted United lost 3–0 at Ipswich, losing control of their own destiny. 'I don't mind winning the Cup and coming second in the league,' laughed Docherty after the game, recklessly cocking a snook at fate.

On the same day, Derby bowed out of realistic contention after going three down inside 20 minutes at Manchester City, eventually losing 4–3, while Liverpool were held to a goalless draw at Aston Villa. QPR took advantage. They had been a goal down at home to Middlesbrough, having toiled for the best part of an hour, when referee Jack Taylor – who had awarded two penalties in the World Cup final between West Germany and Holland a couple of years earlier, one for Bernd Hölzenbein's opportunistic tumble over Wim Jansen's outstretched leg – pointed to the spot. Boro defender Willie Maddren had taken the role of Jansen; Rangers midfielder Dave Clement was the Hölzenbein of the piece.

Gerry Francis converted the spot-kick, and a relieved Rangers went on to register a 4–2 victory. 'I didn't make contact,' fumed Maddren afterwards, though he was big enough to add that easy-on-the-eye Rangers had 'won a lot of friends this season. I hope they go on to win the title.' Clement insisted that he had done nothing wrong – 'I used to be a bit of a swimmer but I am not clever enough to produce a dive like that out of nothing' – but his own manager Sexton wryly confessed he'd seen nothing like it since Brian Phelps won bronze in the ten-metre platform at the 1960 Rome Olympics.

Rangers were in the box seat with just three matches to go. They were the form horse, too, having won 11 of their last 12. But they lost their discipline on a visit to Norwich City, going down 3–2 as Stan Bowles rolled around theatrically on the floor, claiming to have been knocked into a semi-conscious state by Tony Powell. 'Bowles elbowed me, and I thought he was coming after me again,' explained Powell afterwards, admitting partial responsibility but nothing more. 'I swung at him but only the tips of my fingers caught him in the face.' Liverpool meanwhile came out on top in an Anfield goalfest against Stoke, Ray Kennedy strutting around the midfield not so much evading tackles but ignoring them, the inspiration behind a 5–3 victory. Now Liverpool were in control – just – as the rollercoaster careered towards its final turn, picking up speed at a hysterical pace. With two games to go Paisley's team were a point ahead of Rangers and four ahead of United (though Docherty's men had a further two matches in hand and therefore retained an outside chance despite their inferior goal average). Rangers were held at home in their penultimate match by Arsenal until the 87th minute, when Bowles dribbled his way into the box and drew a challenge from Richie Powling. The whistle blew for a controversial decision. 'It was a disgrace,' fumed Gunners coach Bobby Campbell. 'Bowles was acting all through the match.'

Designated penalty taker Gerry Francis was faced with a dilemma. 'There was a picture slap-bang on the front of the matchday programme showing me scoring from the spot by putting the ball to the keeper's left,' he explained.' I thought if Arsenal keeper Jimmy Rimmer has seen that, he'll know which way to go. So this time I placed it to his right. I've got to admit, it was a most nerve-wracking moment.' Liverpool also had to show extreme patience at Manchester City, waiting until the 73rd minute before 19-year-old striker David Fairclough set up Steve Heighway for the opener then scored a couple himself in the last two minutes. The 3–0 scoreline suggested a level of ease and comfort that wasn't totally warranted.

United had kept winning to stay in theoretical touch, but the jig was up for Docherty's free-scoring entertainers when they surprisingly went down 1–0 at home to Stoke, veteran defender

Alan Bloor heading past Alex Stepney with three minutes to go. It was a classic defensive smash-and-grab by the visitors, and it had Docherty spitting feathers: 'The way Stoke refused to play amazed me. I'll tell you this. If they play that way next season they could be relegated. It's no wonder they're drawing home crowds of just 16,000.' Some prognosis by the Doc: Stoke did indeed go down the following year, scoring just 28 goals in 42 matches.

Two teams and one game remained. Liverpool's final match at relegation haunted Wolves was postponed due to their involvement in the first leg of the Uefa Cup final against Bruges. Rangers did what they had to do in their remaining fixture, beating Leeds United 2–0 at Loftus Road in a tense end-to-end thriller. Dave Thomas put the Rs one up just after the hour with a diving header. Duncan McKenzie thought he'd equalised seven minutes from time, but Phil Parkes saved brilliantly, allowing the home side to launch one of their famous counter-attacks. Frank McLintock – so nearly a League champion with Leicester in 1963 and the Double-winning captain of Arsenal in 1971 – sprayed a ball down the right for Bowles, who rounded Norman Hunter and curled one home from the tightest of angles.

Rangers, having taken 27 points from the last available 30, started popping champagne corks in the changing room. 'Wolves will beat Liverpool and we'll take the title,' insisted defender David Webb, leaning back in the hot tub, sipping bubbles from a flute. His manager was more hesitant. 'At this moment I feel we are champions whether we finished first or second,' rationalised Dave Sexton. Rangers faced an agonising ten-day wait to discover their fate, and anxiety quickly bubbled to the surface. As the squad prepared to depart for a week-long tour of Israel, Bowles – his mind a-whirl with a possible £250,000 transfer to Hamburg as well as a fear of flying – walked out after a blazing row with

Sexton at Heathrow. Sexton responded by flying off the handle at some nearby photographers: 'Take one more photo and I'll wrap those cameras round your necks.'

The news, when it eventually came, wasn't good. Liverpool only needed a draw at Molineux. They were a goal down until Kevin Keegan equalised in the 76th minute; John Toshack and Ray Kennedy added a couple more in the 85th and 89th minutes, whereupon the travelling Kop tumbled joyously onto the pitch. Wolves were condemned to relegation, though they'd have gone down even if they'd held onto their lead anyway, seasoned escapees Birmingham having secured a decisive point in a draw at Sheffield United. 'I always felt Liverpool would win,' sighed wise old Frank McLintock.

Liverpool's victory over Wolves was notable for the eerily calm nature in which they'd kept plugging away, even when the clock was beginning to whirl round at an alarming rate. Ray Kennedy, noted Frank McGhee, the *Daily Mirror*'s voice of sport, 'spread his own composure like a cloak around the rest of his colleagues'. Which is not to say their manager was always so sure of victory, Bob Paisley admitting afterwards that he'd compared his team's run-in with QPR's, and decided 'it probably wasn't on. I didn't of course let anyone know what I felt, but that was the main reason I rearranged the closing match against Wolves for after the season had finished. I thought it would be a good way of keeping the team in shape for the Uefa Cup final. I thought we would lose the title but win the Cup.' As it turned out, Liverpool landed both.

Paisley's side were not universally adored. The manager preached a sophisticated, possession-based game, the result of lessons learned when Red Star Belgrade handed Bill Shankly's side a lesson in control during the second round of the 1973–74 European Cup. Liverpool had done most of the attacking in that tie, and nearly all of the running, but were easily contained and lost both legs. Now their new, patient, continental style was beginning to reap rewards, though plaudits were harder to come by when up against crowd-pleasing, kitchen-sink-flinging outfits like QPR and Manchester United. In the *Guardian* David Lacey had admitted that 'the heart' wanted to see a United victory in the title race, while Norwich manager John Bond opined that it would be a bad thing for English football if Liverpool prevailed, expressing a preference for Rangers. 'I've got to be grateful to John,' smiled Paisley, whose avuncular, cardigan-and-slippers image belied an inner steel. 'I didn't have to motivate our players after that. He did it for me.'

With their ninth title, Liverpool became the most successful side in the history of the Football League, one win ahead of Arsenal, two clear of Manchester United and Everton. It wasn't too long before they made it to double figures on the roll of honour. They were the dominant team of 1976–77, winning a second title in a row without the fingernail-bothering narratives of the previous season. Not that it was *totally* plain sailing. They went to Aston Villa in December as leaders only to find themselves 5–1 down at half-time; that remained the score at the full-time whistle. 'I haven't let in five since I was playing for the Scunthorpe A team 12 years ago,' wailed disconsolate keeper Ray Clemence.

But this was the humiliation that proved a rule. Ron Saunders's emerging Villa, powered by the goals of 21-year-old Andy Gray, top-scored in the division with 76, but let in 50. Liverpool by comparison could only find the net on 62 occasions – Kevin Keegan scored just 12 League goals to Gray's 25 – but conceded a miserly 33. The difference between first and fourth in a nutshell. Liverpool saw off their closest challengers, Manchester City and Ipswich, during a serene run-in, coasting home in unspectacular style. It was a masterclass of control, one they'd hone to near-perfection by the end of the decade. It was also the first leg of a potential Treble for Paisley's side, but they lost the FA Cup final, Tommy Docherty finally earning tangible reward for turning Manchester United around. Liverpool had the not-insignificant consolation of becoming the second English club to win the European Cup, seeing off Borussia Mönchengladbach in Rome.

Liverpool's regal carry-on meant the big end-of-season drama was played out at the other end of the table. Tottenham had been in precipitous decline since the departure of Bill Nicholson. New manager Terry Neill had been one game away from leading Spurs to relegation at the end of 1974–75, but his team saved themselves with a final-day 4–2 win over European Cup finalists Leeds. A ninth-place finish in 1975–76 suggested some improvement, though Neill was engaged in a harmful long-running battle with his board over the provision of money for transfers. He'd threatened to quit over the matter a mere two weeks into the job, prompting one joker to ask: 'What took him so long?' Now the row escalated in hilariously petty fashion ahead of a close-season tour. Neill had promised a septuagenarian supporter a lift to Heathrow on the team coach, only for club chairman Sidney Wale to turf the pensioner off. Neill arranged and paid for a taxi for the old man, but that wasn't really the point. The manager's authority had been deliberately undermined. When Neill promised his players a cash bonus from the pot generated by the tour, the board refused to cough up. Neill resigned in high dudgeon. Three weeks later, that lofty vehicle dropped him off at Arsenal.

Spurs, under new boss Keith Burkinshaw, made bids for Newcastle striker Malcolm Macdonald and Ipswich's David Johnson. Macdonald joined Neill's Arsenal instead and scored 29 goals, while Johnson chose Liverpool where he became a League and European champion. In October Spurs went down 8–2 at Derby, a particularly sensational result given the Rams hadn't won a game all season and, panicking at the first sign of trouble, would soon get rid of Dave Mackay. (They've never had a serious look at the title since.) 'I have a deep sense of shame and regret,' admitted Burkinshaw, who wasn't able to halt the decline. A 5–0 humbling at Manchester City in their penultimate game effectively packed them off to the Second Division, ending a 27-year unbroken membership of the First. At the time, that spell was only bettered by Arsenal, ever-present since 1919.

Bristol City, however, did manage to avoid the drop. In the top flight for the first time in 65 years, the 1906–07 runners-up won their opening match of the season at Arsenal. Paul Cheesley ruined Terry Neill and Malcolm Macdonald's welcoming party by pinging two headers off the woodwork then finding the net with a third. After a subsequent nine months of struggle City survived by dint of being in the right places at the right time. In their penultimate game of the season they faced newly crowned champions Liverpool who, with the title tucked safely away and FA Cup and European Cup finals on the horizon, understandably took it relatively easy. Chris Garland scored twice in a precious 2–1 win.

The Bristolians then visited fellow strugglers Coventry in their final match, with the situation precariously balanced. Either of the teams, plus Sunderland who were playing their final game at Everton, could go down; all were level on points. Sunderland's season had been hellishly strange: at one stage they had gone on a nine-game losing streak, scoring one goal in the process; another run saw them hand out consecutive thrashings of 4–0, 6–1 and 6–0. It wasn't enough to get them out of bother, though, and here they were, scrabbling around in desperation.

Sunderland lost 2–0 at Everton. A rumour spread among their fans that Coventry had beaten Bristol City 3–1, a result which would have kept the Mackems up on goal difference. But it proved false. In fact, the Coventry–Bristol showdown had kicked off late due to traffic congestion before the match. (One Bristol judge had adjourned his court 40 minutes early so several jurors could catch a coach to the game.) As a result, the teams were still playing. And when word of Sunderland's defeat got round, Coventry chairman Jimmy Hill ran to the announcer's booth screaming: 'Get it on the board! Get it on the board!' Hill's thought process was super-cynical, manipulative and borderline unfair, but devilishly clever. The two Cities were drawing 2–2 at the time and, upon seeing the Sunderland result flashed up, suddenly realised the scoreline would save them both. With the clock running out, both sets of players effectively declared a ceasefire. Neither team launched a single meaningful attack during the final five minutes.

Sunderland's fate was sealed. Their manager Jimmy Adamson responded with astonishing magnanimity under the circumstances: 'You've got to make your own luck in this game, but we could not.' Coventry remained in the top flight for the next 24 years, earning a reputation as relegation escape artists. Bristol City enjoyed three more years in the top flight before, as a result of overreaching themselves financially by offering players ludicrous contracts lasting up to ten years, they became the first club to drop from the First to the Fourth in consecutive seasons.

In February 1977 Nottingham Forest lost a fourth-round FA Cup replay at Southampton, then a Second Division fixture at Wolves, then another League match at home to Luton Town. It didn't take a genius to work out why the team had hit a sticky patch. Derby County, having sacked Dave Mackay, were in protracted negotiations to entice Forest boss Brian Clough and his assistant Peter Taylor back to the Baseball Ground.

Southampton then came to the City Ground for a League fixture, hoping to once again benefit from the uncertainty. The Saints soon found themselves a goal to the good, with Peter Osgood giving Forest's Larry Lloyd a rare old runaround. 'We were terrible, we wouldn't have scored if we'd played until midnight,' admitted Lloyd. But then the mist trundled in from the Trent, Lloyd took the opportunity to 'sort out' Osgood under cover of fog – 'I bet he still remembers it!' chortled the big defender years later – and the referee abandoned the game after 47 minutes.

A week later, Clough reneged on a verbal promise to rejoin Derby; a month further on, and Forest beat Saints when their game was rescheduled. And so an extremely likely fourth defeat on the spin, one which would surely have shattered Forest's momentum beyond all repair, had been transformed into a vital win. The fog-assisted victory was priceless, because at the end of the season, Forest scraped the third and final promotion place by a single point. Oh, and they had kept hold of Clough.

On his return to the big time after two-and-a-half seasons in the second tier, Clough insisted publicly that Forest's modest priority during 1977–78 was to 'stabilise and build'. His newly promoted side were not expected to become champions, understandably so, given only four teams in 85 years had pulled off that particular trick, and Liverpool 1906, Everton 1932, Tottenham 1951 and Ipswich 1962 had all, unlike Forest, come up as Second Division champions. Liverpool were hot favourites to make it three titles in a row, with Manchester City, Manchester United, Aston Villa and Everton tipped as their closest challengers. Only David Miller in the *Express* displayed any sort of prescience – 'Clough's Forest could surprise us all!' – and even that support was conditional, the pay-off to a piece in which he unequivocally tipped Liverpool.

But it became clear fairly quickly that Clough was in no mood simply to consolidate, and instead wanted to make up for lost time. Forest won their opening game at Everton, and followed it up with five victories in their next six. Clough bought Archie Gemmill from Derby and, crucially, Peter Shilton from freshly relegated Stoke. 'Shilton makes us look like a team,' he crowed, and Forest were on their way. They went top in early October when Peter Withe scored all the goals in a 4–0 win over Ipswich. Forest put another four past Middlesbrough a few weeks later, though Clough wasn't yet content. 'He's unbelievable,' panted Gemmill. 'He wanted three more goals and suggested we had let it go. He was moaning. Can you imagine any other manager chewing up his team after they had won 4–0 and gone four points clear at the top? But that's Clough. I can't tell you how he does it.'

The signature victory of the season came at Old Trafford just before Christmas, when Manchester United, now managed by Dave Sexton in the wake of a scandal involving Tommy Docherty and the physiotherapist's wife, were steamrollered 4–0. It was an all-round performance bordering on perfection. Clough insisted that captain and midfielder John McGovern was the best man on the pitch; the press made various claims for the effervescent Tony Woodcock, Archie Gemmill and scruffy wing genius John Robertson. 'United really had no right to be occupying the same pitch as Forest,' opined the *Guardian*. Sexton could only agree. 'People keep telling me Forest's bubble will burst. I can only say that it is a big bubble. They don't play with 11 men – they seem to have 16 or 17 on the field all the time. When they are attacking they have about seven of them at you. When they are defending, there are about nine of them stopping you even getting anywhere near Shilton.' United responded by winning their next match 6–2 at Everton, a result which further emphasised the different plane Forest were operating on: Everton were second in the table at the time.

Gemmill was ordered by Derbyshire police to cease regular street kickabouts with his young son Scot (later to turn out for Forest and Everton). 'I'm not a soccer fan and I'm sick to the teeth with the sound of a football, never mind the sight of one,' seethed the pinch-faced neighbour who'd shopped him. But otherwise Forest's players could not be stopped. They barged their way to the title with four games to spare, seven points clear of eventual runners-up Liverpool, who were beginning to find Forest rather problematic. Bob Paisley's new-look side had been able to maintain their continental dominance, Graeme Souness and Kenny Dalglish delicately deconstructing Bruges in the 1978 European Cup final at Wembley. But they were suddenly second best domestically: Forest also beat them in the League Cup final. Worse was to come for Liverpool early in 1978–79, as the pair were drawn together in the first round of the European Cup. Forest prised their fingers off the big jug – 22-year-old striker Gary Birtles scored one and set up another, earning a GARY GLITTERS! headline in the *Daily Express* that wouldn't fly these days – and went on to win the competition twice in a row themselves.

Could Liverpool respond by clawing back some ground on the home front? Their opening salvoes in 1978–79 served as serious statements of intent. Kenny Dalglish scored twice in a 3–0 win at Ipswich. Graeme Souness grabbed a couple in a 4–1 victory over Manchester City described by their manager Tony Book as 'out of this world'. Tottenham Hotspur, back up and with Argentina World Cup winners Ossie Ardiles and Ricky Villa adding glitz and glamour, were spanked 7–0 at Anfield, Terry McDermott finishing off a famous pitch-long move of zigzag Hollywood passes by guiding a bullet header into the top corner while running at full pelt. Liverpool took up residence at the top.

Manchester United, whose play under Dave Sexton was overly studious for some tastes, suffered another miserable Christmas. Twelve months on from being defenestrated by Forest, they endured a horrific run of festive form, losing 3–0 at Bolton, then going down by the same scoreline on Boxing Day at home against Liverpool. But if they thought they had bottomed out with that one, the worst was yet to come: a 5–3 thrashing by Ron Atkinson's easy-on-the-eye West Bromwich Albion.

That eight-goal thriller was the signature performance of a fondly remembered and culturally significant team. Until the late 1970s there had been no significant black presence in the Football League, although ground had been broken relatively early in the story when half-Ghanaian, half-Scottish goalkeeper Arthur Wharton stood in for Sheffield United's Fatty Foulke against Sunderland at Roker Park back in February 1895. Wharton's best years were way behind him at this point – those came at Preston North End, just before the formation of the League – and so his trailblazing First Division bow proved something of an assortment. The Blades lost 2–0 against the champions-elect, and Wharton was reportedly at fault for one of the goals. Still, according to the *Manchester Guardian*, he also saved 'several shots in nice style' and 'dealt effectively' with other efforts, despite at one point being deliberately clattered, the game having descended into the rough house after a Sunderland player suffered a dislocated shoulder. Nevertheless, Wharton's staunch performance was not enough to dislodge Foulke from his permanent berth.

Another mixed-race Scot, Willie Clarke, became the first non-white player to score in the top division in a 3–2 win for Aston Villa at Everton on Christmas Day 1901; the outside-right went on to register Bradford City's first-ever First Division goal against Bury in 1908. Jamaican forward Lindy Delapenha played in Portsmouth's title-winning teams of 1949 and 1950. South African winger Albert Johannson and mixed-race full-back Paul Reaney starred for Don Revie's Leeds, while midfielder Stan Horne was part of Manchester City's 1967–68 title-winning squad.

A glacial advance through the decades, then. But progress became more rapid during the seventies. On the first day of April 1972, West Ham named three black players in their starting XI: regular striker Clyde Best was joined by up-and-coming forward Ade Coker and left-back Clive Charles. The Nigerian-born Coker scored a late goal in a 2–0 win over Spurs. 'His transports of delight gave the game the happiest of endings,' reported the *Observer*. Ron Greenwood's selection was a radical statement during an era in which the BBC, in prime time, still considered it acceptable to transmit *a minstrel show*. By 1978 Forest full-back Viv Anderson became the first black player to be picked for England, while West Brom were earning righteous fame for building their team around three black superstars.

Striker Cyrille Regis, winger Laurie Cunningham and defender Brendon Batson were nicknamed 'the Three Degrees' by Atkinson, a clumsy yet affectionate and well-meaning reference to the contemporary black US soul troupe. They were forced to cope with torrents of abuse from thousands of unreconstructed fools around the country, but millions of others fell for their talent and verve: this pioneer side earned its rightful place in a stylish West Brom lineage alongside the free-scoring title winners of 1920 and Vic Buckingham's nearly men of 1954.

They would narrowly miss out on glory too. At Old Trafford, Regis and Cunningham were inspired, their power and grace too much for hapless hosts. Both created a couple of goals; both scored one themselves. When Regis sent Cunningham clear for his, United defender Stewart Houston took a wild rake at the winger's ankles, but only connected with fresh air. Cunningham had been tutored as a young player at Orient by Arthur Rowe, the aesthete-architect of Tottenham's 1950–51 push-and-run side. 'Tell you the truth, nothing much in our game now turns me on,' he said at the time, 'but this boy Cunningham excites me more than anyone I can remember. When I turn up for training and little Laurie's off sick, or with another batch of players, I'm always terribly disappointed, you know, really terribly.'

Albion went top in early January, but a series of postponements caused by a cold snap robbed them of momentum. Their first game back after an enforced hiatus was a trip to Anfield; yet to thaw out, they lost 2–1. Liverpool took over the leadership. Alongside Forest and Everton, Albion did their best to keep Liverpool honest in the subsequent chase, but it was always a forlorn effort. Liverpool clinched the title by beating Aston Villa 3–0 at Anfield on Bob Paisley's 40th anniversary at the club. 'Happy birthday, Bob Paisley!' their supporters sang, adding an ironic blast of 'what a waste of money'. His team ended the season eight points clear of Forest, the European champions elect, having scored 85 goals and let in just 16, the latter a record for a 42-game season. West Brom ended a memorable campaign in third.

Liverpool kept possession of their League title in 1979–80, holding off late charges by Manchester United, improved under Sexton if still not exhilarating, and Bobby Robson's Ipswich Town. Robson's side were rock bottom in October, a 1–0 defeat at Manchester United their sixth in a row. But by the time the teams met again at Portman Road on the first day of March, Ipswich had embarked on a run of 12 wins and three draws in 18 games, their Dutch midfielders Frans Thijssen and Arnold Muhren imperious, Alan Brazil and Paul Mariner dependable up front. They had risen to third in the table. United meanwhile were second, level on points with Liverpool but having played a game more.

United's standing was rendered something of a sick joke as Ipswich won 6–0. It was United's most humiliating defeat since Aston Villa had beaten them 7–0 in 1930, and could easily have been a whole lot worse. United keeper Gary Bailey saved *three* penalty kicks in eight minutes: a weak Thijssen sidefoot, a Kevin Beattie lash that had a little more oomph, and finally, having been penalised for moving too soon for Beattie's effort, a retake by the same player. On the same afternoon, Liverpool won at Everton. Dixie Dean passed away in the Goodison stands, having enjoyed a last lunch with Bill Shankly beforehand, the pair reminiscing over their playing days before the war.

Ipswich finished the season in third, seven points off the pace, an undefeated run of 23 League matches coming to an end on the final day against Manchester City. Their poor early form had cost them dear. United too mourned a slow start: they won six of their last seven matches, but it still wasn't enough to reel in Liverpool, who secured the championship with a game to go, Avi Cohen scoring at both ends in a comfortable 4–1 victory over Aston Villa. For a second time in four years, Paisley's side would have a shot at a title hat-trick. Perhaps the grand old order wasn't in so much tumult after all.

18

Helenio is turned away from the door (1980–81)

Ampfield is a small Hampshire village situated midway, give or take a couple of miles, between Winchester and Southampton. A civil parish with a population barely into four figures, it was never expected to make much of a contribution to world culture. But it has more than pulled its weight. In 1911 the Rev. W. Awdry, author of the Thomas the Tank Engine children's books, was born in the local vicarage. Then, 69 years later, Ampfield played host to one of the most jaw-dropping press conferences in the entire history of the Football League.

On a brisk morning in February 1980 journalists and broadcasters were summoned to the three-star Potters Heron hotel – thatched roof, log fire, real ale, conference facilities, all a stone's throw from junction 12 of the M3 motorway – for a hastily convened press conference. The Southampton manager Lawrie McMenemy, taking the role of mine host, pressed flesh, then chuntered on awhile about how his small south-coast club were progressing. A second-tier outfit only three years previously, they were doing rather well: third in the First Division table as things stood, with only Liverpool and Manchester United ahead. But all of this was nothing that couldn't be gleaned from a quick shufty in the back of the paper. Why had everyone been summoned?

McMenemy, a showman to his bones, an old-school theatrical tease, was setting up the big unveil. Saints were going along nicely, yes, but it was time for the next stage in their development. Please, he asked his audience, will you welcome Southampton's new signing? And to incredulous gasps, in walked Kevin Keegan, formerly of Liverpool, now a Bundesliga champion with Hamburg, and the reigning two-time European footballer of the year.

Safe to say, none of the industry experts in the room had expected *that*. Keegan was one of the hottest properties in world football. Chelsea had been dangling large sums of money they didn't really have in front of his nose, though glamorous foreign giants Juventus, Barcelona and Real Madrid, all seriously interested, were considered more likely destinations. But only Saints could guarantee Keegan a regular starting place in the English First Division – Chelsea were a Second Division club at the time and, with Geoff Hurst as manager, not coming back up either – and so, with his England place and the 1982 World Cup in mind, he brokered a £450,000 deal that would take effect in the summer.

Could Keegan have found a bigger First Division club? Possibly, though Liverpool, who retained a buy-back option from his original 1977 sale to Hamburg, weren't interested, while Manchester United were beyond the pale given his Anfield background. 'The thing that brought me to Southampton,' Keegan insisted, 'was the progress they had made and the quality of players they have. Southampton will give me the challenge I want because I really think they've got the potential to win the championship.' At which point he got up, paused politely for a few photos, then scuttled off to board a private jet back to Hamburg. He spent the rest of the season working his tail off to help *der Dinosaurier* in their quest to retain the Bundesliga title and win a first European Cup. A relentlessly cheerful team player with a good engine and a high work ethic he was not a million miles away from Thomas. The Rev. Awdry would doubtless have approved.

Keegan's return was not the only eye-opening piece of transfer news ahead of the 1980–81 season. Arsenal, having lost the previous season's FA Cup and Cup Winners' Cup finals without scoring a goal, decided they needed to bolster their attack. So they paid Queens Park Rangers £1.2 million for 19-year-old Clive Allen, whose seasonal haul of 30 goals in the Second Division had him lumbered with a great weight: the new Jimmy Greaves. Allen became England's first million-pound teenager. Arsenal ran stringent checks to ensure they weren't buying an upstart troublemaker. The only evidence of a flash lifestyle they unearthed was the fact he drove a Ford Capri, and had bought his parents a new-fangled video cassette recorder. He was in.

And then he was out. On a pre-season tour of Scotland, Allen failed to score in friendlies against Rangers and Aberdeen. 'Allen's a loser!' screamed the *Express*, presumptuous even by tabloid standards. Or maybe they felt something on the breeze. Two days before the start of the season, Terry Neill made the gloriously Arsenalesque decision to trade his teenage-sensation striker for a full-back. Allen was bundled off to Crystal Palace in a swap deal for Kenny Sansom. The teenager's reaction betrayed a bemused, wide-eyed innocence. 'I don't hold any resentment. I don't think Arsenal bought me simply to use as bait later on. They spent a lot of money and had obviously thought about keeping me for a long time.'

Sansom, scuttling past in the other direction, gaze averted, insisted that Allen 'won't be disappointed with Palace. They have a good set-up! I still think they will do well this season.' Allen was indeed soon in the goals, scoring a hat-trick in Palace's early season 5–2 evisceration of Middlesbrough. On the same day, Arsenal went down 3–1 at Coventry, their manager Neill having chosen to brazenly vacate the dugout that weekend in favour of a late summer holiday. But it soon became clear that Samson had got the better of the switch. By mid-October Arsenal were just four points behind pacemakers Ipswich Town. Palace's thumping of Boro, meanwhile, proved to be their only win in the first ten. The other nine games had ended in defeat.

Admittedly one of those could be written off to outrageous ill fortune. Allen sent a screamer into the top right of Coventry City's net, only for the shot to hit a stanchion at the back of the goal frame and rebound out. Both referee and linesman, thoroughly confused but winging it, waved play on with staged authority. But bad luck or no, Palace were bottom, which is where they would end a dismal campaign, well adrift of the rest of the division. So much for the self-styled 'Team of the Eighties'. They made it back to the top flight just before the decade ended, and were belted 9–0 at Liverpool in September 1989. It's fair to say the nineties were more to Palace's liking.

Keegan had not, on his sortie back to Germany, been able to help Hamburg retain their Bundesliga title. Bayern Munich, equipped with their own all-action hero in Karl-Heinz Rummenigge, prevailed by two points. He did get them to the 1980 European Cup final, though, where they faced the holders Nottingham Forest. 'We know he runs the show for Hamburg, he has the freedom to do what he likes, but we've no special plans for him,' yawned Brian Clough before the match. 'If he plays in midfield, he'll be picked up in midfield. If he goes wide, then we'll have people who can pick him up there. We're just waiting to get his feet back on the floor when he plays for Southampton next season.' So Forest picked him up in midfield, and picked him up when he went wide. And they isolated him when he ventured up front. Keegan thus neutered, Forest retained their Cup.

As reigning two-time European champions, Forest were one of the teams expected to challenge hard for the 1980–81 title, tipped alongside Liverpool, Manchester United, Arsenal and Ipswich Town. But it soon became clear they were all over the place. Star striker Trevor Francis was a long-term injury. John Robertson, who set up Francis for the winner in the 1979 European Cup final and scored the only goal against Hamburg, was agitating for more money. Raimondo Ponte, a £250,000 statement signing from Grasshoppers of Zürich, had his pre-season preparation ruined by a work-permit struggle – detained on arrival at Birmingham Airport, the Swiss striker's Forest career never really took off. Scotland striker Ian Wallace was signed from Coventry for £1.25 million, the biggest deal of the summer, and became a qualified success. Set against that, Garry Birtles, described by Forest and England right-back Viv Anderson as 'the best centre-forward I have ever seen', fell out of favour in farcical style. Coming back in the summer from Euro '80 the England international asked Clough for an extra week's holiday to move house. Clough wasn't having any of it, and in a wild tantrum slapped the striker on the transfer list. Birtles joined Manchester United for £1.25 million on 22 October; he scored his first goal for United on 19 September the following year. Any reassessment made by Viv Anderson after that 333-day wait was never recorded for posterity.

Forest lost possession of the European Cup by the start of October, CSKA Sofia quietly prising it from their fingers in the first round with a pair of sleepy 1–0 victories. They ended the season in seventh, a shockingly average performance given their domination of England and Europe between 1978 and 1980. In the two years that followed, Forest's greatest team was broken up with reckless efficiency: Trevor Francis was moved on to Manchester City, Peter Shilton to Southampton, Martin O'Neill to Norwich, captain John McGovern to Bolton. By the end of 1981–82 only Anderson and Robertson remained of the players who had started Forest's two European Cup finals.

Manchester United and Birtles finished a place below Forest in eighth. Having been runners-up the season before, the regression cost manager Dave Sexton his job. Yet in some respects it was a strangely timed sacking: United won their last seven games of the season, a redemptive run which included victories against Ipswich, West Bromwich Albion and Liverpool. But it was too little, too late: before that giddy sequence, Sexton's team had tasted League victory just three times since the start of November. 'Seven wins at the end made us give the decision a little more thought,' admitted chairman Martin Edwards candidly, before adding bluntly: 'If we had lost them, sacking Dave would have been easy.'

United took a good look around at the managerial talent on offer. With Clough's *modus operandi* not in keeping with the United Way, they offered the job to Southampton's McMenemy, then Bobby Robson of Ipswich. But it was West Bromwich Albion's Ron Atkinson who ended up grabbing the opportunity. He would quickly find himself under instant pressure, failing to win any of the first four games of the 1981–82 campaign, United rooted at the bottom of the table. Relief finally came when United won 1–0 at home to newly promoted Swansea City. The goalscorer? Birtles, sure enough, with that long-awaited first goal.

Atkinson had landed his glamour job thanks to the impressive attacking chops of his West Bromwich Albion side. McMenemy had been in the frame thanks to Southampton's continued ability to punch above their weight. Saints made a confident start to the 1980–81 campaign, quickly proving they were more than Keegan plus ten. Veteran striker Mick Channon scored twice on the opening day to see off Manchester City at the Dell. Graham Baker rifled in a 30-yarder to earn a draw at much-fancied Arsenal. Sunderland were then defeated 2–1 at Roker Park. Helenio Herrera, manager of Internazionale's 1964 and 1965 European champions, and now in charge at Barcelona, came along to see how Keegan was doing, and what his side were missing. He was initially refused admission, only to be rescued by McMenemy, who happened to be walking through the foyer at the time. The Saints boss set the doorman straight, and one of the game's legendary figures was allowed in. Herrera warmly shook McMenemy by the hand, as if greeting an old friend – then congratulated him on Sunderland's recent spectacular 4–0 win at Manchester City. McMenemy took the case of mistaken identity with Mackems boss Ken Knighton in good grace.

Southampton's season continued along a faintly surreal path. Charlie George scored twice in a breezy 4–0 second round, first leg League Cup victory over second-tier Watford. Back in the First Division, Keegan scored his first goal for Saints in a 3–1 breeze against Birmingham, before limping off with a tweaked hamstring. 'Kevin is adjusting to a new style,' insisted McMenemy. 'Over here there's only one pace, flat out, while over in Germany it's like Mantovani.' Southampton then performed with all the intensity of 11 James Lasts in the League Cup return with Watford: taking a four-goal lead into the second leg, they lost 5–1 on the night, then shipped a couple more goals in extra-time. A staggered

McMenemy locked his team in the Vicarage Road dressing room after the aggregate 7–5 defeat to offer them some beneficial advice, then appeared before the press pack to deliver a maxim that never caught on, but nonetheless contained a kernel of unquestionable truth: 'When you are 4–0 up, you should never lose 7–1.'

McMenemy's men clearly took something positive from their trenchant post-match debrief, turning over Brighton & Hove Albion 3–1 the following weekend in the League. They were joint top with Ipswich. 'I thought the team last season was the best I'd played in,' mused Mick Channon, 'but now I look at this team and I wonder. I don't think we're quite ready for the championship, but it's up to the other teams to stop us.' Channon was quickly proved bang on the money, though he'd gain no pleasure in finding this out. Saints certainly weren't ready for the championship: they only won one of their next 11 games and slipped to 14th in the table. They rallied to finish sixth, thanks to a tally of 76 goals, the second-best in the division. But while Keegan, Channon and George sparkled in attack, the defence that buckled against Watford continued to let Saints down, shipping 56 goals, by far the worst total of the leading contenders.

Ipswich, the one side who would end the campaign having scored more than Saints, had more staying power. Having won six of their first seven games, they didn't taste defeat until their 14th match, a narrow loss at Brighton. Teams were unable to cope with the pace on the turn of Eric Gates, or the direct power of John Wark, a gallivanting midfielder who ended the season with a barely credible 36 goals in all competitions. By mid-October they led Liverpool at the top by a point and with a game in hand, having briefly threatened to become the first team to win at Anfield since Birmingham City in January 1978: Frans Thijssen scored midway through the first half and Gates very nearly bundled home a second, but Thijssen lunged in on Kenny Dalglish and Terry McDermott put away an equalising penalty. Ipswich deserved their 1–1 draw. 'Without boasting,' Robson boasted, 'we've got a bloody good side. We've now lost only one League game in 34. If we were going to find out about ourselves, it was going to be here at Anfield. For years we've had the feeling that we were a coming team. Now I feel that we've arrived.'

Liverpool kept with the pace for a while: the reigning champions led the division going into the New Year. But there was a sense of complacency in the air at Anfield. An early-season defeat at newly promoted Leicester had sparked one of Bob Paisley's rare but explosive apoplexies: 'My players didn't deserve anything the way they strutted around out there! Our attitude was wrong and our success has probably caused it. If complacency has crept in, I will quickly stamp it out.'

He didn't quite manage it, and their title charge came apart in January. That proud unbeaten home run came to an abrupt end after 85 games when Leicester, bottom of the table but a bogey team ever since the days of Shankly, came from behind to complete a League Double. Epochal enough, though the most significant damage had been done a couple of weeks earlier. In the first round of fixtures in the New Year, Paisley's table-topping side travelled to second-placed Aston Villa. Ron Saunders's team were saddled with a slightly prosaic reputation – 'We have got where we are by having a lot of players pulling together,' shrugged their famously deadpan manager – but they undid Liverpool with a couple of delicious slices of skill: Tony Morley Cruyff-turned on the left to dazzle Richard Money and set up Peter Withe's opener, then Tommy Swain hared down the right, split Liverpool's defence apart with a back-flick inside to Gary Shaw, who set captain Dennis Mortimer clear to score a brilliant pitch-long second. Villa replaced Liverpool at the top.

Liverpool only lost eight matches in 1980–81, the equal-best record in the division, but 17 draws scuppered their hopes of a title hat-trick. They ended the season in fifth place, their lowest finish for a decade. The consolation prizes of a first League Cup and third European Cup would have to suffice.

Villa had not been considered relevant at the beginning of the campaign. They had only finished seventh the previous season, after all, and hadn't won the title since the days of George Ramsay back in 1910, an awfully long time ago. Still, they would have started out with four straight wins had they managed to hang on to a two-goal lead at Manchester City. Villa then travelled to Ipswich. 'They will provide the first real test of our potential,' opined Dennis Mortimer. 'It is important that we go to a place like Ipswich and show we can play. If we only get a draw, we will have done well.' The results of the experiment were inconclusive: Villa were the better team but went down to a scrappy Frans Thijssen goal scored against the run of play. They remained 16-1 long shots behind Liverpool, Ipswich, Southampton, Forest, Manchester United and Arsenal.

But they began to earn more respect after a 12-match unbeaten run took them five points clear by mid-November. 'Those who are waiting for the bubble to burst are in for a big surprise,' observed Jim Smith, manager of city rivals Birmingham. 'If they can finish above Liverpool, then I cannot see any way they will not win the title. The only other team for them to worry about this season is Ipswich. But I suspect they have just not got the strength in depth to become a major concern.' Which proved frighteningly cogent analysis with more than six months of the season still to go. By the start of February, Ipswich and Villa were level on points, and in hot form. Each tore through the month with win after win. But come March, Villa became the first team to blink. A five-game winning streak ended with a 3–3 draw at home to struggling Manchester United. It was a thoroughly miserable experience: they let a two-goal lead slip then conceded a last-minute penalty against a side who hadn't scored a single goal in their previous five matches. Ipswich, meantime, stretched their winning run to six with a rough-and-ready 3–0 win over Tottenham Hotspur that saw poor Mick Mills separated from one of his shoulders by a rugger player's lunge from Don McAllister.

Spurs made an apology of sorts by beating Villa the following week. Ipswich failed to take full advantage, going down at Old Trafford. 'It's not a disaster for us,' insisted Robson. 'We are quite capable of starting another good run next week.' In fact, as Ipswich had only lost 2–1 while Villa went down 2–0, they came out of the afternoon a goal to the good. And the following week they won convincingly, 4–1 at home to Sunderland. But in a hideous echo of the start of the previous season, losing suddenly became a habit again for Ipswich. They were comprehensively outplayed 3–0 by a team of Leeds United reserves at Elland Road, whereupon Jim Smith's prediction began to ring true. Robson's small squad was battling on three fronts: League, FA Cup and Uefa Cup. Injuries started to take their toll. Niggling knocks befell Footballer of the Year Thijssen and Paul Mariner. They went down 3–1 at West Brom, with Ron Atkinson suggesting he 'got the impression that they're already feeling sorry for themselves'. Villa, having beaten Southampton and Leicester, took over the leadership and never relinquished it.

Ipswich lost the FA Cup semi-final, at neutral Villa Park, to Manchester City. They responded to that particular setback heroically, returning to Villa Park and beating their title rivals 2–1. But the win failed to breathe new life into their championship bid. Having pegged Villa back to within a point – and still having a game in hand – they immediately surrendered their 47-match unbeaten home record to Arsenal. The pivotal moment in a one-goal defeat came when Mariner flashed a header wide from close range. 'He's the England centre-forward!' cried an exasperated Robson after the game. 'You just can't miss chances like that if you're going to win the championship. It's his responsibility to put away chances like that. If it had fallen to my missus I could have understood it, but I couldn't believe it when he didn't knock it in. At three o'clock all we had to do was win our remaining games and we'd win the championship.' It was the impotent wail of a man who knew his race was run.

Villa were meanwhile dispatching Forest, now a husk of the team that conquered Europe. 'I think we have the right blend,' mused Dennis Mortimer. 'The hard workers, and the people with skill. We are a team of energy. Football is not just about skill and I think we have more physical strength than Ipswich. They have played a lot more games than us.' Sure enough, a leggy Ipswich lost three of their final four games. Villa could afford to go down 2–0 at Arsenal on the last day, and still gambol across the Highbury pitch at the final whistle, in celebration of their first League title since 1909–10.

A shame for Ipswich, though at least their older fans had 1961–62 to keep them warm at night. As for the younger crowd, there was ample consolation in the Uefa Cup final, which they won 5–4 on aggregate over AZ 67 of Alkmaar. Villa were still, rather unfairly, cast in the role of roundheads to the Ipswich cavaliers, not that Saunders cared too much. 'We've ended up with 60 points and won 26 matches. If anybody knocks that, then they don't know what they're talking about. We have played some tremendous football. I've not only got tremendous players with tremendous ability, but they're also very good people. They've sweated blood and put up with me. Give the lads what they deserve. They're a little bit special.'

They were special, all right. Villa went on to win the European Cup a year later, at the expense of Bayern Munich and Karl-Heinz Rummenigge, though the money shot wouldn't feature Saunders. The boss, assuming he'd be given a pat on the back for being the only man other than George Ramsay to win a title at Villa, asked chairman Ron Bendall for a pay rise. He was brusquely denied. He flounced off to take over at Birmingham, and took a deliberately excessive amount of time to hand back the keys to his company Mercedes. A slightly unsatisfactory ending to the fairytale was exacerbated when the name of his successor, Tony Barton, was omitted in the official 1982 European Cup final match programme in favour of Roy McLaren, the club kitman. In fairness, the white shirts Villa wore on that famous Amsterdam evening were crisp, pristine and very worthy of the occasion.

19

Chas & Dave wheel out the old Joanna (1981–82 to 1986–87)

In early 1978 John Toshack, out of favour at Liverpool, attracted £80,000 bids from Norwich, Newcastle and Anderlecht. The big Welsh striker seriously toyed with the idea of moving to Belgium – 'I am definitely interested in the prospect of playing in Europe!' – but had his head turned by an offer from Fourth Division promotion hopefuls Swansea City. Their manager Harry Griffiths had very nearly got the Swans into the Third the previous season, but his attack-minded side (92 goals scored) had an Achilles heel (68 conceded) and a 4–1 home defeat to Watford on the penultimate weekend of the campaign put the kibosh on their dream. That near-miss sowed doubt in Griffiths. With a couple of months of the 1977–78 season to go, and with Swansea's latest promotion push threatening to falter, he was happy to step aside for a new man if it guaranteed fresh impetus and an increased chance of success.

Liverpool waived their fee to facilitate the move, and player-manager Toshack hit the ground running. A crowd of 15,000 – the biggest at the Vetch Field in seven years – saw him make his debut against Watford. He scored in the 44th minute to give

Swansea a two-goal lead at half-time, but the Hornets, now managed by Graham Taylor and on their way to the Fourth Division title, once again provided a sting in the tail, fighting back for a 3–3 draw. Still, Toshack soon got Swansea playing. A run of eight wins in nine games pushed them to the brink of promotion. They made it over the line, though Griffiths tragically missed the celebration, succumbing to a heart attack in the Vetch treatment room before the second-to-last game of the season against Scunthorpe. An urn containing his ashes was buried under the pitch in recognition of a lasting legacy: five members of his team would find themselves playing in the First just three years later.

Swansea introduced themselves to top-flight football in some style. A bullish Toshack insisted his Swans were 'delighted at the prospect of pitting our wits against the best teams in Britain', pointing out that he could call on six Welsh internationals, two Yugoslav caps, and one from England. 'The whole city is bubbling!' It was practically on a rolling boil when Swansea welcomed Leeds to the Vetch on the opening day of the 1981–82 campaign and trounced them 5–1, Bob Latchford scoring a nine-minute hat-trick on his debut. There were other eyebrow-bothering results that afternoon. The reigning champions Aston Villa went down at home to another newly promoted team, Notts County. Ron Atkinson lost his first match as Manchester United manager at Coventry, who were sporting shirt designs based on the letter T for Talbot cars, extrapolating the new trend of shirt sponsorship to its inevitable conclusion. Pre-season favourites Ipswich Town (Pioneer audio) could only draw at home against Sunderland. Liverpool (Hitachi electronics) lost at Wolves. Stoke City (Ricoh photocopiers) won at Arsenal (JVC tellies and hi-fi).

The likes of United, Sunderland and Wolves were commended for initially retaining the virgin purity of the front of their shirts, though profit trumps tradition and that prime real estate was sold soon enough to Sharp electronics, Cowie's vehicle hire and Tatung home computers. Romantics of the time were appalled at football's irreversible commercial creep – 'I wish they hadn't had advertising in the ground,' sighed Radio 1 disc jockey and celebrity Liverpool fan John Peel, 'I wish they'd just kept themselves above all that' – though in retrospect sponsorship has contributed to the culture, eras captured in amber by different brands and logos, fans swooning over retro shirts despite the capitalist brashness of it all.

None of the other opening-day surprises had the resonance of the Swansea–Leeds result. Leeds had been champions just eight years previously. Now, in a desperate attempt to recapture fast-fading glories, new boss and Revie-era legend Allan Clarke splashed £930,000 of his £1 million summer transfer budget on West Brom winger Peter Barnes, who repaid him by standing around doing nothing for the entire season. 'We are not asking Peter to run his blood to water,' sighed assistant manager Martin Wilkinson, 'but we do want to see him get a bit of a sweat occasionally.' Leeds made a habit of crashing on the road: a fortnight after the Swansea débâcle they went down 4–0 at Coventry; 11 days later they lost 4–0 again, this time at Manchester City. Before November was out they had shipped three at Liverpool and another four at Southampton. Relegation was inevitable. Barnes ended the season with one goal to his name. Clarke fell under the axe.

Meanwhile the Swans flew off in the other direction. At the start of October they travelled to Anfield. Bill Shankly having passed away four days previously, it was an afternoon of heightened emotion. During the minute's silence, Toshack removed his Swansea tracksuit top to reveal a Liverpool shirt. After his side earned a 2–2 draw against the reigning European champions,

Toshack received a two-minute ovation from the home supporters. 'Any doubt about who will be the next manager of Liverpool was dispelled,' opined the *Guardian*, parroting the received wisdom of the time. Toshack's stock was high, and no wonder: it wasn't long before his side went top after a win at Stoke, their seventh victory from the first ten. Potters boss Richie Barker was in awe: 'They were almost arrogant at times.'

Swansea were still in the mix come March, third in the table having beaten the likes of Manchester United, Liverpool, Arsenal and Tottenham along the way. But they tired over the closing stretch, losing five of their last six, and finished in sixth. Ipswich were best placed to take advantage, an opportunity to right the wrongs of the previous campaign. But once again they stuttered. Nearing the end of January they were top with games in hand on their nearest challengers – another difficult winter had decimated the fixture list – but a home defeat to Notts County, followed by a 4–0 mauling at Liverpool, who made hay in the absence of injured defensive pairing Russell Osman and Terry Butcher, robbed them of precious momentum.

Southampton, with Kevin Keegan still a force in the autumn of his career, took over at the top and stayed there until the end of March. But they'd played a significantly higher number of games than everyone else in the tightly packed table – three more than Ipswich, Liverpool and Manchester United, five more than Spurs – and their position was a little flattering. They won just three of their last 14 and dwindled away to finish seventh. Ipswich and Manchester United finished relatively strongly, but their efforts were all for nothing as a result of an astonishing turnaround in form by Liverpool.

Bob Paisley's side had slipped into the bottom half after a miserable Boxing Day home defeat by Manchester City, their new goalkeeper Bruce Grobbelaar infamously fumbling one into his net on national television. This seemed to mark the end of Liverpool's ascendant phase. The City defeat was their third in the League at Anfield in just over two months; they had only lost 11 home matches during the entire 1970s. Having just finished the previous season fifth, outside the top two for the first time in nine seasons, they were on course to do even worse this time. The end of empire!

But Grobbelaar's mistake turned out to represent the exact point at which Liverpool pulled out of their nosedive. On the Monday after the match, Paisley's mild-mannered right-hand man Joe Fagan delivered an uncharacteristically trenchant soliloquy in training, and the team responded to his incandescent advice. They lost just two more games all season, at one point winning ten on the bounce. Under the brand new system, which awarded three points for a win, such a run proved transformative. Liverpool finished four points clear of Ipswich, landing the title with a game to spare. The final match of the season, an irrelevant evening fixture at Middlesbrough, was contested in a half-cut fug, the players having spent all afternoon in the pub on a celebratory bender officially sanctioned by Paisley and Fagan (who were back in the hotel getting stuck into a bottle of Scotch). The game ended goalless, though Liverpool, operating at walking pace, still managed to hit the woodwork three times.

'I reckon only Brian Clough and Bob Paisley are better managers than me,' announced Toshack in the immediate wake of Swansea's brilliant sixth-place finish. But it didn't take long for perceptions to change. Paisley announced his intention to retire at the end of the following campaign; Liverpool wouldn't name his successor until it was all over. In the interim Toshack's status as new kid on the block was usurped by Graham Taylor, whose

Watford took the First Division by storm in even more spectacular fashion. They opened 1982–83 with victory over an Everton side seemingly going nowhere fast under Howard Kendall, and kept troubling opponents with a mix of lump-it-long basics and fast, intricate wingplay, a concoction that was far smarter than Taylor was usually given credit for. Watford put four past Arsenal and Southampton, five past Luton Town and Notts County, and eight past a Sunderland team featuring future Scottish and English title winners Ally McCoist and Barry Venison. The frame of the goal was also rattled on four occasions.

Watford claimed second spot behind Liverpool, who had torn away in Paisley's valedictory season to such an extent that they were able to lose five of their final six matches, cigar already on, and still finish 11 points clear of the pack. Swansea, falling apart as fast as they had got it together, financial worries a factor, were relegated along with Manchester City, whose latest addition to the canon saw them concede a late Raddy Antić goal at home to Luton on the last day, allowing the Hatters to leapfrog them to safety. Joe Fagan took over the reins at Anfield, having unknowingly passed the audition with his Boxing Day bollocking of 1981. Swansea went down again the following year, whereupon Toshack left for Sporting Lisbon, his managerial destiny lying on the Iberian Peninsula, not Merseyside, after all.

Modernity came crashing into football's comfortable world at the start of 1983–84. The Football League was to be sponsored for the first time in its history. A major Japanese camera and electronics concern coughed up £3 million for the rights to put its name to William McGregor's 95-year-old fixity of fixtures: the Canon League it was, then. Meanwhile the League's highly ambivalent relationship with television took a step closer to consummation, as a £5.2 million two-year deal with the BBC and ITV was agreed for two years' worth of live matches. The television companies had wanted to show 62 games in total; instead, they got five each per season. In turn, they conceded their opposition to shirt sponsorship, providing letters and logos were no taller than two inches. It was on!

And so 23 years and 24 days after ITV's farcical transmission of Blackpool versus Bolton, not starring Stanley Matthews, the nation's third channel gave live Football League action another whirl. Tottenham Hotspur versus Nottingham Forest was their first pick for a Sunday afternoon kick-off. Spurs, still worried that attendances would suffer, put on some extra pre-match entertainment to entice the punters to White Hart Lane. Cockney warblers Chas & Dave wheeled out the old Joanna for a couple of boogie-woogie numbers; skydivers poured from the heavens onto the pitch; the world-record holder for stilt-walking plodded around the touchline in lofty fashion. Taking advantage of the cutting-edge vibe, Spurs took the opportunity to hand out copies of a 35-page prospectus for their upcoming flotation on the London Stock Exchange, a Thatcherite wheeze designed to wipe out the debts accrued in building their new West Stand. 'They are going to be the best Bar Mitzvah present in north London this year!' one unnamed board member cheerfully oy-veyed, brazenly pandering to stereotype. Tottenham manager Keith Burkinshaw noted dryly that the match itself was 'a little item down at the bottom of the bill'.

Forest's Colin Walsh scored the first goal of this brave new world after five minutes, turning in Viv Anderson's cross from the right. Spurs did absolutely nothing until an out-of-sorts Alan Brazil was substituted for wide man Garry Brooke, who set up Gary Stevens to equalise with a diving header, then sent in a free-kick which resulted in Steve Archibald's late winner. ITV's coverage was an endearing muddle, with presenters and pundits caught between two stools, ordered to cheerfully hype the new multimillion product to the hills, to an audience of football fans for whom weary realism was a crucial part of the fun. The former Liverpool striker Ian St John, adding a splash of in-game colour by channelling the spirit of Danny Blanchflower, told it like it was: 'It's better to be here than sitting at home yelling at your TV!' The remark earned him immediate rebuke from commentator Brian Moore. 'I'm not sure you should be saying that.'

Erstwhile Spurs striker Jimmy Greaves did a better job of shilling the sport to his viewers, informing the ITV nation he was off home to watch Robert Mitchum vehicle *The Winds of War* on the same channel later that evening. 'And I already know what bloody happened in that! You never knew what was going to happen out there today.' Tottenham chairman Douglas Alexiou, clipping his vowels nervously while gripping his thigh for dear life, expressed satisfaction at the 30,000-plus crowd. His plummy but well-meaning observation that 'it was entertaining for us to listen to the crowd enjoying themselves' wouldn't have sounded out of place in one of the BBC's early broadcasts from the patrician 1930s.

Also proving that the more things change the more they stay the same were Liverpool, who under Joe Fagan finally landed a title hat-trick. They completed their third championship in a row with an unremarkable draw at Notts County. 'Maybe by our standards we didn't deserve the League this time,' shrugged captain Graeme Souness. 'But by everybody else's standards, we did.' Southampton finished second – their historical high – while Queens Park Rangers ended up fifth, Clive Allen in the goals on their excitable Omniturf plastic pitch, manager Terry Venables earning himself a ticket to Barcelona. But neither could get close enough when it mattered. Ron Atkinson's Manchester United were perhaps best positioned to challenge, but they failed to last the pace; they won just two of their last ten while Liverpool ground out the necessary. Big Ron would surely get something going soon?

Manchester United were highly fancied going into 1984–85. Liverpool might have won the three previous titles, and were the reigning European champions to boot, but midfield life-force Graeme Souness had left to earn some serious money in Italy with Sampdoria. Fagan considered bids for one-time Arsenal legend Liam Brady, now at Internazionale, and Paul McStay of Celtic, but neither fancied the move. Another deal that didn't come off concerned Ian Rush, who had rattled up a thoroughly old-fashioned tally of 47 goals the previous season. Napoli offered the best part of £5 million for the striker, but Liverpool, though sorely tempted, decided they couldn't let another major cog in the wheel fly off. His chance to pair up with Diego Maradona gone, Rush spent the pre-season in a mild funk, and went into the new campaign injured. Fagan meanwhile required a replacement captain in the wake of Souness's departure, so tossed the armband to Phil Neal. The long-serving right-back, one of those dependable seven-out-of-ten types, was picked ahead of Kenny Dalglish. The decision was made with a future coaching role in mind. Maybe management.

While Liverpool were in mild turmoil, United felt good about their chances of ending their 17-year title drought. They'd flirted with the title twice in three seasons under Big Ron; four times in the last nine if you factored in the Sexton and Docherty years. They were certainly due. Problem was, so were Everton. Few made claims for Howard Kendall's side before the start of the campaign, which was slightly strange seeing as they'd won the previous season's FA Cup against Taylor's Watford, their first trophy since the League championship of 1969–70. That was followed up by a buoyant victory over Liverpool in the Charity Shield. These successes represented a spectacular turnaround for Kendall and Everton, because the manager's job had been dangling by a thread just a few months earlier.

According to well-worn legend, Kendall had been saved from the axe in January 1984 when Adrian Heath capitalised on a poor Kevin Brock backpass to equalise in a League Cup quarter-final at third-tier Oxford United. Everton went on to win the replay and made it to the final, buying Kendall time to get things right. But captain Kevin Ratcliffe has argued that a previous League Cup tie, played a couple of months earlier, was the real pivotal moment of Kendall's reign. Everton had just been thrashed 3–0 by Liverpool in the League at Anfield, were 17th in the table, and found themselves a goal down at home in the League Cup against Coventry City. Barely 9,000 paying punters had turned up at Goodison, but they made enough noise to register extreme disgust. 'If we had lost that night I'm sure Howard would have gone,' said Ratcliffe. 'There was pressure from the board and the fans. Obscenities had been daubed on the training-ground walls.' Kendall sent on little-used midfielder Peter Reid, whose busy influence turned the game; Everton won 2–1. Within a week Kendall brought in another alumnus from the 1970 title-winning side, Colin Harvey, as his right-hand man, and signed striker Andy Gray from Wolves. The near-defeat at Oxford proved the Coventry experience hadn't erased all the problems in one fell swoop, but by the end of the season Everton had recovered to seventh in the League, winning their last three fixtures, as well as the FA Cup final in which Gray scored. Now they had the wind at their back.

Even so, Manchester United initially looked like making good on their promise during the early months of the 1984–85 season. At the tail end of October, ahead of their visit to Everton, they were tucked in behind pacesetters Arsenal, having conceded just nine goals in 11 matches. They were equally efficient in attack, and their mood was approaching giddy: after a 5–1 win over West Ham, defender Gordon McQueen joked that his busiest moment of the afternoon came when he had to 'flick the ash off my cigar', while the *Guardian* described Danish winger Jesper Olsen as 'the most exciting newcomer to Old Trafford since the early days of George Best'. Ron Atkinson suggested that nobody would put on a better display all season.

But Everton were beginning to click. The first signs came in an astonishing 5–4 win at Watford in late September. Graham Taylor, playing it for laughs at the post-match press conference, entered the room by crawling on all fours. A few weeks later, Everton crossed Stanley Park and won at Anfield, Graham Sharp sending a dipping screamer over Bruce Grobbelaar from 35 yards, the BBC's goal of the season. Liverpool were two points off the relegation zone, having won just two of their first 11. Another opposition manager was forced to genuflect. 'It was a bloody good goal,' admitted Joe Fagan, whose crestfallen response was nothing if not sporting. 'Worth winning any game. It would almost have been a shame if we had scored after that.'

And then came the visit of United, whose previously miserly defence was cut to ribbons. Kevin Sheedy scored twice in the first 23 minutes; Adrian Heath, Gary Stevens and Graham Sharp completed a 5–0 hiding that could easily have been two or three goals more. Joe Mercer, one of the stars of Everton's 1938–39 team, watched from the stand. 'I have never seen an Everton side play better,' the septuagenarian legend announced. So much for Big Ron closing the book on the season's best performance.

Everton went on one of the great title romps. After the rout of Manchester United they proved unstoppable, winning 21 of their remaining 30 games. They lost five, though three of those defeats came after the championship had been wrapped up on Easter Monday with five games still to play. Everton also secured their first European trophy in the Cup Winners' Cup, though failed to secure a treble when Atkinson's side gained a modicum of revenge in the FA Cup final.

One of the great campaigns was soured by the grimmest denouement to any season. On the final day of the League, 56 fans were killed as the main stand burned down at Bradford City, while a 14-year-old boy was crushed to death under a wall as Leeds fans rioted at Birmingham. The latter tragedy was an eerie foreshadowing of Heysel, 18 days later. Liverpool had recovered from their early slump to snatch second place in the League and reach the European Cup final, but the club and their fans ended the season in disgrace. English teams were banned from Europe indefinitely. Everton – the best team on the Continent according to Bayern Munich coach Udo Lattek, whose side had been soundly defeated in the semis of the Cup Winners' Cup – wouldn't get to compete for the European Cup. English football had reached its pitiful nadir. It desperately needed a campaign to sweeten the soul.

Attendances plummeted at the start of the 1985–86 season, partly as a reaction to the tragedies of the spring, but also because, for the first time since *Match of the Day* was launched in 1964, there was no television exposure whatsoever, either live or in highlight form. The TV blackout was the result of big-leggy posturing by the Big

Five clubs of the day. The clique was led by Tottenham Hotspur plc and an increasingly ambitious Manchester United; Arsenal, Everton and Liverpool also fancied a larger slice of the pie. At the time of the 1983 agreement which ushered in live coverage, all TV money was split equally between the 92 League clubs. A few years on and the Big Five demanded a renegotiation of terms to reflect their pulling power. They made noises about breaking away to form a Super League, and turned up their noses at the £4.5 million deal offered jointly by the BBC and ITV, operating as a duopoly in the pre-satellite era. The smaller clubs pushed back. Deadlock. And so the first six months of the season went by untelevised, before the smaller clubs caved in to the Big Five's brinksmanship. But when the League went back to the TV companies to finally accept their deal, ready for a resumption of transmission in the New Year, they found the offer had been reduced to a take-it-or-leave-it £1.5 million. The League had no choice but to accept. The big clubs had their increased share, but by the time the smaller pot was divvied out, they collected exactly the same amount of cash as the previous deal on the old terms. The humiliated Big Five went off to lick their wounds and seethe, waiting for the day someone would smash apart the BBC–ITV cosy cartel.

All of which was something of a shame for fans of Manchester United, a club who finally looked to have found the answers. They thrashed Aston Villa 4–0 on the opening day, then won the next nine games as well, scoring three against Nottingham Forest, Newcastle, Oxford and Manchester City, five at West Brom, and enough to win at Arsenal. They were nine points clear of Liverpool and 13 ahead of champions Everton. It all looked very promising: they were even managing to get a tune out of Peter Barnes, the former Leeds winger having joined from Coventry in the summer. But it couldn't last: United failed to match Tottenham's record opening streak of 1960–61, drawing game number 11 at Luton. After stretching their unbeaten run to 15 matches, they went down at Sheffield Wednesday then lost nine of the remaining 26. Recurring hamstring and shoulder injuries to midfield hero Bryan Robson cost them dear. They eventually trailed home in fourth; only the miserable second portion of their season had been available to view on TV.

The TV blackout also robbed the nation of their chance to witness West Ham's rip-roaring start to the season. Frank McAvennie had joined from St Mirren in the summer, and the young playboy wasted little time in gorging on defences with the sort of relish he would later reserve for champagne, page-three models and jazz salt. He topped the early goalscoring charts, with his partner Tony Cottee not far behind, and earned himself an invite onto the BBC's *Wogan* chatshow, so viewers could at least put a face to the name. West Ham stayed in the title race to the bitter end.

Everton had added Leicester striker Gary Lineker to their already high-functioning side. When they worked over Liverpool at Anfield in late February to go three points clear of crumbling Manchester United with a game in hand, they looked a shoo-in to retain their title. They didn't do much wrong from there on in, but Liverpool's response to defeat was little short of exceptional. Ian Rush scored a last-minute equaliser on an ice rink at Spurs the following week, sparking a previously spluttering campaign to life. Kenny Dalglish – chosen to take over as manager from a distraught Joe Fagan in the wake of Heysel (ahead of a miffed Phil Neal) – put himself back in the team. They won ten of their final 11 games, drawing the other. After Everton surprisingly went down 1–0 at Oxford in their third-last game the door swung open for Liverpool. Dalglish bolted through it, chesting down and steering home the only goal at Chelsea to secure the title. Everton

– despite Lineker's seasonal tally of 30 – had to make do with second. West Ham finished third, their historical high-water mark. Liverpool also denied Everton the FA Cup, turning around a half-time deficit in the final – a microcosm of a campaign that gave English football a restorative shot in the arm.

The 1986–87 race wasn't one of the most memorable, though the scene was certainly livened up by the sprightly introduction of Wimbledon, who had been playing in the Southern League only nine years previously. The Dons made their top-flight debut at Manchester City, where Andy Thorn scored their first top-flight goal, a curling fluke of a free-kick from out by the touchline. Within ten minutes, the Dons were 3–1 down. After the loss, a 'skinny Moss Side adolescent' made off with one of their kitbags. 'It's still better than playing at Rochdale,' ho-hummed manager Dave Bassett.

Wimbledon responded by beating Aston Villa – European champions just five years earlier – at Plough Lane, then knocking over Leicester and Charlton. 'My mum will want this season to finish tomorrow,' chirped Bassett, looking at a table with his team on top and Manchester United at the very bottom. 'I'm not saying this is two fingers to Ted Croker,' he added, referencing the high-handed FA secretary who had questioned whether a small club like Wimbledon should have been admitted into the First Division at all, 'but we have shown that football does need clubs like us.' Wimbledon ended the season in sixth, and knocked aristocratic Everton out of the FA Cup to boot.

That Cup defeat was the only significant low point of Everton's season. They had lost Lineker to Barcelona in the summer, a legacy of his Golden Boot-winning exploits at the Mexico World Cup. But they walked the title anyway, this time by spreading the goals around, Kevin Sheedy top-scoring with 13 from midfield. They hoped to effectively seal the title at Anfield in April: a win over the old enemy would have taken them nine points and at least 16 goals clear of Liverpool, who had just three other matches left. But Ian Rush scored twice to equal Dixie Dean's record of 19 goals in Merseyside derbies, and Dalglish's side won 3–1 to at least delay the inevitable, thus denying Everton the chance to celebrate a first title at Anfield since their days as tenants in 1890–91.

The visitors still had something to take away. After arrowing a free-kick into the top left, Sheedy ran about flicking Vs at the Kop. A very memorable celebration was met with an eruption of laughter rather than anger. 'Despite crossing the great Mersey divide I'd always got on well with the Liverpool fans,' explained Sheedy years later. 'They were always fine with me. I think they recognised me as a good player and respected me for that. I can honestly say now, though, that it was just a spur of the moment reaction and I wasn't being disrespectful. To this day, I still don't know what made me do it. It wasn't something I planned and it wasn't meant to cause offence because there was also a fair number of Evertonians on the Kop that day!' Sheedy was given a rap over the knuckles by the authorities, but otherwise it was quickly forgiven and forgotten. Different times.

Everton wrapped it up nine days later at Norwich, Pat van den Hauwe bashing in the decisive goal from close range after 45 seconds. But success sowed seeds of downfall. The club had managed to fend off Barcelona's interest in Howard Kendall the previous summer; now, with another title on his CV, the manager was an even hotter property. He craved a crack at Europe, and left when Athletic Bilbao came calling. The chance to build a new empire, taking advantage of an unprecedented period of success at Goodison, went with him. Someone else would have to take up the job of knocking Liverpool off their perch. Anyone interested?

20

Howard tucks into his Sunday roast (1987–88 to 1991–92)

♫ Happy birthday, dear Football Lee-ee-eague . . . happy birthday to you! ♫ But when the birthday boy starts drinking way too early, you know the party is destined to fall flat long before the end. William McGregor's fixity of fixtures was due to turn a hundred in 1988, but the first bottle of bubbly was cracked open in August 1987 when the centenary celebrations officially got underway with a match between a Football League XI and a team representing the Rest of the World, at Wembley. Whether the game would be worth attending or not hinged on the availability of Argentina genius Diego Maradona, who had been offered £100,000 to strut his stuff but was reportedly overweight and unfit after a pleasant summer holiday. He was so out of condition that, upon returning to his club Napoli for pre-season prep, he had only been allowed to sit and watch his teammates train. A plan counterintuitive to whipping him back into shape, but that's what they went with.

Maradona eventually did roll up, and 61,000 paying punters took the opportunity to come along and verbally abuse the great man, the Hand of God goal at the 1986 World Cup still a raw memory. Maradona responded by holding the ball high in the air with the very same paw that caused all the fuss in Mexico, then not giving the crowd very much bang for their buck. He played a couple of cute lay-offs, but otherwise did very little to justify his fee. He went back to his hotel and ran up a £2,000 phone bill before heading back to Italy on a private jet laid on by the Football League. The Rest of the World side, also starring Gary Lineker, Josimar, Michel Platini and, er, Glenn Hysén, looked the hastily constructed rabble they were. Bryan Robson scored twice and Norman Whiteside once on a good day for the Football League XI and Manchester United. Brian Clough later faced an FA disciplinary charge for suggesting that League goalkeeper Peter Shilton, the injured party in the Hand of God psychodrama, should take the opportunity to punch Maradona in the face.

The Football League's actual hundredth birthday fell the following spring, on 17 April, the date the 12 original members passed their famous resolution in the Royal Hotel in Manchester. Normal fixtures were suspended for the weekend, and a Centenary Festival was held at Wembley. A knockout competition saw sixteen teams from all four divisions playing 40-minute matches. Liverpool, on the brink of the title and with the FA Cup final to look forward to, sent a reserve squad. Brian Clough didn't bother turning up with his Nottingham Forest team. But Forest did go on to win the trophy, albeit in less than memorable style, beating Sheffield Wednesday 3–2 on penalties in the final after a 0–0 draw. A celebratory concert starring blues crooner Elkie Brooks and baroque synth shredder Rick Wakeman could only half fill the Albert Hall. A game between Everton and Rangers, the respective champions of England and Scotland, was nixed by the police, who simply couldn't be bothered with any potential hassle.

Celebration fatigue was setting in. Come autumn 1988 it was time for the Centenary Trophy, games timed with rough reference to the very first fixtures a hundred years previously. Those original matches had been played on 8 September; the final of the Centenary Trophy, held symbolically at Villa Park, Old Mac's stately pile, was fixed for 9 October. (Near enough, huh?) Arsenal beat Manchester United 2–1, the game and result utterly unmemorable save for marauding midfielder Michael Thomas romping clear to score the winner. As portents go, it was the sort that only comes around every hundred years or so.

The Centenary Festival got in the way of a title procession worthy of the League's big birthday. In the summer of 1987, two years after nearly losing Ian Rush to Napoli, Liverpool saw the focal point of their attack leave for Juventus. Kenny Dalglish responded with one of the most effective high-profile transfer rebuilds in history, signing Watford and England winger John Barnes for £900,000 and paying a British-record £1.9 million to Newcastle for Peter Beardsley. The pair would bounce off striker John Aldridge, local lad and mustachioed Rush lookalike who had been an integral part of Oxford's mid-eighties rise from the Third Division to the First, and to 1986 League Cup glory. Within nine minutes of their first match together at Liverpool, the three combined for Aldridge's opening goal of the season at Arsenal, a game eventually won by full-back Steve Nicol's absurd long-range header from outside the area. Dalglish's new-look side were up and running with indecent speed.

Even so, they weren't able to take control of the 1987–88 race until December. A collapsed sewer under the Kop at Anfield led to the postponement of a couple of early home matches. Just how intensely contractors worked to get the stadium fit for purpose in time is a moot point: the BBC's *Football Focus* transmitted pictures of a works project consisting of a couple of blokes in hard hats casually throwing about a plank of wood, while an engineer surveyed the scene while drawing hard on a fag. And so Liverpool were forced to play catch-up first with early surprise leaders Queens Park Rangers, then an Arsenal side beginning to work things out under their 1971 Double-winning hero George Graham.

Liverpool stuck four past QPR when they arrived at Anfield, John Barnes hipshaking his way down the middle of the park for two solo efforts that stood as mini-manifestos. This more attractive Liverpool was a different proposition from the clinically relentless Paisley sides of the late seventies and early eighties. When Arsenal came to town in early January Liverpool scored two outrageous goals to showcase their new individualism. The first move began when Steve McMahon retrieved a ball that looked like disappearing into the stand, trapping it on the line, bouncing back off an advertising hoarding, skipping past two desperate challenges and taking out three other men with one pass to Beardsley, whose shot-cum-cross was turned in at the far post by Aldridge. Then in the second half Beardsley went on an elaborate slalom down the inside-right channel before chipping gently into the net.

'I never thought I'd see an English team playing like this,' said former France and Juventus star Michel Platini, watching in the stand in his new role as Uefa executive. 'It was a continental performance. Beardsley's goal could have been scored by a top French or Italian player.' At a time when Serie A was in its pomp, and the reigning Football League champions Everton had just been stuffed 6–1 in a friendly by the Real Madrid of Emilio Butragueño and Hugo Sánchez, this was high praise. As was Sir Tom Finney's expert review of a late-season 5–0 takedown of Nottingham Forest: 'That's one of the finest exhibitions of football I've ever seen in my life. It'll never be bettered, I don't think.'

Barnes, Beardsley and Aldridge won the bulk of the plaudits as Liverpool eventually won the League at a canter, losing just two games all season. But special praise should be reserved for Steve Nicol, who set the tone early in the season with performances that demonstrated how Dalglish's new Liverpool were capable of coming at teams from all angles. As well as his long-range headed winner at Arsenal, he scored twice from the left-back position in a 4–1 win at Coventry, then hit a hat-trick from right-back in another 4–1 victory, this time at Newcastle. That latter game should be seen as the signature performance of this side. The famous felling of Forest came when the League was practically done and dusted; the Newcastle rout was a clear announcement of something special unfolding, live on a Sunday lunchtime. As if to further emphasise the dawn of a new era, Ian Rush made his debut for Juventus on the same afternoon. Juve lost 1–0 at Empoli, Rush touching the ball a mere 17 times. Liverpool eventually missed out on the Double after a rare collective misfire in the FA Cup final against Wimbledon, but the prevailing wisdom suggested that, over the long haul of a League season, it would take something out of the ordinary to stop them retaining their title next time round.

For a little while it seemed as though Norwich City might have that special something. The Canaries had never been part of a title race before, but Dave Stringer's side, with Mike Phelan and Andy Townsend sturdy in midfield and Robert Fleck busy up front, won their first four matches of 1988–89 and defied general expectation by stubbornly refusing to collapse back into the pack. Phelan and Townsend secured a 2–1 win with fine goals at Manchester United; Phelan dropped into the back four at Liverpool, soaking up the pressure as Townsend smashed and grabbed a 1–0 victory over the champions. Norwich led the League at Christmas, deep enough into the season for comparisons to be drawn with the similarly unheralded Ipswich side of 1961–62.

But Alf Ramsey's title winners benefited from big boys Burnley and Tottenham stumbling along the home stretch. Norwich were up against Arsenal and Liverpool, and both locked into a metronomic groove around the New Year. Arsenal had started the season brilliantly with a 5–1 win at Wimbledon, Alan Smith scoring a hat-trick, Brian Marwood excelling on the wing, George Graham's team earning plaudits as the most attacking Gunners since the Double days of Bertie Mee. (The club had served up some turgid fare in the interim under Terry Neill and Don Howe. Had they followed through with their 1976 plan to install Real Madrid coach Miljan Miljanić as Mee's successor, or succeeded in enticing Brian Clough from Nottingham Forest the same summer, history might have taken a drastically different course. But here they were. Arsenal fans would have to wait a while longer for an enigmatic foreign coach to implement some exotic new ideas.)

Arsenal stayed on Norwich's shoulder, then turned on the jets over Christmas. A five-game winning streak, including impressive victories over Manchester United, Aston Villa, Tottenham and Everton, sent them top. The reigning champs Liverpool meanwhile had started the season in a lukewarm manner few had predicted, despite the popular re-signing of Ian Rush. The returning hero was, by turns, ill, injured and out of form, and by the end of the calendar year Liverpool had scored just 22 goals in 18 games. John Barnes made it 23 at Old Trafford on New Year's Day, but Manchester United youngster Russell Beardsmore responded by scoring one and setting up two more in a frenetic six-minute burst of illusory, career-defining activity. Liverpool were nine points behind leaders Arsenal, who had played one game fewer while scoring 17 more goals.

At this point the influential Danish international Jan Molby returned to the Liverpool team, having recently spent a spell in the jug after a drink-driving bender. Though injury would rule him out again soon enough, he stayed long enough to coax Liverpool out of their staid, pragmatic trance and back into a mood of exhilarating creativity. Barnes, Aldridge and Beardsley were soon in their pomp once more, as the team won 11 of their next 13 games. The final victory in that sequence, at Millwall in early April, edged them back to the top on goal difference. With all the momentum behind them, and both Arsenal and Norwich suddenly shipping points, a content Liverpool support began dreaming of another joyous title celebration.

In its place came a nightmare on a scale almost beyond comprehension. On the afternoon of 15 April 1989, with both Liverpool and Norwich on FA Cup semi-final business, Arsenal beat Newcastle 1–0 at Highbury thanks to a borderline-offside Brian Marwood goal. Arsenal were three points clear again. But the mood in the Arsenal dressing room – normally bouncing after a crucial victory – reflected tragic events elsewhere. 'Everyone's stunned, people were sitting in the bath saying nothing, it completely overshadows the joy of being top of the League,' reported striker Niall Quinn. Numb and anxious, he quickly made his way home to make phone calls about friends who had attended the ill-fated cup semi-final between Liverpool and Nottingham Forest. The Hillsborough disaster claimed 96 lives, the tragic result of gross negligence by the authorities. Nothing, it seemed, had been learned from the Burnden Park disaster all those years ago.

The rest of the season was played out in a state of hazy emotion, and produced a denouement to match. Arsenal stuck five past

Norwich, only to pick up one point from two home matches against Derby and Wimbledon. Liverpool, after picking themselves up again with a goalless draw at Everton, won four in a row to reclaim pole position. Their penultimate fixture was a 5–1 win over relegation-bound West Ham in which they scored three times in the last ten minutes. The late goal rush was crucial: Arsenal were coming to Anfield for the final match of the season, rearranged in the wake of Hillsborough, and would now need to win by two clear goals if they were to pip the hosts on goal difference. West Ham's Mark Ward summed up what most people were thinking: 'They haven't got a chance.'

But Liverpool were playing their eighth match in 23 days, a sequence that had included extra-time in a draining FA Cup final victory over Everton. They had also been dealing with the unbearable aftermath of Hillsborough. The team reverted to the defensive tactics of earlier in the campaign. Arsenal, given permission to play on the front foot, took the lead on 52 minutes, Alan Smith scoring his 23rd of the season. Liverpool dug in, and nearly did enough to see the job through. But as the game moved into injury time John Barnes lost the ball near the corner flag, Arsenal keeper John Lukic threw to Lee Dixon, the ball was desperately shuttled upfield to Smith, who slipped it forward for Michael Thomas. It was the Centenary Trophy writ large: Thomas clear on goal, silverware in his sights. He gently scooped it over the advancing Bruce Grobbelaar, and the most astonishing conclusion to a Football League season in a century was complete.

'At the end of the day, Arsenal deserved it,' said Dalglish, putting everything into perspective. The Kop, heartbroken and weary, were equally magnanimous, staying on to applaud their victors and the new champions. It was the ovation they had given 20 years previously to Leeds United, replayed for a new generation.

Aston Villa had managed to get themselves relegated in 1987. Their manager Billy McNeill was instantly given the boot, to be replaced by Graham Taylor of Watford. It hadn't been a good year for McNeill. He'd travelled south after winning three titles with Celtic to take over at Manchester City, where he won promotion in 1985. But City struggled back in the First, and he left them for Villa early in the 1986–87 season. A run of only three wins in 27 matches sealed his and Villa's fate. City went down that season as well, McNeill suffering an unwanted double whammy, destined forever to be a pub-quiz staple. If that wasn't enough, while at City he was refused permission to manage the Republic of Ireland on a part-time basis, then overlooked for the Scotland job in favour of Andy Roxburgh, despite the SFA having tipped him 'a series of nudges and winks'. Another Scottish title back at Celtic, in their 1988 centenary season, salved the Lisbon Lion's wounded pride.

Villa had been champions of Europe just five years previously; theirs was a decline even more precipitous than Manchester United's six-year fall from European Cup grace to the Second Division in 1974. But like United before them, Villa bounced back to the First Division at the first attempt. They only stayed up in 1988–89 by the skin of their teeth, though, and didn't start 1989–90 particularly well either. After one win in their first seven games they were two points off the bottom, the vultures gently swirling around Taylor's noggin. But Villa's squad was better than that: a couple of heroes of 1982 in Gordon Cowans and Nigel Spink; former Everton title winner Derek Mountfield; the balletic Manchester United reject Paul McGrath; and England Under-21 stars David Platt, Ian Olney and Tony Daley. Ian Ormondroyd, tall and ungainly on the wing, yet strangely effective, added a little cult appeal.

They responded to their plight by winning five on the bounce, the final match in that sequence a spectacular 6–2 rout of Everton, who with two championships still fresh in the memory, had yet to lose their cachet as contenders. Platt in particular was outstanding, an irrepressible whirl of nature announcing himself live on ITV. Completely unknown at the time, he'd end the season as one of England's semi-final heroes at Italia '90. Villa doubled down on their promise over the Christmas holidays with two big wins at Villa Park: a 3–0 victory over highly inconsistent Manchester United – whose manager Alex Ferguson still hadn't got it going since taking over from Ron Atkinson in late 1986, and was beginning to feel a little bit of pressure – and a 2–1 win against an Arsenal side making an unconvincing fist of retaining their title ever since losing 4–1 on the opening day at Old Trafford.

Villa reached the top in late February: a 2–0 win at Spurs was their 15th in 18 games, a storming run. But looking down from the top made them awfully dizzy. Wimbledon came to Villa Park and turned them over 3–0, and nothing was quite the same again. Their 20-year-old striker Ian Olney had lost a little form since a fine first half of the season, so Taylor spent a club record £1.5 million on big Tony Cascarino from Millwall. (The south Londoners were caught in something of a downward spiral. Having just finished their maiden First Division campaign in tenth spot, they started their second by reaching the top after four games with a draw at Wimbledon, the highlight of a poor match being a shot during the warm-up which knocked a policeman's helmet clean off his startled head. Millwall consolidated their position with a 4–1 thrashing of Coventry, whose diminutive striker David Speedie was forced to take over in goal from injured regular Steve Ogrizovic. But Manchester United hammered them 5–1 the following week, they won only two more games all season, and were relegated in last place, 17 points adrift of safety.)

'With someone like Tony Daley on the wing and crossing the ball for me, I can't really go wrong!' simpered Big Cas as he put pen to paper. On his first appearance for his new club, at Derby, he forced Peter Shilton into an ersatz restaging of the famous Gordon Banks save from Pelé. But that was as good as it got during his first eight games. Cascarino, by his own admission, got 'lazy and complacent' in the wake of his breakthrough transfer, although in fairness to the striker, Cowans and Platt had lost a little of their earlier creative edge, and weren't exactly showering him with chances.

By the time Cascarino finally scored for Villa, in a 3–3 home draw against Norwich at the end of April, it was way too late. Liverpool had made a late-season signing of their own in Ronny Rosenthal, who scored a perfect hat-trick on his full debut at Charlton: left foot, right foot, head. He scored four more during the run-in as Liverpool hit the front and tore off into the distance. On the afternoon Cascarino billowed the net, Liverpool were sealing their 18th title with a garden-variety 2–1 home win over QPR. Hardly as dramatic as the previous season's Anfield title decider, Kenny Dalglish felt the need to explain that his side won the League 'because we have been the best team this season, and not because Norwich held Aston Villa to a draw'. Few begrudged Liverpool a little succour after all their suffering.

Arsenal came straight back at Liverpool in 1990–91. What else did anyone expect from such an entertainingly bellicose bunch? In November 1989, on the day David O'Leary broke their all-time appearance record, they became embroiled in a glorious hoedown with Norwich at Highbury. Lee Dixon's injury-time goal, scored on the rebound from a ludicrously generous penalty, sealed a 4–3 comeback win for the hosts and sparked a 19-man free-for-all. The old-school television pundits Ian St John and Jimmy Greaves tried to play it down on their ITV show. 'It's been dubbed a brawl, but there's been less scuffles in the January sales,' observed the sideways-glancing Saint, while Greavsie dryly noted that 'they were all having a pint in the bar afterwards, and that should be the end of it'.

It probably would have been. But eleven months later, Arsenal were throwing hands again, this time in the middle of a 21-man brouhaha at Manchester United. The teams had recent history. In 1987, Arsenal midfielder David Rocastle walked at Old Trafford for a retaliatory lunge on Norman Whiteside which had emptied both dugouts in one fell swoop. A year later, United striker Brian McClair missed a late penalty at Highbury that would have forced an FA Cup fifth-round replay, and was theatrically mocked by Nigel Winterburn, who pursued his man all the way back to the halfway line. But this one, coming hot on the heels of the Norwich affair, was the biggest of the lot. Winterburn was involved again, sliding in on his old friend McClair. The collective fuse lit, Paul Ince dispatched Anders Limpar, who had been brawling with Denis Irwin, into the advertising boards. McClair put Tony Adams on his ass. There were no red cards, though, in a landmark decision, the League docked Arsenal two points for their trouble, United just the one.

Arsenal suffered a second blow when captain Adams was packed off to the slammer for a drink-driving offence. It appeared Liverpool were on course to retain their title. But it soon became apparent that Kenny Dalglish had been running on empty since Hillsborough. Emotionally spent, he resigned one February morning after a see-saw fourth-round FA Cup replay at Everton ended 4–4. Ron Yeats, Bill Shankly's captain from the 1960s, swept Dalglish away from the press conference for a game of golf. Graeme Souness arrived from Rangers to take control, but the shock of Dalglish's departure had knocked Liverpool out of their stride, and they couldn't keep up with a relentless Arsenal over the final furlongs.

On the May Day bank holiday, Souness's side were totally outplayed at Nottingham Forest, Ian Woan scoring a pearler to send the title back to Highbury. Arsenal celebrated that evening by beating their old sparring partners Manchester United 3–1, then trounced Coventry 6–1 on the last day of the season to become the first champions in 102 years to go through an entire full-length campaign with just one defeat. Preston's Invincibles had gone through the card unbeaten in 1888–89, of course, but they'd played 16 fewer matches. Another 13 years on, Arsenal would go one better in the 38-game Premier League, becoming the greatest Invincibles of all. But for now, this was unprecedented supremacy.

A Super League had been mooted for quite some time, ever since ITV arrived on the scene in the mid-1950s and started dangling large wads of cash in front of the era's Big Five: Manchester United, Newcastle, Wolves, Arsenal and Spurs. The lifting of the maximum wage in 1961 threatened to accelerate the process: the transfer of Tony Kay to Everton a year later caught the *Mirror*'s chief football writer Frank McGhee in rhapsodic mood: 'My belief is that the Kay deal – and incidentally the signing of Jimmy Greaves by Spurs, Denis Law by Manchester United, and George Eastham by Arsenal – is an indication that the day of the Super League is nearer. The day when all the top talent in the country is concentrated in, perhaps, a dozen clubs. And it will be a great thing for English football.'

The majority resisted the self-serving wishes of the elite until satellite television arrived in the mid-1980s, offering an alternative to the BBC and ITV duopoly. The new kid on the block didn't have enough reach to influence the 1986 TV talks, at which the Big Five – now starring Everton and Liverpool – were comically humiliated. But ITV sensed something on the breeze, and stumped up £44 million for four years of exclusive rights in 1988, their immediate reward *The Michael Thomas Show*. Now, with the rights up for grabs again in 1992, and satellite channels firmly established in the UK, the elite clubs had a lot more leverage. They promised the smaller clubs in the First Division a slice of a much more substantial pie, and gained the backing of the FA, who sensed checkmate in their century-old power struggle with the Football League. The 22 First Division clubs resigned en masse to set up the FA Premier League, which would begin in August 1992. Promotion and relegation between the new competition and the remaining three divisions of the Football League would still occur; the only real difference in the set-up was that the Premier League clubs no longer had to share their TV booty with the lower orders. Sky offered £304 million for five years, knocking ITV's offer of £200 million into a cocked Amstrad dish. So the 1991–92 edition of the Football League would be the last to determine the champions of England. The famous old competition deserved nothing less than a spectacular send-off, and the last hurrah didn't disappoint.

Arsenal went into the 93rd and final campaign as favourites, though that status didn't last too long. On the opening day they welcomed QPR to Highbury. On 15 minutes, new Rangers signing Dennis Bailey met a corner from the right on the volley, guiding a cute shot into the top left. The previous season Bailey had struggled to hold down a place at Third Division Bristol Rovers.

Paul Merson equalised late to salvage a draw, but Everton turned Arsenal over 3–1 at Goodison in midweek, and Aston Villa repeated the scoreline at Villa Park the following Saturday. The season was eight days old: Arsenal had already lost twice and shipped seven goals. An unfavourable comparison to the previous season, in which they were defeated just once and took four months to concede seven, was unavoidable. The pressure of being the first English team back in the European Cup since the Heysel ban also took its toll. Benfica came to Highbury in the second round and dismissed the Gunners with contemptuous ease, sparking a slump in which George Graham's side won just two League games out of 12 and were knocked out of the FA Cup by Fourth Division Wrexham, a seismic shock in an era when these things really mattered.

Liverpool started out as second favourites, expected to rebound strongly from adversity, as they always did during the sixties, seventies and eighties. But it was over. During their last title-winning season they had stuck nine past Crystal Palace at Anfield. Now they went down 2–1 in the same fixture. Ian Rush, Steve McMahon and Jan Molby were getting old, John Barnes was injured and out of condition, Peter Beardsley had been inexplicably sold to Everton. Graeme Souness's new-look side, with the basic £2.9 million Dean Saunders up front, languished in mid-table. The *Guardian* referred to them, with a straight face, as 'relegation candidates'. The aura had vanished in a flash. They ended up in sixth spot, their lowest finish since 1965.

Manchester United, by contrast, were on a clear upward curve. Alex Ferguson had kept hold of his job despite their harsh winter of 1989, subsequently delivering the FA Cup and European Cup Winners' Cup. The general consensus was that United might have to wait another season to scratch their 25-year title itch. But

Ferguson's side flew out of the traps, winning eight and drawing two of their first ten games. 'We've all grown up after winning the Cup Winners' Cup,' said the manager after a 2–1 win at Spurs sent his side six points clear at the top before September was out. 'We haven't been carried away by it, and are still hungry to achieve things.' Typifying this desire, 34-year-old Bryan Robson retained the enthusiasm and drive of a teenager. Andrei Kanchelskis and Ryan Giggs were causing all manner of speedy havoc on the wings. The arrival of Peter Schmeichel in goal and Paul Parker at right-back shored up a defence that conceded just three goals during that ten-game run. A first League title since 1967 was suddenly a realistic prospect.

Unfortunately for United, Leeds were resurgent, too. The playing legends of the Revie era hadn't passed muster as managers: Allan Clarke led them to relegation in 1982, after which Eddie Gray and Billy Bremner spent the remainder of the decade flailing around in the Second. Sheffield Wednesday boss Howard Wilkinson arrived in 1988 and pointedly made a break with the past, taking down all the photographs of the glory years. He added silk and steel to the midfield in Gordon Strachan and Vinnie Jones, and got the club back up in his first full season. Jones was immediately offloaded, his purpose served, and replaced by the more refined Gary McAllister. With Gary Speed and David Batty coming through the youth team, Leeds suddenly had quite an engine room. They finished fourth in their first season back, then signed Southampton striker Rod Wallace for a club-record £1.6 million. Could they go even higher? The pundits predicted a near miss.

Leeds didn't get off to quite as spectacular a start as Manchester United – four wins and five draws – but consistency soon turned into something a little more persuasive. A run of seven wins in eight games took them to the top. A 4–1 victory at Aston Villa – Wallace and his strike partner Lee Chapman both in the goals, Strachan and McAllister imperious – was the first sign that a serious challenge might be on. By the turn of the year both Uniteds had lost just one game each and were clear of the pack: the title race would be a two-hander. Manchester United held a two-point and two-game advantage over Leeds; any glasses of Scottish wine raised at Hogmanay to celebrate Alex Ferguson's 50th birthday would have had a particularly satisfying kick.

But Manchester United suffered one hell of a hangover the day after. Live on New Year's Day television, they stumbled around at Old Trafford like festive revellers. Queens Park Rangers went two goals up within five minutes. Andy Sinton was given time to score the opener despite the presence of *seven* sleepy United players in the box. Dennis Bailey, tormenter of Arsenal on the opening day, completed a hat-trick in a scarcely believable 4–1 win. Rangers manager Gerry Francis sent for six bottles of champagne to be delivered to the away dressing room. Leeds meanwhile won at West Ham and regained top spot.

Given that United's normally impregnable defence had also conceded three at Oldham on Boxing Day, albeit on an afternoon when they themselves had scored six, Ferguson was surprisingly philosophical in the wake of the Rangers rout. 'Perhaps it has come at an appropriate time to remind us that we have got where we are through hard work, and if we desert that route it could end up in embarrassment. Hopefully this is a one-off and they have got it out of their systems.' The back line did manage to get their act together again, but somewhere along the line precious belief was misplaced.

Leeds made a big statement in mid-January at Sheffield Wednesday, routing a side destined to finish third 6–1, and doing it without the injured Strachan and suspended Batty. But a couple of heavy away defeats – 4–1 at QPR and 4–0 at Manchester City – threatened to jigger their charge as they entered the business end of the campaign. Manchester United won their first-ever League Cup in early April against Nottingham Forest, and as they embarked on their lap of honour around Wembley to celebrate, Ferguson observed that his team 'can go and enjoy the last six games'. The logic was sound: they were a point behind Leeds, but still had two games in hand.

But they didn't enjoy their last six games at all. A nervous one-goal win over Southampton was followed by a disappointing draw at Luton, Gary Pallister's error throwing away the lead and a couple of points. Then, on Easter Monday, Nottingham Forest came to Old Trafford, future legends Roy Keane and Teddy Sheringham combining to set up erstwhile street footballer Scot Gemmill for the winner. 'The chips are down now,' admitted a downbeat Ferguson. 'We've got ourselves into a ridiculous position, considering the way we have played this season. Now we must win our remaining games.' That was easier said than done, given they'd won just five of the previous 16. They were also dealing with a schedule of five games in ten days. Soon after, they lost at West Ham, and opportunity knocked for Leeds.

Wilkinson's team had recovered from the capitulation at Manchester City by beating Chelsea 3–0 at Elland Road. A close game was turned into a rout by new signing Eric Cantona, who trotted on with six minutes to go, set up one for Chapman then juggled the ball awhile before lashing a volley home. Cantona's arrival gave Leeds fresh impetus, a plan B, and the confidence to close out the season. As Manchester United were losing at home to Forest, Leeds saw off Coventry. A week later Leeds won 3–2 at Sheffield United, a manic match settled in absurd style when Brian Gayle, under pressure from the lurking Cantona, sliced the ball into the air with his knee then headed into his own net. United lost 2–0 at Anfield later in the afternoon, and Leeds were champions.

Wilkinson had refused to watch the Liverpool–United match, transmitted live on ITV, instead opting for a quiet Sunday roast with his wife. Upon being informed of the result, his response was typically deadpan: 'When I went into management I had two dreams: to win a title and a Cup in Europe. But I felt it was a bit like a politician saying he wanted to be prime minister.' Ferguson relayed his congratulations, then admitted that 'it's a terribly disappointing end. But it's not been that bad a season. We have won the League Cup and we've had thousands of people coming through the turnstiles to enjoy it.'

His side's last game of the season, a meaningless 3–1 win at Old Trafford over Tottenham, was 'more carnival than wake' according to the *Observer*, 'almost as if it were an act of defiance by Manchester United and their supporters.' There was an unspoken fear, nonetheless: having come so close to ending their 25-year drought, only to implode spectacularly, was the club fated to never again win the English championship? Perhaps the upcoming Premier League era would herald a change of fortune. It promised to be a 'whole new ball game', after all.

And so, for the very last time, the new champions of England raised the Football League Championship Trophy as evidence of their great achievement. Leeds paraded it around Elland Road, ahead of a valedictory win over Norwich, then took it on an open-topped bus tour of the city. Over 200,000 people lined the streets to catch a glimpse of the precious old pot. It was Leeds' third title. They moved up one place on the all-time roll of honour, ahead of Preston North End who, with a little help from Old Mac 104 years earlier, had started the whole thing off.

Afterword

Fifth. Fourth. Eighth. Sixteenth. Fifteenth. Eighth. Eleventh. Seventeenth. Nineteenth. Eleventh. Eighth. Whichever way you slice it, Newcastle United's First Division record during the 1950s wasn't up to much. Yet they unquestionably remain one of the defining teams of that particular decade. Three FA Cup wins, you see. The goalscoring antics of Wor Jackie Milburn, Toon's quintessential number nine, and his exotic sidekick George Robledo still loom large in a way those of, say, Norman Deeley of Wolverhampton Wanderers or Portsmouth's Peter Harris simply do not. And those two lads scooped five League titles between them.

The Cup was the glamour prize, history mapped out by its landmark moments: Billy the off-white charger keeping 200,000 men at bay; Bert Trautmann breaking his neck but playing on; Jim Montgomery making that wondrous double save from Trevor Cherry and Peter Lorimer; Keith Houchen hovering at full stretch to head home. Everyone knows Stanley Matthews finally won a medal one heady afternoon in early May 1953; fewer folk recall how Joe Mercer beat Tom Finney to the League title by 0.099 of a goal just 19 hours earlier.

We've travelled through all this time, only to come slap-bang face-to-face with an inconvenient but elephantine truth: for great swathes of our 104-year journey, the Football League was not considered the most prestigious competition in English football.

The winners of a random six-game knock-out beano were, more often than not, greater revered than the folk who emerged battered, bruised but victorious from the 42-game long haul.

Received wisdom has long insisted we view most of the First Division years through this prism, and weight its importance accordingly. It's just how things were, up until the sixties certainly, maybe the seventies, possibly even the late eighties, Coventry, Wimbledon and all that.

But time will surely be kind to our old friend. Re-evaluations will be made. In the modern age, generations brought up to view the Cup as a sideshow may soon begin to wonder what on earth everyone was thinking. And, at some point, they're going to start redressing the balance. After all, while Billy the horse certainly deserved a sugar-cube treat after his big shift at Wembley, and the whole day made for some mighty fine photos, the truly notable achievements of the twenties were surely Huddersfield's title hat-trick and Dixie's 60-goal season. Bolton's workmanlike win over an average West Ham, once Billy had got round to clearing the pitch? It no longer passes muster.

Similarly, the 1930s weren't shaped by the FA Cups won by West Brom, Preston and Portsmouth, but all-conquering Arsenal and their five League championships. The glory of Tottenham Hotspur's world-famous 1960–61 Double can be found in each and every one of the 115 League goals they scored that season, not in the woefully flat Cup-final win over ten-man Leicester that sealed the deal. Danny Blanchflower couldn't even be bothered to go on a lap of honour after that game, and there was a man who knew what was what.

At the end of the 1992–93 season, Manchester United became the Preston North End of their time, winning the inaugural FA Premier League title, the first champions of a brave new world.

They partied in memorable style: big defender Gary Pallister, the only star who hadn't scored for United all season, drove a free-kick home in the final minute of their final home fixture. Meanwhile the premier edition of the re-booted, second-tier First Division was won by Newcastle, who celebrated promotion in extraordinary fashion, thumping a decent Leicester side 7–1, David Kelly and Andy Cole both claiming hat-tricks. It was Newcastle's first Football League championship since 1927, even if it didn't quite represent the achievement of old.

A couple of weeks later, Andy Linighan scored an uber-dramatic 239th-minute winner in the Cup final for Arsenal. But unlike the resurgence of the Red Devils, or the eventually bittersweet renaissance of Kevin Keegan's era-defining Magpies, nobody talks about that much these days. Seems the title was the thing, after all.

Bibliography

Books

Andrews, David L (ed.): *Manchester United: A Thematic Study* (Routledge, Abingdon, 2004)

Bagchi, Rob and Paul Rogerson: *The Unforgiven* (Aurum, London, 2009)

Barclay, Patrick: *The Life and Times of Herbert Chapman* (Weidenfeld & Nicolson, London, 2014)

Barrett, Norman (ed.): *The Daily Telegraph Football Chronicle* (Carlton Books, London, 2004)

Bateson, Bill and Albert Sewell (ed.): *News of the World Football Annual 1986–87* (Invincible Press, London, 1987)

Belton, Brian: *East End Heroes, Stateside Kings* (John Blake, London, 2008)

Best, George: *Blessed* (Ebury Press, London, 2002)

Biddiscombe, Ross, Patrick Curry and Jonathan Hayden: *The Official Encyclopedia of Manchester United* (Simon & Schuster, London, 2011)

Blows, Kirk and Tony Hogg: *The Essential History of West Ham United* (Headline, London, 2000)

Brown, Jim: *Huddersfield Town, Champions of England* (Desert Island Books, Westcliff-on-Sea, 2003)

Buchan, Charles: *A Lifetime in Football* (Mainstream, Edinburgh, 2010)

Butler, Bryon: *The Football League, the Official Illustrated History* (Blitz Editions, Leicester, 1993)

Charlton, Sir Bobby: *My England Years* (Headline, London, 2008); *My Manchester United Years* (Headline, London, 2007)

Clough, Brian: *Cloughie, Walking on Water* (Headline, London, 2004)

Crick, Michael and David Smith: *Manchester United, the Betrayal of a Legend* (Pelham Books, London, 1989)

Dalglish, Kenny: *Dalglish* (Hodder & Stoughton, London, 1996)

Dunphy, Eamon: *A Strange Kind of Glory* (Aurum, London, 2007)

Evans, Bill: *A Season To Remember, Burnley 1959–60* (Tempus, Stroud, 2003)

Fagan, Andrew and Mark Platt: *Joe Fagan, Reluctant Champion* (Aurum, London, 2011)

Farnsworth, Keith: *Sheffield Football, A History, 1857–1961* (The Hallamshire Press, Sheffield, 1995); *Wednesday!* (Sheffield City Libraries, Sheffield, 1982)

Ferguson, Alex: *Managing My Life* (Hodder & Stoughton, London, 1999)

Glanvill, Rick: *Chelsea FC, the Official Biography* (Headline, London, 2006)

Glanville, Brian (ed.): *The Footballer's Companion* (Eyre & Spottiswoode, London, 1962)

Goldblatt, David: *The Ball is Round* (Penguin, London, 2007)

Green, Geoffrey: *There's Only One United* (Coronet, London, 1979)

Hill, Jimmy: *Striking for Soccer* (Peter Davis, London, 1963); *The Jimmy Hill Story* (Hodder & Stoughton, London, 1998)

Hornby, Nick (ed.): *My Favourite Year* (H. F. & G Witherby, London, 1993)

Horrie, Chris: *Premiership* (Pocket Books, London, 2002)

Horton, Steven: *We Love You Yeah, Yeah, Yeah, Yeah* (Vertical Editions, Skipton, 2014)

Imlach, Gary: *My Father and Other Working-Class Football Heroes* (Yellow Jersey, London, 2005)

Inglis, Simon (ed.): *The Best of Charles Buchan's Football Monthly* (English Heritage, London, 2006)

Inglis, Simon: *The Football Grounds of Great Britain* (Collins Willow, London, 1983)

Jackman, Mike: *The Essential History of Blackburn Rovers* (Headline, London, 2001)

James, Gary: *Manchester City, 125 Years of Football* (At Heart, Altrincham, 2006)

Joannou, Paul: *Newcastle United, the First 100 Years* (Polar Print Group, Leicester, 1995)

Keith, John: *Bob Paisley, Manager of the Millennium* (Robson Books, London, 1999)

Kelly, Stephen F: *Back Page United* (Island Books, Menai Bridge, 1997); *You'll Never Walk Alone* (Queen Anne Press, London, 1987)

Kelner, Martin: *Sit Down and Cheer* (Bloomsbury, London, 2012)

Lanfranchi, Pierre, Christiane Eisenberg, Tony Mason and Alfred Wahl: *100 Years of Football, the Fifa Centennial Book* (Weidenfeld & Nicolson, London, 2004)

Law, Denis: *The King* (Bantam Press, London, 2003)

Leatherdale, Clive (ed.): *The Book of Football* (Desert Island Books, Southend-on-Sea, 2005)

Lord, Bob: *My Fight for Football* (The Soccer Book Club, London, 1964)

Lowe, Simon: *Potters at War* (Desert Island Books, Westcliff-on-Sea, 2004)

Mason, Rob: *The Sunderland Story* (Pillar Box Red, Edinburgh, 1999)

Matthews, Tony: *1953–54 West Bromwich Albion* (Tempus, Stroud, 2004); *The Encyclopaedia of Birmingham City* (Britespot, Cradley Heath, 2000); *The Essential History of Wolverhampton Wanderers* (Headline, London, 2000)

McColl, Graham: *The Illustrated History of Aston Villa* (Hamlyn, London, 1998)

McKinstry, Leo: *Jack and Bobby* (Collins Willow, London, 2002); *Sir Alf* (Harper Collins, London, 2006)

Mears, Brian with Ian Macleay: *Chelsea, the 100-Year History* (Mainstream, Edinburgh, 2004)

Morris, Peter: *Aston Villa* (The Sportsmans Book Club, London, 1962)

Mortimer, Gerald: *Derby County, the Complete Record* (Breedon Books, Derby, 2006)

Nawrat, Chris and Steve Hutchings: *The Sunday Times Illustrated History of Football* (Hamlyn, London, 1998)

Neasom, Mike, Mick Cooper and Doug Robinson: *Pompey* (Milestone, Portsmouth, 1984)

Platt, Mark: *The Essential History of Everton* (Headline, London, 2000)

Ponting, Ivan: *Red and Raw* (André Deutsch, London, 1999); *The Book of Football Obituaries* (Know the Score, 2008)

Prestage, Mike: *Preston North End, the Glory Years Remembered* (Breedon Books, Derby, 2000)

Radnedge, Keir: *The Complete Encyclopedia of Football* (Carlton Books, London, 1998)

Redden, Richard: *The History of Charlton Athletic: Valley of Tears, Valley of Joy* (Print Co-ordination, London, 1993)

Riley, Reg and Graeme Riley: *Liverpool FC Match by Match 1892–1900, Volume 1* (Tony Brown, Nottingham, 2012)

Shankly, Bill: *My Story* (Trinity Mirror Sport Media, Liverpool, 2011)

Shaw, Gary and Mark Platt: *At the End of the Storm* (Gary Shaw, 2009)

Smith, Tommy: *Anfield Iron* (Bantam, London, 2009)

Soar, Phil: *Tottenham Hotspur: The Official Illustrated History, 1892–1997* (Hamlyn, London, 1997); *The Official History of Nottingham Forest* (Polar Publishing, Leicester, 1998)

Soar, Phil and Martin Tyler: *The Official History of Arsenal* (Ted Smart, Godalming, 1996)

Taw, Thomas: *Football's War and Peace* (Desert Island Books, Southend-on-Sea, 2003); *West Bromwich Albion, Champions of England* (Desert Island Books, Southend-on-Sea, 2007)

Taylor, Rogan and Andrew Ward: *Kicking and Screaming* (Robson Books, London, 1995)

Taylor, Rogan and Andrew Ward with John Williams: *Three Sides of the Mersey* (Robson Books, London, 1994)

Ticher, Mike and Andy Lyons (ed.): *When Saturday Comes, the First Eleven* (WSC Books, London, 1998)

Tomsett, Pete and Chris Brand: *Wembley, Stadium of Legends* (Dewi Lewis Media, Stockport, 2007)

Tyrrell, Tom and David Meek: *The Illustrated History of Manchester United* (Hamlyn, London, 1994)

Walvin, James: *The People's Game* (Mainstream, Edinburgh, 1994)

White, Rob and Julie Welch: *The Ghost of White Hart Lane* (Yellow Jersey Press, London, 2011)

Williams, John: *Red Men* (Mainstream, Edinburgh, 2010)

Willmore, G. A.: *West Bromwich Albion, the First Hundred Years* (Readers Union, Newton Abbot, 1980)

Wilson, Alan: *Team of All the Macs* (Vertical Editions, Skipton, 2011)

Wilson, Jonathan: *Inverting the Pyramid* (Orion, London, 2008); *Brian Clough: Nobody Ever Says Thank You* (Orion, London, 2011)

Wilson, Jonathan with Scott Murray: *Anatomy of Liverpool* (Orion, London, 2013)

Wolstenholme, Kenneth: *Kenneth Wolstenholme's Book of World Soccer* (World Distributors, Manchester, 1972)

Newspapers, magazines, periodicals and fanzines

The Blizzard, Boy from Brazil, Daily Express, Daily Mail, Daily Mirror, Daily Telegraph, Guardian, Lancashire Telegraph, Liverpool Echo, News of the World, Observer, Sunday Express, Sunday Times, The Times, When Saturday Comes

Websites

BBC, BFI Screen Online, Blue Moon, British Pathé, Football and the First World War, ITV, ITV Football 1955–1968, Ken Aston, LFC History, MUFC Info, RSSSF, Set Pieces, Soccerbase, Spartacus Educational, Stat Cat, Statto, Stretford End, YouTube

Appendices

Roll of Honour: First, Second and Third by Season

The Football League

1888–89: Preston North End, Aston Villa, Wolverhampton Wanderers
1889–90: Preston North End, Everton, Blackburn Rovers
1890–91: Everton, Preston North End, Notts County
1891–92: Sunderland, Preston North End, Bolton Wanderers

The Football League, First Division

1892–93: Sunderland, Preston North End, Everton
1893–94: Aston Villa, Sunderland, Derby County
1894–95: Sunderland, Everton, Aston Villa
1895–96: Aston Villa, Derby County, Everton
1896–97: Aston Villa, Sheffield United, Derby County
1897–98: Sheffield United, Sunderland, Wolverhampton Wanderers
1898–99: Aston Villa, Liverpool, Burnley
1899–1900: Aston Villa, Sheffield United, Sunderland
1900–01: Liverpool, Sunderland, Notts County
1901–02: Sunderland, Everton, Newcastle United
1902–03: The Wednesday, Aston Villa, Sunderland
1903–04: The Wednesday, Manchester City, Everton
1904–05: Newcastle United, Everton, Manchester City
1905–06: Liverpool, Preston North End, The Wednesday
1906–07: Newcastle United, Bristol City, Everton
1907–08: Manchester United, Aston Villa, Manchester City
1908–09: Newcastle United, Everton, Sunderland
1909–10: Aston Villa, Liverpool, Blackburn Rovers
1910–11: Manchester United, Aston Villa, Sunderland
1911–12: Blackburn Rovers, Everton, Newcastle United

1912–13: Sunderland, Aston Villa, The Wednesday
1913–14: Blackburn Rovers, Aston Villa, Middlesbrough
1914–15: Everton, Oldham Athletic, Blackburn Rovers
1915 to 1919: League suspended due to First World War
1919–20: West Bromwich Albion, Burnley, Chelsea
1920–21: Burnley, Manchester City, Bolton Wanderers
1921–22: Liverpool, Tottenham Hotspur, Burnley
1922–23: Liverpool, Sunderland, Huddersfield Town
1923–24: Huddersfield Town, Cardiff City, Sunderland
1924–25: Huddersfield Town, West Bromwich Albion, Bolton Wanderers
1925–26: Huddersfield Town, Arsenal, Sunderland
1926–27: Newcastle United, Huddersfield Town, Sunderland
1927–28: Everton, Huddersfield Town, Leicester City
1928–29: The Wednesday, Leicester City, Aston Villa
1929–30: Sheffield Wednesday, Derby County, Manchester City
1930–31: Arsenal, Aston Villa, Sheffield Wednesday
1931–32: Everton, Arsenal, Sheffield Wednesday
1932–33: Arsenal, Aston Villa, Sheffield Wednesday
1933–34: Arsenal, Huddersfield Town, Tottenham Hotspur
1934–35: Arsenal, Sunderland, Sheffield Wednesday
1935–36: Sunderland, Derby County, Huddersfield Town
1936–37: Manchester City, Charlton Athletic, Arsenal
1937–38: Arsenal, Wolverhampton Wanderers, Preston North End
1938–39: Everton, Wolverhampton Wanderers, Charlton Athletic
1939–40 (abandoned after three matches): Blackpool, Sheffield United, Arsenal
1939 to 1946: League suspended due to Second World War
1946–47: Liverpool, Manchester United, Wolverhampton Wanderers
1947–48: Arsenal, Manchester United, Burnley
1948–49: Portsmouth, Manchester United, Derby County
1949–50: Portsmouth, Wolverhampton Wanderers, Sunderland
1950–51: Tottenham Hotspur, Manchester United, Blackpool
1951–52: Manchester United, Tottenham Hotspur, Arsenal
1952–53: Arsenal, Preston North End, Wolverhampton Wanderers
1953–54: Wolverhampton Wanderers, West Bromwich Albion, Huddersfield Town
1954–55: Chelsea, Wolverhampton Wanderers, Portsmouth
1955–56: Manchester United, Blackpool, Wolverhampton Wanderers
1956–57: Manchester United, Tottenham Hotspur, Preston North End
1957–58: Wolverhampton Wanderers, Preston North End, Tottenham Hotspur
1958–59: Wolverhampton Wanderers, Manchester United, Arsenal
1959–60: Burnley, Wolverhampton Wanderers, Tottenham Hotspur

1960–61: Tottenham Hotspur, Sheffield Wednesday, Wolverhampton Wanderers
1961–62: Ipswich Town, Burnley, Tottenham Hotspur
1962–63: Everton, Tottenham Hotspur, Burnley
1963–64: Liverpool, Manchester United, Everton
1964–65: Manchester United, Leeds United, Chelsea
1965–66: Liverpool, Leeds United, Burnley
1966–67: Manchester United, Nottingham Forest, Tottenham Hotspur
1967–68: Manchester City, Manchester United, Liverpool
1968–69: Leeds United, Liverpool, Everton
1969–70: Everton, Leeds United, Chelsea
1970–71: Arsenal, Leeds United, Tottenham Hotspur
1971–72: Derby County, Leeds United, Liverpool
1972–73: Liverpool, Arsenal, Leeds United
1973–74: Leeds United, Liverpool, Derby County
1974–75: Derby County, Liverpool, Ipswich Town
1975–76: Liverpool, Queens Park Rangers, Manchester United
1976–77: Liverpool, Manchester City, Ipswich Town
1977–78: Nottingham Forest, Liverpool, Everton
1978–79: Liverpool, Nottingham Forest, West Bromwich Albion
1979–80: Liverpool, Manchester United, Ipswich Town
1980–81: Aston Villa, Ipswich Town, Arsenal
1981–82: Liverpool, Ipswich Town, Manchester United
1982–83: Liverpool, Watford, Manchester United
1983–84: Liverpool, Southampton, Nottingham Forest
1984–85: Everton, Liverpool, Tottenham Hotspur
1985–86: Liverpool, Everton, West Ham United
1986–87: Everton, Liverpool, Tottenham Hotspur
1987–88: Liverpool, Manchester United, Nottingham Forest
1988–89: Arsenal, Liverpool, Nottingham Forest
1989–90: Liverpool, Aston Villa, Tottenham Hotspur
1990–91: Arsenal, Liverpool, Crystal Palace
1991–92: Leeds United, Manchester United, Sheffield Wednesday

Summary of League Title Wins by Club

18: Liverpool
10: Arsenal
9: Everton
7: Manchester United, Aston Villa
6: Sunderland

4: Newcastle United, Sheffield Wednesday

3: Huddersfield Town, Wolverhampton Wanderers, Leeds United

2: Preston North End, Blackburn Rovers, Portsmouth, Burnley, Tottenham Hotspur, Manchester City, Derby County

1: Sheffield United, West Bromwich Albion, Chelsea, Ipswich Town, Nottingham Forest

Most Goals Scored in a Single Season

60: Dixie Dean (Everton, 1927–28)

49: Pongo Waring (Aston Villa, 1930–31)

44: Dixie Dean (Everton, 1931–32)

43: Ted Harper (Blackburn Rovers, 1925–26), Dave Halliday (Sunderland 1928–29)

42: Ted Drake (Arsenal, 1934–35)

41: Vic Watson (West Ham United, 1929–30), Jimmy Greaves (Chelsea, 1960–61)

All-Time Goalscorers

357: Jimmy Greaves (Chelsea, West Ham United, Tottenham Hotspur)

310: Dixie Dean (Everton)

309: Steve Bloomer (Derby County, Middlesbrough)

287: Gordon Hodgson (Liverpool, Leeds United, Aston Villa)

258: Charlie Buchan (Sunderland, Arsenal)

255: Nat Lofthouse (Bolton Wanderers), David Jack (Bolton Wanderers, Arsenal)

248: Joe Bradford (Birmingham City)

247: Hughie Gallacher (Newcastle United, Chelsea, Derby County, Grimsby Town)

243: Joe Smith (Bolton Wanderers)

Miscellaneous

Highest win: West Bromwich Albion 12–0 Darwin (1892); Nottingham Forest 12–0 Leicester Fosse (1909)

Highest away win: Newcastle United 1–9 Sunderland (1908); Cardiff City 1–9 Wolverhampton Wanderers (1955); Wolverhampton Wanderers 0–8 West Bromwich Albion (1892)

Highest aggregate goals total: Aston Villa 12–2 Accrington (1892); Tottenham Hotspur 10–4 Everton (1958)

Highest scoring draw: Leicester City 6–6 Arsenal (1930)

Most goals scored in a season (team): Aston Villa (128; 1930–31)

Acknowledgements

It's been a long old trek, and I couldn't have carried the bags on my own. Thanks to Rob Smyth, Rob Bagchi and Paul Doyle for being sounding boards extraordinaire. Thanks to James Dart and Philip Cornwall at the *Guardian* for not forgetting about me. Thanks to Ian Preece for his eagle eye. Thanks to Nicola Barr at Greene & Heaton for her patience, advice and support. Thanks to Charlotte Atyeo at Bloomsbury for her belief, guidance and expertise. Thanks to Holly Jarrald and Charlotte Croft for guiding the ship into the harbour. Thanks to Neal and Brenda Mitchell for all the encouragement, golf and pimento cheese. Thanks to my mum, for reasons too obvious to explain. And thanks to Wendy for the love that makes me the richest man in town. Thanks, everyone!

Index